Every Firm for Itself

Economists have modeled the economic rationale for intra-industry trade, yet political scientists largely have neglected it until recently. *Every Firm for Itself* explores how dramatic shifts in the way countries trade have radically changed trade politics in the US and EU. It explores how electorally minded policymakers respond to heavy lobbying by powerful corporations and provide trade policies that further advantage these large firms. It explains puzzling empirical phenomena such as the rise of individual firm lobbying, the decline of broad trade coalitions, the decline of labor union activity in trade politics, and the rising public backlash to globalization due to trade politics becoming increasingly dominated by large firms. With an approach that connects economics and politics, this book shows how contemporary trading patterns among rich countries undermine longstanding coalitions and industry associations that once successfully represented large and small firms alike.

Mary Anne Madeira is an assistant professor of international relations at Lehigh University. She was a Jean Monnet Postdoctoral Research Fellow in the Robert Schuman Centre for Advanced Studies at the European University Institute. She is the coauthor, with James A. Caporaso of *Globalization, Institutions and Governance* (2011).

Every Firm for Itself

Corporate Lobbying and the Domestic Politics of Intra-Industry Trade

MARY ANNE MADEIRA

Lehigh University

Shaftesbury Road, Cambridge CB2 8EA, United Kingdom

One Liberty Plaza, 20th Floor, New York, NY 10006, USA

477 Williamstown Road, Port Melbourne, VIC 3207, Australia

314–321, 3rd Floor, Plot 3, Splendor Forum, Jasola District Centre, New Delhi – 110025, India

103 Penang Road, #05–06/07, Visioncrest Commercial, Singapore 238467

Cambridge University Press is part of Cambridge University Press & Assessment, a department of the University of Cambridge.

We share the University's mission to contribute to society through the pursuit of education, learning and research at the highest international levels of excellence.

www.cambridge.org
Information on this title: www.cambridge.org/9781009651264

DOI: 10.1017/9781009651271

First published 2025

A catalogue record for this publication is available from the British Library

A Cataloging-in-Publication data record for this book is available from the Library of Congress

ISBN 978-1-009-65128-8 Hardback
ISBN 978-1-009-65126-4 Paperback

Cambridge University Press & Assessment has no responsibility for the persistence or accuracy of URLs for external or third-party internet websites referred to in this publication and does not guarantee that any content on such websites is, or will remain, accurate or appropriate.

To Adam, Julian and Sacha

Contents

Figures

Tables

Acknowledgments

The ideas that grew into this book began forming during graduate seminars in international political economy with Jim Caporaso at the University of Washington (UW), and specifically, while reading a seminal contribution to the canon, *Commerce and Coalitions* by Ron Rogowski. I was fascinated by Rogowski's elegant use of economic theory to explain important patterns in trade politics across time and space. Yet the nature of trade has changed dramatically since the time periods on which Rogowski focused, and I wondered how more contemporary features of and patterns in international trade would affect today's political cleavages and coalitions. Under Jim's superb, generous and supportive supervision, these half-formed ideas grew into a dissertation, and eventually into this book. I owe Jim the deepest gratitude for his unwavering support, excellent mentorship, first-rate and constructive criticisms and advice, and, now, a lasting friendship. Our work together has taken us as far as Rome and Seoul where I made some of the best memories. Thank you, Jim, for everything.

Most recently, I am indebted to the invited reviewers at the Textor Book Workshop generously hosted by the International Relations Department at Lehigh University. Ida Bastiaens, Tim Peterson, and Gary Winslett devoted considerable time to reading and discussing my manuscript, and their brilliant critiques and insights strengthened the manuscript to the point that it was ready to submit for publication. Similarly, I thank two anonymous reviewers of Cambridge University Press for their rigorous, detailed feedback. The final version of this book is enormously improved, thanks to their close reads and incisive comments. At Cambridge University Press, I thank Robert Dreesen for his enthusiasm for this project and editorial expertise, as well as Laura Blake for shepherding this expertly through production.

The long journey from seminar paper to dissertation to book would not have been possible without the intellectual contributions of many other scholars along the way, first and foremost the other members of my dissertation committee, Victor Menaldo, Aseem Prakash, and Christine Ingebritsen. Victor preferred to walk during our meetings rather than sit in his office, resulting in afternoons strolling through UW's beautiful campus, talking animatedly and gesticulating wildly, honing and shaping ideas. Just what an education should be. This is now a tradition, as I do the same with my students at Lehigh University. Aseem and Christine's contributions to the project also were critical to its development not only as a dissertation but also as a book, and I am grateful to Aseem for his always generous professional advice over the years.

Upon leaving UW, I was fortunate to spend a year as a Jean Monnet Fellow at the Robert Schuman Centre of Advanced Studies at the European University Institute in Fiesole, Italy. There I conducted research on the European cases presented in this book and benefited from the supervision and constructive feedback of Bernard Hoekman. At EUI, I thank other colleagues who provided excellent feedback on this project, most notably Phillip Ayoub, Adriana Bunea, and Timea Pal. It was also wonderful to reconnect with Chad Damro, my former professor and mentor from the University of Edinburgh, who overlapped with me at EUI and continued to provide encouragement and insight formative to my professional development.

I owe much gratitude to my colleagues in the Political Science Department at the City University of New York – Queens College and at Lehigh University's International Relations Department, my present home. At Queens, I thank John Bowman, Peter Liberman, and Pat Rachal for their mentorship and guidance during my first years as a professor. At Lehigh, I thank Dinissa Duvanova and Norrin Ripsman for expert mentorship and support of my work.

This research was generously funded by Lehigh University's Paul J. Franz Summer Research Award and by the European Union Centre for Excellence Graduate Research Award at the University of Washington. I thank August Rim at Queens College for his excellent research assistance. I am also grateful to the many busy bureaucrats at the European Union that were willing to be interviewed and to staff at trade associations both in Europe and the United States for the same. Writing retreats at Lehigh University, sponsored by the Humanities Center, the Women, Gender, and Sexuality Studies program, and the Office of Research and Graduate Studies (thank you, Kate Bullard) were integral in bringing this book over the finish line by providing time and space for focused writing.

I have been blessed by wonderful friendships with colleagues who have sustained me, challenged me, and directly contributed to my ability to complete this book. My friends in graduate school spent countless hours reading and discussing each other's work, and I remain indebted to Dan Berliner, Amanda Clayton, Loren Collingwood, Sarah Dreier, Yoav Duman, Josh Eastin, Adam Forman, and Milli Lake for all the benefits of their continuing brilliance and love. Since graduate school, I thank Jorge Alves, Phillip Ayoub, Edann Brady, Bill Bulman, Julie George, Keena Lipsitz, Nimah Mazaheri, and Allison Mickel for providing intellectual and moral support as well as encouragement during tough times – and many, many laughs. Outside academia, my dear friends are too numerous to name, but I hope you know who you are and how much I appreciate you (and if you are actually reading this, you get an extra award).

Last but not least, my parents, stepparents, and in-laws have been endlessly dedicated to me, emotionally and financially, and I would not be where I am without the six of them. Finally, my deepest and eternal thanks and love go to my partner, Adam Hoff. He has selflessly supported me every step of the way, from Seattle to Bethlehem, PA, while being the very best dad to our children, Julian and Sacha. This book would not exist without him. I love you, Adam, and am forever grateful.

Introduction

In 2014, a wave of protests swept Europe opposing the mega-trade and investment deal that was being negotiated at that time with the United States and which was called the Transatlantic Trade and Investment Partnership (TTIP). Taking to the streets even in exporting powerhouses such as Germany, many small-business owners participating in the "Stop TTIP" movement expressed their strong opposition to TTIP and other free trade agreements (FTAs) that the European Union (EU) was negotiating, including one with Canada. A small-business owner and organizer of protests in Austria said: "fewer than 1% of European SMEs export to Canada and the US. For the other 99% CETA [the Canadian agreement] and its twin TTIP increase the competition in their main market, which is the European."[1] The largest employer federation in France raised these concerns in a meeting with the European Commission, asking how it could "reassure the 19 million European SMEs which do not export and which will face increased import competition" about the value of TTIP.

Across the Atlantic, a self-described "mid-market domestic manufacturer" of precision machine tools described the existential threats to his firm from another mega-regional trade deal being considered – this one between the US and eleven Pacific Rim countries, the Trans-Pacific Partnership (TPP). In comments to the US Trade Representative (USTR) in 2009, a representative from this firm wrote that "the proposed trade agreement will simply let the multinationals expand production facilities in East Asia to gain more unfair mercantilist trade advantages there. Then they will dump more underpriced foreign goods here to compete with domestic producers like us. And we have

---

[1] See "Small and medium-sized enterprise from across Europe call on European governments to reject the CETA agreement." Joint press release from KMU Gegen TTIP (Germany), KMU Gegen TTIP (Austria), and Ondernemers van NU (Netherlands), September 23, 2016. Available at www.noalttip.org/wp-content/uploads/2016/11/2016-09-23-SME-against-CETA_TTIP-press-release.pdf, accessed March 5, 2023.

neither the money nor the political power to get our government to enforce the law and stop this unfair trade from destroying our business and industry" (Penn United, 2009). Another small-business owner and board member of the National Association of Manufacturers discussed trade politics in similarly existentialist terms in the mid 2000s, as trade between the US and China was booming: "We've got to have a level playing field. But I worry whether there will be enough survivors to put on the pressure."[2]

These anecdotes suggest that trade liberalization is contentious in developed economies today, yet observers of trade politics would not know this by looking at lobbying data. A recent study found that over 99.25 percent of firms that lobbied on US trade agreements since the 1990s lobbied in favor of free trade (Blanga-Gubbay et al., 2024). When USTR solicited societal feedback on the proposed TTIP, very nearly *all* of the 215 comments from business groups were supportive. More recently, in 2022, USTR asked firms for feedback on the Section 301 tariffs imposed by President Trump in 2018 as part of his trade war with China. Seventy-eight percent of firms that provided feedback opposed the tariffs.[3] One study analyzed business coalitions that have formed to either support or oppose US trade agreements over the past three decades and counted fifty-five pro-trade coalitions and only four anti-trade coalitions (Osgood, 2021). Among these politically active business actors, manufacturing firms have spent ten times more than industry associations to influence trade policy since the Lobbying Disclosure Act was passed in 1995 (Blanga-Gubbay et al., 2024), even though historically, most US firms delegated political activity to their industry associations.

Despite the overwhelming dominance of pro-trade lobbying relative to protectionist lobbying, the two most recent mega-trade deals that the US government attempted to conclude – the TPP and the TTIP – both failed. While there was an entire social movement that formed to oppose TTIP in the EU, playing a key role in that agreement's failure, TTIP was virtually unknown among the US public. TPP, on the other hand, inspired widespread public opposition and became a lightning rod in the 2016 US presidential campaign. Lobbying over the two agreements was very different as well. In the US, virtually no firms or industry associations lobbied in opposition to TTIP, while peak labor unions and some powerful industries mounted a passionate campaign to kill TPP, ultimately succeeding when President Trump withdrew the US from the agreement as one of his first acts in office.

The politics surrounding TPP and TTIP highlight puzzles whose answers are central to understanding some recent and fundamental changes in the politics of international trade in developed economies. Specifically, individual firms are now leading political actors. Whereas historically, firms tended to delegate

---

[2] See "Who Lobbies for the Little Guys?" by Samuel Fromartz, *CNN Money*, March 1, 2006.
[3] See www.cfr.org/blog/amid-trade-war-china-few-industries-support-tariffs.

nearly all lobbying to industry associations or even broader cross-sectoral associations, such as the National Association of Manufacturers, today we are very likely to see firms "going it alone" to lobby for their own narrow trade preferences. Additionally, the conventional wisdom among political economists for decades was that protectionists lobby more than free traders. In the US and the EU today, we see far more lobbying in favor of liberal trade rules than of protection.

The domestic politics of recent trade agreements, and the intense activity of individual firms, are also puzzling from a historical perspective. In the US, trade policy coalitions were once well organized, broadly class-based or sector-based, and typically protectionist. Industrialization in the Northern states in the 1800s gave birth to a powerful urban coalition of industrialists and their workers. These infant industries sought protection from competition from European manufactured imports. Protectionist preferences dominated the Republican party of the time, and trade debates with the Democrats, representing the free-trading, export-dependent Southern farmers, were fierce. Protection was a cornerstone of American trade policy through the 1920s, culminating in the infamous Smoot-Hawley tariff in 1930. Since then, the nature of trade policy coalitions has changed dramatically. In the postwar period, broad class-based coalitions have not been a feature of trade politics in the US. Increasingly, coalitions both of industries and labor have dissolved, industry associations and labor unions have become less politically active in many cases, and lobbying today is dominated by individual firms and ad hoc cross-sectoral coalitions in favor of freer trade. Despite heavy corporate lobbying in support of trade liberalization, industry, labor, and political parties were all divided during debates over major pieces of trade legislation such as the North American Free Trade Agreement (NAFTA). More recent bilateral trade deals with South Korea, Panama, and Colombia stalled in Congress for years before being concluded.

Why are firms today much more likely to engage in individual lobbying than in the past, when broader industry and class-based coalitions dominated trade politics? What determines whether they lobby alone or whether they organize for collective action? Why do free-traders lobby so much more than protectionists, a reversal of a longstanding feature of trade politics? In advanced democracies, why are certain sectors and industries deeply divided over trade while others remain united in their positions? Finally, what are the wider implications of the rise of individual firms as leading actors in trade policy debates, particularly in light of the populist backlash to trade that took shape within developed economies in the 2010s and early 2020s?

These questions, which bring us to the nexus of domestic and international political economy (IPE), are the central concern of this book. In the chapters that follow I argue that the leading models of democratic trade politics, while very powerful in explaining historical trade coalitions, lose leverage in their attempts to explain more recent political developments in trade politics and policy. I argue that the majority of political science work on trade politics has not kept pace with important empirical developments in the structure of international trade that have changed the distributional effects of trade and, consequently, the resulting political cleavages and coalitions.

This book makes a major contribution to the field of IPE by showing how the domestic politics of trade in developed economies have changed dramatically as a result of major structural changes in the way that rich countries trade. A significant amount of global trade is no longer founded upon endowments-based comparative advantage, so it does not conform to the economic assumptions underlying classic political economy models. Today, most trade among developed countries is intra-industry, which means two-way trade in similar products, such as when the US exports cars to Germany and also imports German cars. The redistributive implications of intra-industry trade are profoundly different from those of the classic inter-industry, endowments-based trade. I show that due to this changing structure of international trade, classic models of trade politics and trade policy struggle to explain contemporary features of trade politics, such as the rise of firm-centered lobbying. In this book, I develop a model to explain how the move from endowments-based to intra-industry trade affects trade politics and policy in developed democracies.

1.1 THE DOMESTIC POLITICS OF INTRA-INDUSTRY TRADE

What is the link between intra-industry trade and domestic trade politics? This book's claim is that intra-industry trade undermines the longstanding societal coalitions that are traditionally active in trade politics. Intra-industry trade hollows out broad class-based coalitions of workers, farmers, or industrialists, and it also divides industry-based associations made up of firms and employees from the same industry. This is because, unlike classic inter-industry trade, the distributional effects of trade liberalization fall at the level of the individual firm, rather than at the level of the industry as a whole. Larger, more productive, internationalized firms gain from trade liberalization and increased foreign market access. However, smaller, domestic-oriented firms within the same industry may incur significant losses from trade liberalization. For non-exporting firms, freer trade often means losses in market share and stiffer competition from lower-priced imports as well as from the large, leading firms that benefit from trade liberalization. In this way, intra-industry trade undermines industry consensus over trade and generates competing trade preferences among firms within the same industry.

The effect of these competing intra-industry preferences is to hamstring industry-based trade associations. It becomes difficult for industry associations to take strong lobbying positions on trade policy without acting in direct contradiction to the interests of some of their members. Firms may revoke membership or contributions if trade associations take an active lobbying stance for a trade position that is counter to their interests. The result of this, in terms of lobbying, is that trade associations take weaker stances on policy to avoid losing members. They may also stop lobbying for particular trade positions altogether, or they may decrease the amount of resources they spend on lobbying. At the same time, individual firms become more politically active, engaging in direct corporate lobbying instead of collective action.

Despite the way that intra-industry trade undermines industry consensus over trade, I show that the political implications are counterintuitive. Though we might expect an increasingly contentious lobbying landscape, with many more firms lobbying for conflicting trade policies, consider how costly it is to engage in political action. As industry-wide associations become less active due to competing preferences among member firms, not all firms are equally able to mobilize politically on behalf of their own interests. Only the largest firms will be able to put significant resources into political activity, and these firms tend to be exporters (and importers) that prefer liberal trade rules. Internationally oriented firms want access to foreign markets (as well as imported inputs) and are willing to grant foreign firms reciprocal market access. Non-exporting firms, however, do not reap the exporting gains from trade and are harmed by the increased domestic competition that comes with trade liberalization. Yet these non-exporting firms tend to be small- and medium-sized businesses that are the least equipped to mobilize politically. Therefore, they are likely to be massively out-lobbied by the large, competitive exporting firms that lobby in support of trade liberalization. Many opt out of lobbying altogether, expecting that their efforts will not be successful.

These insights form the basis for a second major implication of my argument, which is that trade policy outcomes are affected by the structure of international trade. Specifically, tariffs will decrease in industries with higher intra-industry trade as politically powerful, internationalized firms engage politically in support of liberal trade rules. As large, pro-trade firms dominate the lobbying landscape, policymakers are able to liberalize high-IIT industries more easily than industries where trade is based on endowments and comparative advantage. Although policymakers may have strong domestic support for liberalizing a comparative advantage industry, trading partners may maintain higher levels of protection if they have a comparative disadvantage in that same industry. This means that globally, average tariff levels will be higher in industries where intra-industry trade is low and trade takes place primarily along comparative advantage lines. Yet the intra-industry divisions generated by two-way trade also give policymakers an incentive to respond to demands by large, globalized firms for veiled forms of protectionism via nontariff measures (NTMs). Indeed, I will show that tariffs fall along with intra-industry trade, but NTMs increase.

A third implication of my argument is that some trade agreements will be easier to conclude than others. Intra-industry trade occurs most intensively between developed economies producing similar but differentiated products.

There is public support for increased access to foreign products, and industries as a whole are not threatened with extinction, as labor costs tend to be similar among countries at similar levels of development. Most lobbying on these agreements is likely to come from the large, internationalized firms that support freer trade. On the other hand, trade agreements between countries whose trade is more heavily inter-industry are likely to be more politically contentious. This characterizes trade between developed and developing economies whose labor costs and endowments may be substantially different. The extremely difficult negotiations surrounding NAFTA and the TPP on the one hand, and the low level of salience of the TTIP (at least in the US) on the other hand, illustrates this argument. Trade agreements between countries whose trade is primarily inter-industry are likely to unite more industries around protectionist positions. Thus, an important implication of my argument is that North–South agreements will inspire more protectionist lobbying and will be more difficult to conclude. On the other hand, and counterintuitively, heavy corporate lobbying in support of more liberalization may inspire a public backlash arising from the belief that trade agreements are written to advance firm-specific interests rather than broad societal interests, a dynamic that likely contributed to unexpectedly intense public opposition in Europe to recent North–North trade deals, despite the near absence of protectionist lobbying from industry or labor unions.

A comprehensive analysis of trade politics must consider the role of both economic structure and institutions. Without considering institutions, we risk confusing interests with outcomes. By ignoring economic structure, institutionalists risk misunderstanding underlying interests. This book attempts to incorporate both societal preferences and institutions into the analysis, but nevertheless leans heavily toward the demand-side of the policy process. Even so, my efforts to develop a more comprehensive and testable model of the influence of intra-industry trade on trade politics and policy outcomes is a major step forward and important update of the demand-side models relied upon by political economists who study trade politics. Only when we have a clear understanding of the stakes involved for economic actors in the new trading environment will institutional analyses provide empirically robust explanations. By examining the effect of intra-industry trade on lobbying patterns in the EU as well as the US – two very different institutional contexts – I increase confidence in its independent effect on lobbying patterns.

Overall, this book makes five major contributions to our understanding of trade politics. First, it demonstrates that intra-industry trade radically changes the landscape of trade politics and develops a coherent model of its political implications. Second, in doing so, it provides theoretical explanations for recent empirical phenomena, such as the rise of firm-based lobbying and the rise of pro-trade lobbying, that conventional models have struggled to explain. Third, it advances our understanding of industry-level variation in trade coalitions and trade politics. Explanations that focus on systemic features of the international trading regime or on domestic institutional structures are ill-equipped to account for the ways that coalitions over trade – and the preferences they express – vary at the industry level, within a given country. Fourth, it connects the Americanist and EU literatures on trade politics, which too often remain separate, advancing our understanding of the generalizability of domestic trade politics. Finally, it uses firm-level data to analyze the microfoundations of trade politics and assess a firm-level theory of the political economy of lobbying over trade.

1.2 TRADE POLITICS IN ADVANCED DEMOCRACIES: EXISTING LITERATURE

Most of the literature on the politics of international trade is grounded in neoclassical trade theory, which expects countries will exchange primarily along inter-industry lines and the redistributional effects of trade will affect either entire classes or specific industries. Seminal work such as that of Frieden (1991); Hiscox (2002b) and Rogowski (1990) are based on these assumptions, as are the numerous studies that have built on their theoretical and empirical contributions.[4] These studies are similar in that they expect coalitions to form among economic actors with shared preferences over trade policy outcomes, yet they differ in their expectations about whether coalitions will be broad and class-based (e.g., labor unions or cross-sectoral business associations) or narrow and industry-based (e.g., industry associations). Factor mobility plays a central role in determining these coalition patterns.

Two major limitations of the factor/sector-based approaches above are that (1) their assumptions are based on inter-industry, comparative advantage-based trade models that are less relevant in today's advanced economies where trade is largely intra-industry, and (2) they assume firms will organize themselves into coalitions of various forms, ignoring the possibility of countercoalitional political activity by individual firms. Notably, Rogowski's seminal book struggles to predict trade politics in advanced democracies in the postwar period, as Rogowski himself noted (1990:126–128). While many studies have sought to improve upon Rogowski's model by developing more sophisticated measures of factor endowments (Midford, 1993), using updated data (Jeong, 2009), or including survey data of individual attitudes (O'Rourke, 2003; Scheve and Slaughter, 2001), factor mobility loses its relevance in a world of intra-industry trade between countries with similar factor endowments (Alt et al., 1999).

New trade theory explains the economics behind shifting global trading patterns and the rise of intra-industry trade (Dixit and Norman, 1980; Helpman, 1981; Krugman, 1981).[5] To explain the rise of firm-based lobbying,

---

[4] For example, Alt et al. (1999); Brawley (1997); Garst (1998, 1999); Jeong (2009); Ladewig (2006); Midford (1993).

[5] I discuss this in depth in Chapter 2.

a puzzling phenomenon given that industry associations have been well organized for decades, the most recent models of trade politics draw on a central finding of new–new trade theory (NNTT) from economics: Intra-industry trade reallocates resources not at the industry level, but at the firm level (Melitz, 2003). Productive, exporting firms within an industry stand to gain from trade liberalization while less productive, typically non-exporting firms expect to lose. This firm heterogeneity within industries is a central factor in explaining why some firms prefer trade liberalization while others in the same industry prefer protection.

Firm-centric approaches to trade politics take this firm heterogeneity as their starting point. This literature argues that within any given industry, firms differ from each other in a number of important ways that affect their engagement with the global economy, their trade preferences, and their political behavior. For example, only a small percentage of firms export and/or import. This "heterogeneity" of firms' exporting/importing status means even firms within the same industry are not likely to benefit in a uniform way from trade liberalization. This, in turn, means that they may not be united as an industry on trade policy. Many recent studies emphasize how firm characteristics such as size, engagement in global value chains, foreign investment, and productivity levels are central to understanding trade preferences and lobbying behavior (Drope and Hansen, 2006; Jensen et al., 2015; Kim, 2017; Osgood, 2016; Osgood et al., 2017; Plouffe, 2017). Taken together, these contributions show how firm-level differences are central to understanding trade politics.

Other models of trade politics are more centrally concerned with collective action and understanding how actors cooperate to influence trade policy. Lobbying is costly, and industries may face collective action problems in their attempts to organize politically. In general, larger firms are more likely to lobby individually than smaller firms (Bombardini, 2008; Drope and Hansen, 2006; Hansen and Mitchell, 2000), while smaller firms are more likely to channel their political activity through associations (Kerr et al., 2013). Thus, many studies have investigated the relationship between firm-level political activity and industry concentration. These studies evaluate the Olsonian argument that members of smaller groups (fewer firms in the industry) will be more politically active, as they are better able to overcome the free-rider problem (Barber et al., 2014; Bombardini and Trebbi, 2012; Drope and Hansen, 2009).[6] Other industry characteristics can affect lobbying decisions as well, such as the level of product differentiation in the sector and whether protection is expected to primarily benefit the lobbying firms' products alone (protection as a private good) or competitors' products as well (protection as a public good) (Bombardini and Trebbi, 2012; Gilligan, 1997b; Kim, 2017; Osgood, 2017).

---

[6] In general, results of studies attempting to link industry concentration with mode of lobbying are quite mixed. Barber et al. (2014) present a thorough review of these studies, their methodologies, and their findings.

Another major factor influencing the politics of trade is the role of domestic institutions. Institutional analyses problematize the supply side of policymaking and theorize that different institutional configurations affect the costs of political action and the likelihood of political success. Similarly, institutions create political incentives for certain types of policy responses by policymakers themselves. A rich literature demonstrates the way that institutional factors such as regime type (Kono, 2008; Milner and Kubota, 2005; Wu, 2020), the location of trade policymaking authority (Bailey et al., 1997; Schattschneider, 1935; Woll, 2009), access to the policymaking process (Ehrlich, 2007; O'Reilly, 2005), party politics (Lohmann and O'Halloran, 1994; Hankla, 2006; McGillivray, 2004; Milner and Judkins, 2004; Weller, 2009), and electoral systems (Betz, 2017; Grossman and Helpman, 2005; Rogowski, 1987) all affect societal decisions to mobilize politically as well as resultant trade policy. Further, nontariff measures that affect trade may provide an alternative pathway through which policymakers can supply protection to firms and industries while maintaining low tariffs (Gulotty, 2020; Mansfield and Busch, 1995; Rickard, 2012).

This book engages with and builds on each of these literatures in the following ways. First, it directly advances the classic IPE literature on societal preferences over trade policy, drawing on new trade theory, and new–new trade theory to show how structural changes in global trading patterns have affected the domestic politics of trade, particularly in developed economies. Second, it integrates insights from the firm heterogeneity and collective action literatures, exploring the ways that diverse preferences within an industry affect that industry's ability to overcome collective action problems to lobby together on trade policy. I show that firm-based lobbying is higher in industries with higher intra-industry trade, and I show that this shift from primarily collective, industry-based lobbying to firm-based lobbying changes the structure of protection (away from tariffs and toward nontariff measures). Third, the comparative framework I adopt allows me to assess my argument in two very different institutional contexts, strengthening confidence in the independent role of intra-industry trade in trade politics and policy. This is a significant contribution, as many leading studies of trade politics are limited to the US context, limiting our understanding of the generalizability of many of the literature's claims.

By focusing on a structural attribute of trade between countries, this analysis can go beyond explaining firm preferences and firm-based lobbying to explain more macro-level trade policy outcomes – such as why certain trade agreements are more easily concluded than others, why some agreements achieve deeper liberalization, and why tariffs are falling globally even as nontariff barriers to trade increase.[7] Only in the presence of exports *and* imports does

---

[7] Thies and Peterson (2015) take a similar approach in their comprehensive analysis of the international political effects of intra-industry trade.

industry-level consensus break down in a manner in which the characteristics of individual firms affect the industry's subsequent political engagement and its trade policy demands. The extent to which two countries' trade is intra-industry changes not only the degree to which firms engage politically and the demands that they make but also the type and level of protection that policymakers are willing to provide. Once we understand this, we can better understand industry-level variation in protection, the varying public salience of particular trade agreements, and why some trade agreements are successfully concluded while others very publicly fail.

Some scholars have argued that intra-industry trade is an artifact of product differentiation and that its effects on intra-industry division and political activity can be captured using product differentiation as the key explanatory variable (Kim, 2017; Osgood, 2017). There is certainly strong evidence from recent work that product differentiation affects the political organization of firms and industries. Yet while product differentiation may be a necessary condition for IIT, it is not a sufficient condition. Some industries with high product differentiation may not experience significant levels of two-way trade. Two-way trade is also a result of factors such as low transport costs, foreign direct investment flows, trade in intermediate goods, and the similarity of trading partners in terms of endowments and competitiveness. Trade in differentiated products is not likely to occur between countries with greatly different endowments or greatly different market sizes. Thus product differentiation and IIT are different phenomena, though related, with one being a feature of industries and the other being feature of international trade.

Finally, this book resolves longstanding tensions within the political science literature on intra-industry trade. An earlier generation of scholarship argued that intra-industry trade was easier to liberalize than inter-industry trade, since two-way trade in similar products tends to occur between countries at similar levels of development with similar factor prices (Lipson, 1982; Milner, 1999; Verdier, 1998). For this reason, adjustment costs are limited to specific firms rather than entire industries. Some recent work corroborates these arguments (Manger, 2014, 2015; Thies and Peterson, 2015), but others find that protection rises with IIT, as firms successfully lobby for protection of their particular product varieties (Gilligan, 1997b; Kono, 2009). The analysis of trade policy in this book makes sense of these conflicting findings by disentangling tariffs and NTMs theoretically and empirically. I show that IIT is associated with falling tariffs, as several analyses have suggested, but that the rise in firm-based lobbying that accompanies IIT incentivizes policymakers to provide alternative, nontariff forms of protection. In this way, I use insights from the more recent firm heterogeneity literature to extend our understanding of the ways that a shift from predominately comparative-advantaged based to intra-industry trade affects political activity, firm demands, and resulting trade policy outcomes.

1.3 THE PLAN OF THE BOOK

I proceed as follows. In Chapter 2, I introduce the concept of intra-industry trade, its economic rationale, its importance in the global economy, and the ways in which it differs from inter-industry trade. I first define the various types of intra-industry trade, discuss measurement issues, and trace its rise in the postwar period. More than half of all global trade is now intra-industry, depending upon how it is measured. Next, I present descriptive statistics on sector- and country-level patterns in intra-industry trade, demonstrating that it tends to occur most intensively among differentiable manufactured goods and among developed economies that specialize in the production of these goods. Third, I discuss the economic rationale for intra-industry trade, drawing on the work of economists who pioneered new trade theory by explaining why countries with similar factor endowments would trade for similar goods. This type of trade dominates global trade today but is a stark departure from the expectations of endowments-based theories that predict inter-industry trade between countries based on comparative advantage. Fourth, I discuss the distributional effects of intra-industry trade and the contributions of new–new trade theory to the crucial point that intra-industry trade causes resources to reallocate *within* industries, rather than across industries. I present an extended example of these effects through discussing the effects of trade liberalization between Canada, Mexico, and the US.

Chapter 3 develops my theory of the political economy of intra-industry trade. I argue that changes in the nature of trade away from endowments-based trade to two-way trade within industries changes the structure of preferences over trade policy and the way that actors mobilize politically in order to influence trade policy. This, in turn, affects trade policy outcomes and the varying ease with which trade agreements are concluded. The argument proceeds in three parts. First, I argue that the distributional effects of intra-industry trade drive a wedge through industry preferences over trade policy. As intra-industry trade increases, exporting and importing firms support openness and less productive, domestic-oriented firms within the same industry support protection. Second, I argue that these heterogeneous firm preferences change the ability of industries to overcome collective action problems and organize politically to influence trade policy. I argue that industry associations are hamstrung in their ability to lobby while individual firms have a greater incentive to lobby alone for their preferred policies. Third, in contrast to the conventional wisdom, I argue that exporters will overwhelm domestic-oriented firms in their lobbying efforts, and as a result, tariffs will be lower in industries with higher intra-industry trade. Finally, I discuss my empirical strategy for assessing my arguments.

In Chapter 4, I examine the role of intra-industry trade in trade policy lobbying in the United States. Using firm-level data on trade policy lobbying expenditures for 459 US manufacturing industries, I show that industry associations are less active in their lobbying efforts, relative to individual firms, in industries with higher two-way trade. Furthermore, I find that this effect is stronger in import-competing sectors than in export-oriented sectors. This suggests that in import-competing sectors, exporting firms break away from more protectionist industry associations to lobby alone for liberalization.

Chapter 5 assesses the generalizability of my argument with an analysis of trade lobbying in the European Union. I first discuss the dynamics of trade politics and policymaking in this very different institutional context, focusing on alternative explanations for the patterns we observe in lobbying activity over trade policy. I present an original dataset of firm-level lobbying during four open consultations on trade policy conducted over the period of 2010–2012. I analyzed nearly 600 responses to the consultations, coding each lobbying actor according to their primary industry and actor type. The results of my statistical analyses provide further support for the argument developed in Chapter 3. Despite the differing institutional constraints and incentives in the EU context, I find that as in the US, industries with lower IIT are more likely to engage in collective action via industry associations, while firms are more likely to lobby alone in industries subject to high IIT.

In Chapter 6, I link my findings in Chapters 4 and 5 to trade policy outcomes. Here I consider not only firm preferences and incentives to lobby, but the receptivity of political institutions to pressure groups, and I consider how different policy options (tariffs vs. nontariff forms of protection) give rent-seeking policymakers two different channels through which to supply large, politically powerful firms with their preferred trade policies. I develop and test hypotheses about the way that intra-industry trade should affect tariffs and nontariff forms of protection in developed economies. I test these hypotheses with industry-level trade data in a cross-national time-series analysis of eleven high-income democracies from 1995 to 2014. I find that average tariff levels are lower in industries with higher levels of intra-industry trade, as my model predicts. Interestingly, however, nontariff barriers to trade increase with IIT, a finding that suggests that firms may seek NTMs as substitutionary forms of protection as tariffs decrease. This is consistent with a key insight in this book, which is that firms in the same industry may have very different preferences over trade, and while some firms may lobby hard for tariff reductions, others may seek nontariff forms of protection. In addition, the same firms that lobby for tariff reductions may simultaneously seek regulatory NTMs that disadvantage foreign varieties.

Chapter 7 presents qualitative case studies of firm and industry lobbying over the TPP and TTIP in the US. These two mega-regional trade agreements were negotiated concurrently and exhibit significant variation on both the key independent variable (IIT) and the dependent variable (political organization), both across and within the agreements. I examine how US firms and industries organized and engaged politically during the negotiations of each agreement, using the content of their public statements, comments submitted to USTR during societal consultations, and testimony provided at hearings of the US International Trade Commission. The case studies in this chapter illustrate the ways that industry associations moderate their political activity in the presence of high IIT and disagreement among their member firms over trade policy. I show how industry associations are able to take much stronger political positions when IIT is low – either in support of or against further liberalization – while they reduce or equivocate their political activity when IIT is high.

Finally, in Chapter 8, I conclude with a summary of this book's argument and findings, and I present some major implications of this study for the future of the global trade regime and for future research on the politics of international trade.

2

The Rise of Intra-Industry Trade in the Postwar Trading Regime

Since the contributions of Adam Smith and David Ricardo, international trade has been explained as a process by which countries specialize in the production of goods in which they have a comparative advantage and trade for the rest. The implication of specialization based on comparative advantage is that trade between different countries is primarily inter-industry in nature. Indeed, from the mid-nineteenth century up until World War I, the time period often referred to as the "first wave of globalization," international trade patterns were primarily driven by comparative advantage. As one economic historian describes it,

The United States exported heavily to Europe while importing tropical raw materials, like jute, sugar and coffee, from the less developed economies of the periphery. The Continental European nations, as a group, balanced imports of temperate and tropical foodstuffs and raw materials primarily by exporting manufactured goods to Britain. Britain, in turn, earned surpluses by selling manufactured goods to the periphery, on shipping and financial services, and from large overseas investment. (Harley, 1996, p. xii)

According to Harley, even the manufacturing trade between the United States, Britain, and the European Continent was inter-industry, with Britain exporting highly processed "old" manufactured goods such as textiles, clothing, ships, and railroad materials while the US and the Continent specialized in "new" industrial goods such as chemicals and steel. But trading patterns changed significantly after World War II with the onset of the "second wave" of globalization. At this time, two-way trade for goods within the same industrial category, also known as intra-industry trade (IIT), became a significant feature of the global economy, but especially for the developed countries. More than half of all global trade is now intra-industry (World Bank, 2009).

In this chapter, I introduce the concept of intra-industry trade with a view toward showing how it generates dramatically different political implications than classic, inter-industry trade. First, I define IIT and explain how it differs from inter-industry trade. I present descriptive statistics demonstrating its importance in the global economy, in aggregate and also at the country and sector level. Second, I discuss important issues related to operationalizing and measuring IIT. Third, I present the economic rationale for the rise of IIT in the postwar period, drawing on new trade theory, the economics literature that emerged to explain this phenomenon. Fourth, I discuss new–new trade theory and its contributions to understanding the distributional effects of IIT. Finally, I present an extended example of these effects using the case of trade liberalization between Canada, Mexico, and the US. These distributional effects have political implications, and understanding these political implications is the purpose of this book.

2.1 INTER- AND INTRA-INDUSTRY TRADE

The vast majority of political science work on the politics of international trade takes neoclassical trade theory as its starting point. According to the standard Ricardian model, comparative advantage drives international trade (Ricardo, 1817). Each country specializes in the production of the good it produces most efficiently (with the least labor) and it trades for the rest. In Ricardo's classic example using two countries and two commodities, Portugal specializes in and exports wine and England specializes in and exports cloth. Each country imports what the other produces. By specializing in what each does most efficiently and trading for the rest, countries maximize their efficiency and their welfare. The Heckscher-Ohlin model builds on Ricardo's formulation by introducing factor endowments as the basis of comparative advantage.[1] Because countries differ in terms of factor endowments, they will each be relatively better at producing different types of goods, depending on what is the abundant factor in each economy. Firms specialize to produce goods exploiting abundant factors, and countries trade for goods that are produced more efficiently in other countries with different mixes of factor endowments. Trade is based on comparative advantage and it occurs between countries with different factor endowments.

During the first wave of globalization, falling transport costs facilitated long-distance, comparative advantage-based trade for "essentials" (Indian tea for British machinery for American cotton, for example). As shown in Table 2.1, in 1910, 80% of Britain's exports were manufactures and only 22% of its imports were manufactures. In the same year in land-rich and labor-scarce Canada, by contrast, manufactures accounted for 56% of

[1] For Ricardo, the basis of comparative advantage lay in the amount of labor required to produce a good. His labor theory of value held that countries would specialize in the production of the goods that required the least amount of labor inputs relative to other goods.

TABLE 2.1 *Manufactures as a percentage of exports and imports, 1910 and 2019*

	Exports: 1910	Imports: 1910	Exports: 2019	Imports: 2019
United Kingdom	80.3	22.2	71.8	66.3
France	25.4	60.0	80.5	76.7
Germany	72.1	20.2	84.8	73.4
Italy	45.9	36.3	82.0	68.6
USA	35.2	37.8	59.1	77.8
Canada	11.3	56.1	47.9	77.3
Japan	49.6	37.2	86.6	58.9

Data source: UN Comtrade Historical Trade Data, 1900–1960 and World Bank World Development Indicators.

imports and only 11% of exports. Less industrialized nations (including many colonies) were important trading partners at this time, serving as sources of manufacturing inputs and receivers of manufacturing exports.

In the postwar period, trading patterns began to change significantly. The United States and Western Europe embarked on a trade liberalization project embodied multilaterally in the General Agreement on Tariffs and Trade (GATT) and regionally within the European Community. At the same time, technological developments allowed transport costs to fall dramatically, facilitating trade among neighbors for similar goods. North–North and two-way manufacturing trade took on a greater importance than in the first wave of globalization (Krugman, 2008). The countries of Europe, especially, began trading with each other to expand variety in types of beer, automotive parts, footwear, and furniture, as just a few examples. These similar goods typically had relatively minor differences driven by diverse consumer tastes. Today, countries trade heavily in different varieties of consumer goods such as mobile telephones produced by firms based in a variety of countries (Apple, Samsung, Nokia, Sony Ericsson, Motorola, and Huawei), computers (Apple, Dell, Sony, Toshiba, Lenovo, and Acer), and of course automobiles (General Motors, Volvo, Mercedes-Benz, Toyota, and Hyundai). As the World Bank puts it, "in the old trade theory and with high transport costs, countries trade only what they need to. In the new trade theory and with scale economies, a love of variety, and low transport costs, countries trade because they want to" (World Bank, 2009, p. 182).

This horizontal, two-way trade in different varieties of similar goods is one type of intra-industry trade. As defined by Krugman, intra-industry trade "consists of two-way international trade within an industry because firms in different countries will produce different differentiated products" (Krugman, 1990, p.30). In all of the OECD economies, trade has become increasingly intra-industry rather than inter-industry (OECD, 2002). Indeed, the developed economies are exceptional vis-à-vis the rest of the world for the high percentage of intra-industry trade in their trading profiles. In terms of the standard trade theories discussed above, the crucial distinction between intra-industry and inter-industry trade is that intra-industry trade occurs between countries with similar factor endowments, countries that Ricardo's model does not predict will have an economic basis for trade.

In addition to horizontal trade in similar but differentiated products, intra-industry trade also occurs for vertically differentiated products of varying levels of quality and price. For example, Italy produces a great deal of high quality, high-priced leather footwear for luxury markets and imports a great deal of lower quality, low-priced synthetic footwear for discount markets. The specialization in high quality leather goods represents Italy's comparative advantage: Italy has an abundance of skilled workers and capital to invest in cutting-edge machinery. Countries such as China that specialize in low-priced footwear have an abundance of lower-skilled workers that assemble less skill-intensive product varieties.

A third type of intra-industry trade is trade in intermediate goods. The rise in trade in intermediate goods used as inputs in production processes was another effect of the falling transport costs during the second wave of globalization. As trade costs fell, firms found it most efficient to specialize in the production of only a subset of inputs in a complete production process and trade for the rest. This is known as the vertical disintegration of production, and it resulted in production becoming increasingly internationalized in the latter half of the twentieth century. Production processes that were once concentrated from start to finish in high-income countries now take place across national borders within global value chains: Certain stages in the production process are outsourced to other countries, often based on comparative advantage. For example, although Boeing airplanes are "made in the USA", Chinese suppliers famously manufacture parts used in the production of every Boeing airplane. With low transport costs, trade becomes less costly and firms have an incentive to specialize in producing fewer goods in order to capture the benefits of economies of scale. Beyond economies of scale, firms as consumers benefit from access to differentiated varieties of intermediate goods. Thus, as transport costs fell in the twentieth century, there was a large increase in trade in intermediate goods relative to final goods. Although IIT and the development of global value chains are linked, they are independent processes: IIT can occur without global value chains and vice versa.

Intra-industry trade in both intermediate and final goods continues to increase. In a comprehensive study of intra-industry trade prepared for the World Bank, Brülhart (2008) found that by 2006, approximately 40% of global trade in intermediate goods was intra-industry, approximately 35% of global trade in final goods was intra-industry, up from about 12% for both types of goods in 1962. By contrast, in 2006, approximately 11% of trade in primary goods was intra-industry, up from approximately 4% in 1962 (Brülhart, 2008). Table 2.1 provides a snapshot of how dramatically trading patterns changed over the course of the twentieth century. We see that in the United Kingdom in 2019, manufactures accounted for 66% of imports (compared to 22% in 1910) and 72% of exports (compared to 80% in 1910). Not only are the advanced economies now importing manufactures as well as exporting them, they are also engaged in this two-way manufacturing trade with each other. In their analysis of historic trade flows, Baldwin and Martin found that 75.5% of European exports were destined for Europe or North America in 1910, but this number had risen to 83.4% by 1996 (Baldwin and Martin, 1999).

2.2 MEASURING INTRA-INDUSTRY TRADE

Before turning to a more detailed look at global patterns in intra-industry trade, I discuss important issues and debates the surrounding measurement of IIT, and I justify the theoretical and empirical rationales for the measurement choices made in this book. I describe the standard operationalization procedure in the literature and then discuss critical questions regarding the appropriate level of product aggregation, the distinction between horizontal and vertical intra-industry trade, and the role of intra-firm trade.

The Grubel-Lloyd Index

Grubel and Lloyd (1975) developed a measure of intra-industry trade at the commodity level that remains standard in the literature:

$$IIT_i = 1 - \frac{|X_i - M_i|}{(X_i + M_i)}, \tag{2.1}$$

where IIT_i is industry i's level of intra-industry trade, and X_i and M_i are measures of exports and imports of industry i, respectively.[2] This measure approaches one as an industry's exports and imports become more balanced, or more heavily IIT, and it reaches zero when there is no two-way trade in the given industry. An important point to bear in mind about this measurement is that it gives no information as to the import versus export composition of trade. In other words, a competitive industry that exports heavily and competes with a small number of imports may have the same level of IIT as a primarily domestic-oriented industry with few exports and heavy import competition. Both these industries would have low levels of IIT, although one is primarily an exporting industry (in other words, a comparative advantage industry) and the other is primarily an import-competing industry (a comparative disadvantage industry). Therefore, the measure truly captures IIT rather than revealed comparative advantage, and it may be important for researchers to include controls for an industry's level of import competition or revealed comparative

---

[2] Brülhart (2008) notes that the G-L index has achieved "near-universal acceptance."

advantage, an issue I will discuss further in Chapter 4. While the Grubel-Lloyd index measures IIT at the commodity level, it is possible to aggregate the measure across all commodities to create country-level or dyadic-level measures of IIT. In this book, unless otherwise noted, I use commodity-level measures of multilateral IIT which capture an industry's combined exports to all countries and imports from all countries. This is a theoretical decision, based on the assumption that firm and industry preferences about multilateral trade policy are driven by the extent of import competition and export orientation generally, rather than within dyads.[3]

Defining an "Industry"

When measuring intra-industry trade, how do we define an industry? Commodity-level trade data is disaggregated at various levels of precision, allowing researchers to choose how broadly or narrowly they define industries. This is a critical decision, as economists caution that measures of IIT vary dramatically depending on how finely disaggregated commodity-level trade data is (Brülhart, 2008; Grimwade, 1989). In order for an IIT measure to be valid, it must accurately measure trade in similar, substitutable products. There are risks to defining industries both too broadly and too narrowly. If industries are defined too broadly, the risk is that the IIT measure is actually capturing trade in different commodities (inter-industry trade). This would lead to a biased measure that overestimates the true extent of IIT. Conversely, when industries are defined too narrowly at a very fine level of disaggregation, there is a risk that differentiated products that are actually reasonable substitutes are misclassified as distinct products, resulting in bias that underestimates true levels of IIT.

It is helpful to examine how traded products are classified statistically. Statistical classification systems disaggregate traded products in a hierarchical structure moving from the broadest two-digit sector level to the most narrowly defined six-digit product level. To illustrate this, Table 2.2 shows how selected apparel items and motor vehicles are classified in the Harmonized Commodity Description and Coding System, maintained by the World Customs Organization.

Table 2.2 demonstrates some of the primary dilemmas confronting researchers deciding which level of aggregation is appropriate for their particular analyses. First, we see that some products defined at the six-digit level are indeed distinct products that are not substitutable, suggesting that the six-digit level is appropriate for accurately measuring intra-industry trade. For

---

[3] Of course, dyadic IIT would be more appropriate when analyzing firm preferences over bilateral trade agreements, and I consider this in Chapter 5's analysis of lobbying in the EU over bilateral and multilateral trade policies. See Thies and Peterson (2015) for a study using a dyadic measure of IIT between countries to capture the extent to which trade between two countries is intra- versus inter-industry trade.

TABLE 2.2 *Example of Harmonized System product classification, selected sectors*

HS code	Description
61	Apparel and clothing accessories; knitted or crocheted
61.01	Coats; men's or boy's; knitted or crocheted
61.01.20	Coats; men's or boy's, of cotton, knitted or crocheted
61.01.30	Coats; men's or boy's, of man-made fibers, knitted or crocheted
61.01.90	Coats; men's or boy's, of textile materials n.e.c. in heading no. 6101, knitted or crocheted
87	Vehicles, other than railway or tramway rolling stock, and parts and accessories thereof
87.03	Motor cars and other motor vehicles; principally designed for the transport of persons, including station wagons and racing cars
87.03.10	Vehicles; specially designed for travelling on snow, golf carts and similar vehicles
87.03.21	Vehicles; with only spark-ignition internal combustion reciprocating piston engine, cylinder capacity not over 1000cc
87.03.22	Vehicles; with only spark-ignition internal combustion reciprocating piston engine, cylinder capacity over 1000 but not over 1500cc
87.03.23	Vehicles; with only spark-ignition internal combustion reciprocating piston engine, cylinder capacity over 1500 but not over 3000cc
84	Nuclear reactors, boilers, machinery and mechanical appliances; parts thereof
84.50	Household and laundry-type washing machines
84.50.11	Household and laundry-type washing machines, fully automatic, (of a dry linen capacity not exceeding 10 kg)
84.50.12	Household and laundry-type washing machines, with built-in centrifugal drier, (not fully automatic), of a dry linen capacity not exceeding 10 kg
84.50.13	Household and laundry-type washing machines, not fully automatic, without built-in centrifugal drier, of a dry linen capacity not exceeding 10 kg
84.50.20	Household and laundry-type washing machines, with a dry linen capacity exceeding 10 kg

Note: Descriptions are paraphrased by the author.

example, vehicles for traveling on snow (HS 87.03.10) are indeed distinct from other types of motor vehicles. However, the vehicles defined in codes 87.03.21, 87.03.22, and 87.03.23 are differentiated by the size of their engine cylinder capacity. Arguably, these are in fact substitutable vehicles from a consumer's perspective, suggesting that separating them at the six-digit level is overly narrow and compromises the validity of the measure by categorizing trade as inter-industry that in fact may be more accurately considered intra-industry. Similarly, washing machines are coded at the four-digit level as HS 84.50. At the six-digit level, washing machines are differentiated by whether they have a built-in drier and whether they are fully or semi-automatic. Again, these products may reasonably be considered substitutable by the consumer, suggesting that the four-digit level of disaggregation better captures intra-industry trade in washing machines. Likewise, men's and boy's coats that are knitted or crocheted get their own four-digit category (HS 61.01). Arguably, even this level of disaggregation is too narrow, as categorizing clothing according to gender is a meaningless distinction for many consumers, not to mention that men's and boy's coats that are not knitted or crocheted get their own four-digit category, which also seems too narrow a distinction. At the six-digit level, men's and boy's coats are categorized according to whether they are made of cotton, man-made fibers, or other textile materials. Surely, these are substitutable goods from a consumer perspective. These dilemmas plague nearly every product category. Additionally, many products are fully disaggregated at the four-digit level, obviating the need for six-digit level disaggregation.

Brülhart (2008) offers one potential way out of this dilemma. He argues that researchers have over time begun to consider that substitutability in production, rather than consumption, is the appropriate criteria to apply. This approach would group goods according to the similarity of their input requirements, not their similarity to consumers. The justification for this approach is that IIT is driven by specialization to capture economies of scale, leading firms to specialize in fewer products and import other products that they nevertheless could theoretically produce themselves from a comparative advantage perspective. This is, in fact, the defining feature of IIT according to Krugman and others that developed new trade theory to explain the rise in IIT. Grouping goods according to production input requirements would suggest that a coarser level of disaggregation is appropriate. Brülhart notes that many empirical studies adopt the three- or four-digit level, depending upon the classification system, though he himself chose the Standard International Trade System (SITC) five-digit product level in his comprehensive analysis, in order to minimize the likelihood of grouping "substantially different activities" under the same industry heading.[4]

Thies and Peterson (2015) make a different argument, but one that reaches a similar conclusion. Emphasizing the importance of designing an IIT measure that is consistent with a given study's theoretical expectations, they define an industry as a group of goods that can be considered substitutable by consumers, even though these goods will not be identical. They justify this choice because their theory centers on the role of consumer demand for variety, rather than on firms' production choices. Using the SITC system, they make the case that goods categorized at the three-digit level would not be considered substitutable by consumers, but at the four-digit level they most often would. We see

---

4 The Harmonized System I use in the above example does not disaggregate at the three- or five-digit level, but other common classification systems do.

this dynamic in Table 2.2, where cars disaggregated at the HS four-digit level are in all likelihood considered reasonable substitutes by consumers, whereas at the six-digit level, they are disaggregated on the basis of rather minor differences in engine size. This means that in many cases, using the finest level of disaggregation treats goods that most consumers would consider substitutable as goods from different industries altogether, biasing the measurement toward underestimating levels of IIT. Thies and Peterson (2015) make another crucial point, similar to that made by Brülhart. Disaggregation to the product level (five or six digits) rather than the industry level (four digits) is more likely to classify intra-firm trade within global value chains as IIT (e.g., when a product is imported, value is added, and then re-exported while retaining the same product code), even though the internationalization of production in global value chains is driven by differences in factor endowments, and thus is more similar to classic, Heckscher-Ohlin trade than IIT. By using trade data disaggregated at the broader four-digit level instead, they argue that this better captures IIT reflecting consumer demand for product variety rather than trade that is actually driven by differences in factor endowments. Kono (2009), on the other hand, emphasizes that many products have high IIT scores even when classified at the six-digit level, implying that there is an indeed substantial product differentiation even at the six-digit level. He advocates the use of six-digit product data to avoid classifying inter-industry trade as intra-industry.

In the end, political scientists have approached this problem in different ways, often driven by pragmatic considerations as much as theoretical ones. Existing studies use three- to six-digit categories. In this book, I justify my choice of industry aggregation level with both analytical and practical considerations. This book's theoretical focus is on firm and industry lobbying over trade policy, rather than on consumers. Therefore, it is more important for me to capture the extent to which trade liberalization affects the competition firms face in both domestic and foreign markets. Because most firms make a variety of products that map onto multiple six-digit codings, the advantage of four-digit level data is that it is more likely to capture the competition firms will face from a variety of similar products that may nevertheless be categorized into separate six-digit categories due to relatively minor differences. In other words, grouping goods at a slightly broader level, along the lines Brülhart described, should allow me to best capture the extent to which firms are affected by competition by similar product varieties.

Additionally, I am interested in industry lobbying and the extent to which firms in an industry are able to overcome collective action problems to lobby together over trade policy. Since firms within an industry make a range of goods, not all of which are close substitutes (some members of the United States Footwear Manufacturers Association make work boots and others make running shoes), my measure should capture the extent of IIT in the broader industry and not simply in very specific product categories. An American manufacturer making steel-toed work boots faces stiff competition from imports and may urge the industry association to take a protectionist stance, while exporters of high-end, luxury shoes may push the association to take a more liberal stance. An industry-level focus requires a measure that captures the extent to which two-way trade affects the industry as a whole, suggesting that data disaggregated to the four-digit industry level is most appropriate for the present study. Practically speaking, the SITC four-digit data – employed by the United Nations Comtrade system – is the most widely available cross-nationally and over time (available from 1962 to the present), which is another advantage of using this system. In the end, I conduct several different empirical analyses in this book focused on different countries and different time periods. Data availability differs for each of these analyses, and I at times use different classification schemes, always at the four-digit industry level. I discuss data sources and availability for each analysis in Chapters 4–7. In Appendix A Figure A.1, I graph US multilateral IIT over time, as measured by the four classification systems used in different analyses in this book. While IIT levels vary somewhat across the different systems, changes in IIT track fairly closely across classification systems.

Horizontal versus Vertical Intra-Industry Trade

Another important theoretical issue is the distinction between horizontal and vertical intra-industry trade. As discussed above, horizontal IIT refers to two-way trade in different varieties of similar goods. While horizontal IIT results in the exchange of goods that are differentiated by variety, vertical IIT results in exchange of goods that are differentiated by price and quality. Horizontal IIT occurs primarily among countries with similar factor endowments, while vertical IIT is more common among countries with different factor endowments and thus different factor prices. Because of this, two-way trade in goods differentiated by price and quality (vertical IIT) can take on some of the characteristics of inter-industry trade driven by comparative advantage (Fontagné et al., 1998). However, vertical IIT will not cause the elimination of a relatively unproductive industry altogether. The presence of varieties, differentiated by cost and quality, means that vertical IIT may shrink a company's or industry's market share, but there will remain room in the export market for a range of varieties. Firms from a high-wage country can produce and export high quality, high-priced goods, while importing lower-quality, lower-priced goods that satisfy a certain segment of consumers. Still, vertical IIT generates distributional effects closer to those of inter-industry trade, benefiting some firms while being very costly to others.

This book is focused on intra-industry division among firms regarding trade policy preferences, particularly in developed economies, and how IIT changes the ability of firms within an industry to engage in collective action. Within industries, some firms will be more threatened by low-cost imported varieties than other firms will. Some firms will have an interest in easing access to export markets or to imported inputs, while others will not. In other words, firm heterogeneity means that there is the potential for political conflict stemming from both horizontal and vertical IIT, and from the simultaneous occurrence of both. For example, a firm that imports components for further processing and re-export (vertical IIT) is likely to support trade liberalization. This preference may conflict with a domestic-oriented firm in the same industry that will be harmed by more liberal trade policies and the presence of more foreign varieties (horizontal IIT). Disaggregating trade data to the four-digit industry level encompasses both horizontal and vertical IIT within an industry, while disaggregating to the six-digit level would better isolate vertical IIT while obscuring horizontal IIT among similar varieties (Thies and Peterson, 2015).

Intra-firm Trade

Intra-firm trade makes up a significant part of total global trade, facilitated by the spread of global value chains. Global data on intra-firm or related-party trade are not available, but UNCTAD estimates that a third of global exports are intra-firm transactions (UNCTAD, 2016). About half of all US trade with Canada and Mexico is intra-firm trade (Lakatos and Ohnsorge, 2017). Similarly, a report on EU–US trade found that in 2020, intra-firm exports made up 65% of EU plus UK exports to the US and 39% of US exports to the EU plus UK (Hamilton and Quinlan, 2022). The role of intra-firm trade is important theoretically, but it does not require special treatment in terms of operationalizing the IIT variable. Intra-firm trade spans the spectrum in terms of type of trade: It can be inter- or intra-industry in nature, consists of trade in intermediates or final goods, and takes the form of horizontal or vertical IIT. Most often, it consists of vertical IIT, wherein firms import intermediate inputs from foreign affiliates, add value, and re-export, all within the same product code (Peterson and Thies, 2012). Economists view the rise of global value chains as driven more by comparative advantage and differences in factor endowments, rather than the gains from increasing returns to scale and demand for variety, as is the case with IIT. Because the distributional effects of comparative advantage-based trade differ from those of IIT, it may be important to control for related-party trade where data availability allows, and I discuss this in more depth in Chapter 4.

2.3 SECTOR-LEVEL AND COUNTRY-LEVEL PATTERNS IN INTRA-INDUSTRY TRADE

To examine the empirical importance of IIT in global trade, I begin by constructing a dataset using data from the Atlas of Economic Complexity, which

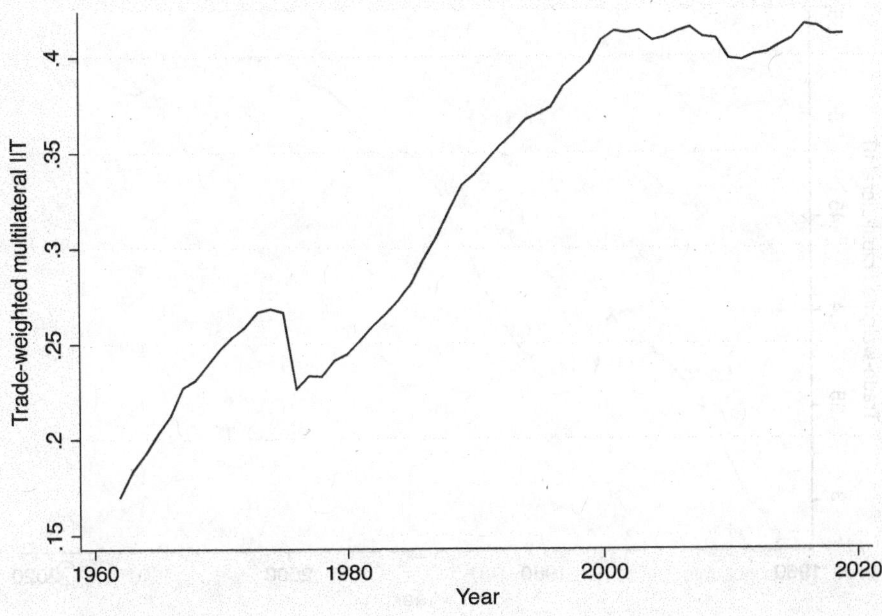

FIGURE 2.1 Global IIT as a proportion of total trade, 1962–2019, long coverage sample
Data source: Author's calculations based on data from the Atlas of Economic Complexity.

uses raw data from the United Nations Comtrade database.[5] Using import and export data measured in thousands of US dollars, I construct multilateral IIT measures for a sample of countries covering the period from 1962 to 2019. In order to maximize temporal coverage, I follow Brülhart (2008) and limit the sample to a "long-coverage" set of fifty-six countries with the most complete industry-level import and export data extending back to 1962, the first year of Comtrade's data. This minimizes the likelihood that changes in global IIT are driven by temporal variation in country-level data availability. I specify this list of countries in Appendix A. I construct the IIT measure using industry-level trade flow data disaggregated to the four-digit level, classified according to the SITC system, Revision 2. For each industry at each country-year in the sample, I calculate IIT using the Grubel-Lloyd measure described above. This long-coverage sample includes 2,475,472 observations of intra-industry trade for SITC four-digit industries within these fifty-six countries over the fifty-eight-year time period. There are 781 industries per country per year. To get a picture of the rise of intra-industry trade as a proportion of global trade

---

[5] The advantage of the Atlas trade data is that it has been cleaned, yielding trade flow estimates that are much more consistent and reliable.

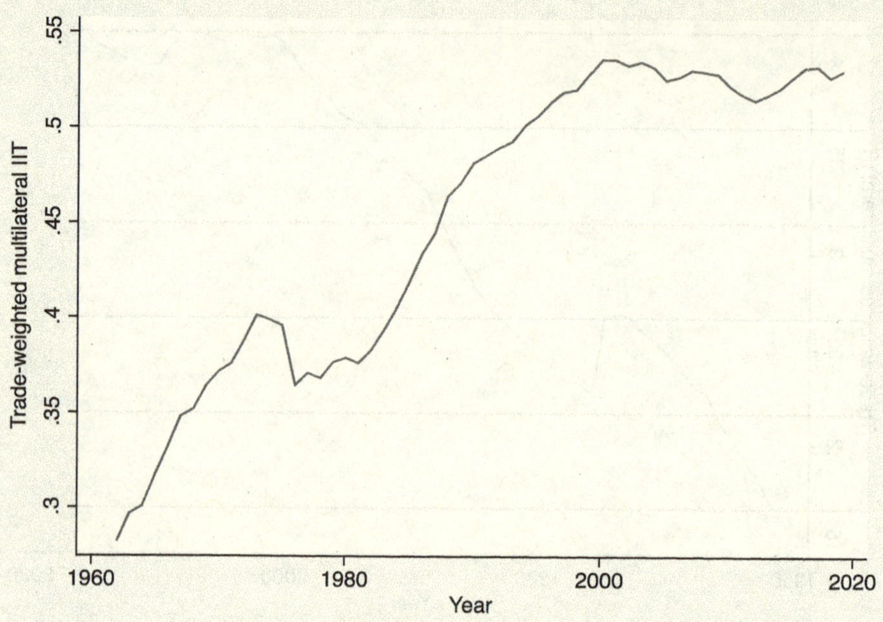

FIGURE 2.2 Global IIT as a proportion of total trade, 1962–2019, high-income countries
Data source: Author's calculations based on data from the Atlas of Economic Complexity.

in the postwar period, I created a country-level IIT measure for each country at each time period in the dataset. To do so, I took the weighted average of each industry's proportion of a country's total grade in a given year:

$$IIT_c = \sum_{i=1}^{n} IIT_i * \frac{(X_i + M_i)}{(X_c + M_c)}, \tag{2.2}$$

where IIT_c is country c's trade-weighted average level of IIT across all industries i, X_i and M_i are the values industry i's exports and imports, and X_c and M_c are the value of country c's total trade that year. Next, I aggregate the country-level measures by year to create a global measure of trade-weighted multilateral IIT. Figure 2.1 shows the proportion of global trade that was intra-industry over time.

We see that IIT has increased markedly over time, from around 17% of global trade in 1962 to over 40% in 2019, among the countries in the sample. Though IIT has grown dramatically in importance in the postwar period, it varies significantly at the country level. IIT has increased between countries in all income groups, but it occurs at the highest levels among high-income countries. Figure 2.2 shows how IIT has changed in high-income countries (as

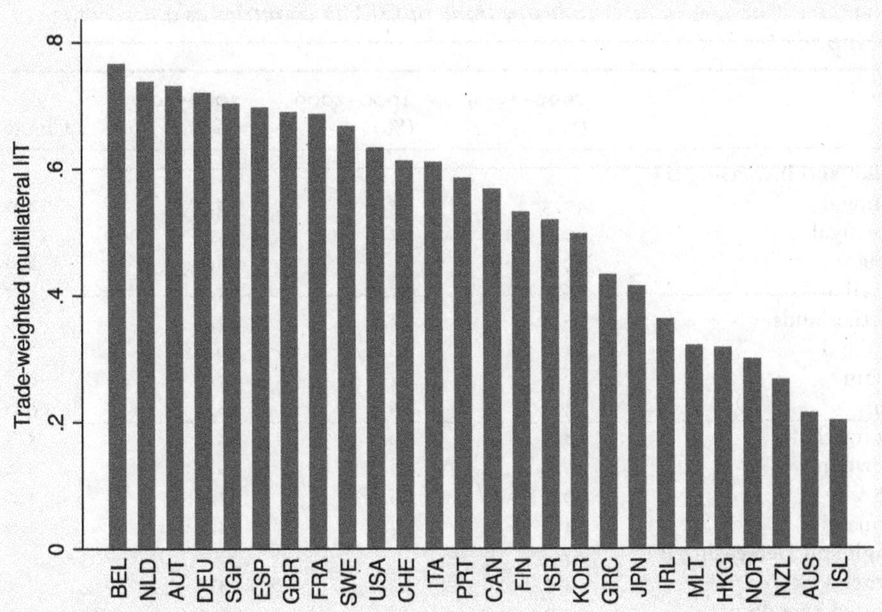

FIGURE 2.3 IIT as a proportion of total trade, high-income countries, 2019
Data source: Author's calculations based on data from the Atlas of Economic Complexity.

defined by the World Bank) over the same time period. Here we see that trade-weighted IIT makes up an even higher proportion of rich countries' trade: IIT has increased in this group from around 28% of total trade in 1962 to nearly 53% of total trade.

Even among high-income countries, however, there is substantial variation in trading structure. Figure 2.3 shows trade-weighted IIT for high-income countries in 2019. Among the major advanced economies, South Korea and Japan are notable for their relatively low levels of intra-industry trade, although IIT is on the rise in both countries. Intra-industry trade is low in these countries for a few reasons. First, heavy export orientation (and import restrictions, especially in South Korea) kept imports low relative to exports. Second, much of Japanese manufacturing has traditionally been vertically integrated, minimizing the importation of production inputs. As import restrictions are lifted and Japanese firms increasingly source from affiliates throughout Asia, intra-industry trade is increasing in both these countries.

In general, countries that are highly dependent on trade also tend to have very high levels of intra-industry trade, which we see reflected in the 2019 data presented in Figure 2.3. Highly open, "supertrading" economies such as Belgium, the Netherlands and Austria engage heavily in two-way trade. Table 2.3

TABLE 2.3 *Changes in intra-industry trade in OECD countries as a percentage of total trade*

	1990–1999 (%)	2000–2009 (%)	2010–2019 (%)	Change
High and Increasing IIT				
Hungary	47.3	57.7	65.3	18.0
Portugal	40.6	52.5	55.7	15.1
Belgium	69.5	77.2	78.5	8.9
Sweden	56.8	61.6	65.5	8.7
Netherlands	66.7	73.8	74.6	7.9
Finland	43.2	46.4	50.7	7.5
Spain	59.3	64.6	65.7	6.3
Italy	53.0	56.3	58.9	6.0
Switzerland	58.1	60.7	63.9	5.8
Germany	65.3	68.7	69.6	4.2
USA	60.2	58.2	61.4	1.2
Canada	54.7	59.0	55.7	1.0
High and Decreasing IIT				
Israel	54.2	57.8	53.1	−1.1
United Kingdom	71.9	70.8	69.3	−2.7
France	71.2	71.9	68.3	−3.0
Low and Increasing IIT				
Turkey	26.8	37.3	43.6	16.8
Greece	30.9	34.1	41.0	10.2
Japan	29.9	36.8	38.6	8.7
Korea	40.8	45.1	47.1	6.3
Iceland	10.8	17.3	16.6	5.7
Mexico	48.7	51.0	49.9	1.2
Chile	13.8	17.4	14.9	1.2
New Zealand	27.9	32.3	28.9	1.0
Low and Decreasing IIT				
Norway	33.4	29.2	29.1	−4.3
Australia	29.0	33.5	24.6	−4.4
Ireland	49.6	41.8	39.3	−10.5

Data source: Author's calculations based on data from Atlas of Economic Complexity. Countries are classified as having "high" or "low" IIT according to whether trade-weighted IIT is above or below 50% of total trade in the most recent time period (2010–2019), and "increasing" or "decreasing" according to change in IIT between the earliest and latest time periods.

shows changes in levels of intra-industry trade for individual OECD countries since 1990. The countries in Table 2.3 with low and stable intra-industry trade tend to be those that are least reliant on manufacturing exports and most reliant on exporting agricultural and marine products (Australia, New Zealand, Iceland) as well as oil (Norway) and other raw materials (Iceland).

TABLE 2.4 *IIT among high-income economies, top ten traded goods by volume,* *2018*

SITC code	Industry description	IIT
7810	Passenger motor cars	.602
5417	Medicaments	.799
3340	Refined petroleum products	.996
3330	Crude petroleum oils, and crude oils obtained from bituminous minerals	.920
5416	Glycosides, glands, antisera, vaccines, and similar products	.904
7849	Motor vehicle parts	.925
7764	Electronic microcircuits	.454
9710	Gold, non–monetary	.817
5156	Heterocyclic compounds, nucleic acids	.858
7643	Television, radio-broadcasting, radiotelegraphic transmitters, and receivers	.825

Data source: Atlas of Economic Complexity. Calculations by the author based on multilateral industry-level trade among high-income countries, trade-weighted.

In terms of variation across industries, intra-industry trade tends to be highest for manufactured goods, as these goods tend to be more differentiable than primary goods or raw materials. Among manufactured goods, those with the highest IIT are the more sophisticated manufactured products such as transport equipment, chemicals, and machinery, although this varies by country. More complex manufactured goods are not only more differentiable, but they also may be most subject to economies of scale in production (leading firms to specialize in fewer products) as well as vertically disintegrated production across countries. All these factors increase the likelihood of two-way trade within an industry. Table 2.4 shows the level of IIT of the top ten traded goods by volume (defined at the four-digit SITC level) among high-income economies in 2018.

In sum, a fundamental difference between the first and second waves of globalization is that in the first wave, countries traded with dissimilar countries for dissimilar goods, and in the second wave, they began trading with similar countries for similar goods. In other words, in the first wave they traded for things they could not produce efficiently (or at all) according to factor endowments and comparative advantage, and in the second wave, they also trade for things that they could theoretically produce themselves, sometimes quite efficiently. Trade between countries with similar factor endowments and similar levels of development is now part and parcel of international trade. The World Bank calls intra-industry trade "perhaps the most important economic development since World War II" (World Bank, 2009, p. 171), but until the 1980s, as Krugman (2008) observes, existing trade theories could not explain this "new" trade. In the early 1980s, economists set about developing new theories to understand the economic rationale for trade in similar goods.

2.4 NEW TRADE THEORY AND THE LOGIC OF INTRA-INDUSTRY TRADE

The economists that pioneered new trade theory, such as Dixit and Norman (1980); Helpman (1981) and Krugman (1981) all argue that the primary economic basis for trade between similar countries is increasing returns to scale and consumer demand for product variety.[6] These two phenomena are related in that both derive from product differentiation, but they are different in that increasing returns to scale is a producer-driven cause of intra-industry trade, while demand for a variety of differentiated products is consumer-driven. I explain how each generates intra-industry trade in turn.

First, when products are similar but differentiated, firms have some control over pricing, and market structure becomes that of monopolistic competition. Under monopolistic competition with differentiated products, it is assumed that firms enjoy increasing returns to scale. When there are increasing returns to scale (IRS), producers have an incentive to specialize in their particular product variety and increase output of that product. Increasing returns to scale is a property whereby an expansion of input use raises output more than proportionately, and IRS usually result from production that has high fixed costs (pharmaceuticals, jet airliners). These are typically development costs, or setup costs of production lines. The high fixed costs associated with developing a new product line cause firms to specialize in a subset of products rather than produce a full range of product varieties within an industry. Firms specialize and then seek increasing returns to scale by producing for an international market. Exports of differentiated, manufactured goods with IRS properties often go to countries whose firms produce similar goods, because as firms specialize, each country is limited in the types of products available. There is likely to be a large market for additional product variety, as well as for intermediate good inputs.

Consider an example from a classic IRS industry, motor vehicles. When trade in automobiles was liberalized between Canada and the US through the 1965 US–Canada Auto Pact, one of the first moves by Canadian producers was to rationalize plants and cut the number of automobile models they produced in half. By specializing in fewer automobile models, but maintaining output, Canadian manufacturers were able to capture increasing returns to scale and better compete with larger, more efficient US manufacturers. Another example is Boeing, which increasingly outsources the manufacture of aircraft parts to China, even though final assembly and additional part manufacture remains in

---

[6] Paul Krugman received the Nobel Prize in Economics in 2008 for his pioneering contributions to the "new trade theory."

TABLE 2.5 *Scale economies in manufacturing industries*

Large economies of scale	Petroleum
	Coal products
	Pharmaceuticals
	Motor vehicles and machinery
	Electronic components
	Computer and office equipment
Medium economies of scale	Electric machinery
	Engines and turbines
	Tires and inner tubes
	Household appliances
	Petroleum refineries
Small economies of scale or constant returns to scale	Instruments
	Nonelectric machinery
	Apparel
	Footwear
	Textiles

Data source: Antweiler and Trefler (2002) and Chase (2009).

the US. By specializing in the production of fewer intermediate parts and trading for the rest, Boeing captures increasing returns to scale. Table 2.5 provides some examples of industries with various levels of returns to scale.

Intra-industry trade between the US and Canada in the first example, and the US and China in the second example, is a result of firm-driven moves to specialize and enhance productivity. In this way, scale economies are a source of specialization, independent of factor endowments or comparative advantage, which induces countries to trade (Helpman, 2011; Krugman, 1990). Firms seek trade liberalization in order to capture increasing returns through the expansion of the market (Dixit and Norman, 1980). This model contrasts with classic trade theory, which assumes constant returns to scale when trading homogeneous goods. With identical goods and constant returns, identical countries (in terms of factors or technologies) have no incentive to trade with each other. With increasing returns and differentiated products, producers have an incentive to specialize and expand production in order to export overseas.[7]

A second, though related, source of intra-industry trade is consumer demand for variety. As discussed above, the variety of products available in

[7] The only incentive to trade, under the classic trade theories, is to capture gains due to relative factor price differences in countries with different factor endowments. Firms reap productivity gains from specializing according to comparative advantage; specializing in production of goods that use abundant factors intensively produces enough cost-saving gains for firms to induce them to specialize and export surplus production.

one industry in a country will be limited by the gains firms can achieve by creating economies of scale in a smaller set of products. This country then has a consumer-driven incentive to trade for different goods in the same industry. For example, pharmaceutical companies invest heavily in the production of certain drugs and cannot produce a full range of drugs. Heavy investment in a subset of drugs leads to intra-industry trade with other countries whose pharmaceutical firms produce another subset of drugs. In order for consumers in one country to have access to a full range of pharmaceuticals, countries must engage in intra-industry trade with other pharmaceutical-producing countries. Thus, IIT is also driven by consumer preferences for a variety of products within the same industry (Helpman, 2011). In a globalized economy, manufacturers seek to differentiate their products not only from those produced by other domestic manufacturers, but from goods produced by manufacturers around the world. As a result, in each country there is a limited product variety but there is demand for all the different brands produced in the world economy. With greater product variety, prices fall as well, an added consumer benefit of trade in similar goods.

As Helpman and Krugman (1985) show, if all countries produced homogeneous products, then intra-industry trade would be zero and trade volumes would be better explained by differences in factor endowments. When there are differentiated products, however, intra-industry trade increases. As factor similarity across countries increases, intra-industry trade will increase at the expense of trade in homogeneous products. In the OECD countries, where the capital–labor ratio is similar relative to other countries, intra-industry trade of differentiated products should be higher, and the data confirm this. Helpman (1987) sampled fourteen OECD countries and found that the share of intra-industry trade was larger in time periods when factor endowments were more similar. He argues, "differences in factor proportions are less important and intra-industry specialization is more important for trade between rich countries" (Helpman, 2011, p.87).

Another feature of intra-industry trade is that, as Krugman noted, the direction of trade is arbitrary when economies of scale are the source of trade. However, an effect of increasing returns to scale is that the country that happens to produce the larger volume of a good becomes an exporter. No country needs special characteristics to gain a comparative advantage in an increasing returns sector (Helpman, 2011), yet Krugman argues that there may be such thing as a "home-market effect" that affects the direction of trade. The "home-market effect" means that countries will export goods for which they have a large domestic market (Krugman, 2008). Firms will disproportionately locate production for export in countries with greater volume of demand for those products to minimize trade and transport costs. If there are trade impediments and/or transport costs, it is more cost-effective for firms to locate production in the larger market.

In sum, increasing returns to scale, consumer love of variety, and lower prices under expanded competition are all drivers of intra-industry trade. Economies of scale create barriers to entry, which means a limited array of goods will be produced in each country. Thus, trade will increase variety of differentiated but similar products. These products will come most often from countries with similar factor proportions and similar technologies. Intra-industry trade is also likely to be highest among high-income countries that manufacture differentiated products, while it is likely to be lowest among low-income countries that export homogeneous goods. Finally, it is important to emphasize that models of intra-industry trade are complementary to classic trade models, rather than competing.[8] Comparative advantage explains inter-industry specialization and inter-industry trade: It explains why Germany specializes in high-tech manufactures while Argentina specializes in beef production, and it explains why these countries trade with each other for these goods. Increasing returns to scale, however, explain intra-industry specialization: They explain why German firms specialize in a subset of manufactures (luxury sedans, for example) and seek to export these products. Consumers in countries whose firms make a similarly limited range of products will demand access to additional foreign varieties. In short, new trade theories explain trade between similar countries, while classic trade theories explain trade between different countries.

2.5 NEW-NEW TRADE THEORY AND THE DISTRIBUTIONAL EFFECTS OF INTRA-INDUSTRY TRADE

The development of new trade models to explain the rise of intra-industry trade in the postwar period was a major, Nobel-prize winning advancement in economics, but why does it matter to the political scientist? Krugman argues that intra-industry trade is politically interesting because it is, in his words, "surprisingly non-disruptive" relative to endowments-based trade (Krugman, 2008, p. 339), a conclusion reached by many of the economists who pioneered the new trade theory. Yet a new generation of scholars working within new-new trade theory (NNTT) has located where disruptions do indeed lie. In this section, I discuss the contributions of NNTT to our understanding of the distributional effects of IIT. All of this matters to the political economist because if IIT generates different distributional effects than classic, inter-industry trade, then political economists need to update our models of the politics of trade, the vast majority of which are based on classic trade models.

In the political economy literature, the two leading models of the income effects of trade, the Stolper-Samuelson and Ricardo-Viner theorems, are derived from endowments-based trade models. The redistributive effects of endowments-based trade are clear: The owners of abundant factors gain

---

[8] This was formally modeled by Helpman and Krugman (1985).

as trade expands, while the owners of scarce factors suffer income losses. When factor mobility is high, the Stolper-Samuelson theorem predicts that trade returns will accrue across classes: Classes that own the abundant factor (whether landowners, industrialists, or workers) will enjoy higher returns, while classes that own the scarce factor will suffer income losses. When factor mobility is low and one or more factors is "specific" to an industry, the Ricardo-Viner theorem predicts returns from trade will accrue to sectors that use the abundant factor intensively while sectors that use scarce factors intensively will suffer losses.

A primary argument from early contributions to new trade theory is that the economic adjustment costs of intra-industry trade are lower than inter-industry, endowments-based trade.[9] The argument is that IIT is generally welfare-enhancing and less redistributive within the economy, as it provides greater product variety and lower prices to consumers and allows firms market access both at home and abroad. The benefits to consumers are clear, but workers and industry face lower adjustment costs with intra-industry trade for one key reason: This trade most often takes place between countries with similar factor endowments and similar skills and technology profiles. Similarity between trading countries is key. If trade is not based on factor scarcity and abundance, it does not result in decreasing demand for scarce factors and heightened demand for abundant factors. When two trading countries are similar, scarce factors are scarce in both countries, and trade liberalization won't cause declining demand for this factor and demise of industries that use scarce factors intensively.[10] Even if the scarce factor does incur losses via trade liberalization, Bernard et al. (2007b) show that this decline will be less than in a Stolper-Samuelson setting. Part of the reason for this is that both scarce and abundant factors will be better off due to the gains from a wider variety of goods (Krugman, 1981).

As countries become less similar in terms of factor endowments, product differentiation must increase if intra-industry trade is to have minimal adjustment costs: If products are identical (or close to identical), then consumers will prefer goods from the country where production is relatively cheaper. But when goods are sufficiently differentiated, even less efficient firms can survive because consumers love variety, and some consumers will be willing to pay slightly more for their favorite variety of product. In short, the crucial difference between intra-industry and inter-industry trade is that because intra-industry trade typically occurs between countries with similar endowments, it does not redistribute wealth or resources away from entire sectors. Thus, its

---

[9] This argument dates back to Balassa's seminal study of trade liberalization within the European Community (Balassa, 1966).

[10] Under inter-industry trade, resources are redistributed from scarce factors to abundant factors (or from industries using scarce factors to industries using abundant factors) as trade liberalization makes scarce factors less competitive.

adjustment effects, at least at the industry level, are less severe than those of inter-industry trade.

The rise in IIT among OECD countries in recent decades has often been cited as a major factor in the smoothness of market liberalization among these countries in the postwar period (notably, in Krugman, 1981; Lipson, 1982). It has also been cited as an explanation for why trade liberalization with Japan has been so much more controversial in the US than trade liberalization with other OECD states (Gawande and Hansen, 1999). US trade with Japan is primarily inter-industry, while US trade with other wealthy countries, such as Canada, is much more intra-industry. For example, the US receives about the same amount of automobile imports from Canada ($38 billion) as from Japan ($39 billion), but the US exports many more cars to Canada ($14 billion) than it does to Japan ($1 billion).[11]

Greater similarity between the US and Canada might also explain the ease of negotiating the US–Canada Free Trade Agreement, while the significant factor differences between the US and Mexico contributed to the highly contentious negotiations to conclude the North American Free Trade Agreement. The controversies surrounding NAFTA were revived under the administration of President Donald Trump, who made renegotiation of NAFTA a centerpiece of his campaign and focused his criticisms on NAFTA's effect on offshoring of US manufacturing jobs, primarily to Mexico. The political difficulty liberalizing North–South trade, as evidenced not only by conflicts over NAFTA but also in multilateral negotiations such as the World Trade Organization's failed Doha Round, is a key corollary to claims about IIT. Because North–South trade is predominately inter-industry and endowments-based, this trade should be more politically difficult to liberalize, and this appears to have been largely the case in the postwar era.

While the earlier wave of new trade theory emphasized the harmonious effects of intra-industry trade, this has been challenged by recent literature with access to newer firm level data. Scholars working within new-new trade theory argue that there are real losers of trade in similar products, and these losers are individual firms. While IIT does not reallocate resources away from an entire industry, it does reallocate resources away from less productive to more productive firms within a given industry (Melitz, 2003). Assuming that trade liberalization is reciprocated by trading partners, IIT is likely to benefit the most productive firms that can compete successfully both in export markets and in the newly liberalized domestic market, while less productive firms are unlikely to export and also face intensified pressure from imports. Without trade protection, many inefficient firms are forced to exit. Though political economists frequently speak of "export sectors," NNTT emphasizes the fact that within these sectors, only a small percentage of firms actually export (Bernard et al., 2003; Mayer and Ottaviano, 2008; Melitz, 2003). The

---

[11] 2019 trade data from UN Comtrade.

TABLE 2.6 *Summary comparison of classic versus new trade theories*

	Endowments-based trade/classic trade theory	Intra-industry trade/NNTT
Economic basis for trade	Comparative advantage Differences in factor endowments	Increasing returns Economies of scale Product differentiation
Explanation for specialization	To take advantage of differences in relative factor endowments	To take advantage of economies of scale
Direction of trade	Determined by endowments	Indeterminate or based on size of home market
Production for export	Determined by endowments	Goods for which countries have large domestic markets IRS industries
Effects of trade on income	Scarce factors lose Industries using scarce factor intensively lose	Income-distribution effects out-weighed by gains from the larger market Less productive firms lose
Effects of trade on scarce factors	Relatively worse off	Gains from trade
Market structure	Competitive	Imperfect competition

majority of firms are small, non-exporting, and less productive. IIT places considerable pressure on these firms. Greater exposure to trade forces smaller firms to adjust or exit, and it decreases the number of domestic firms within an industry, while raising the overall productivity of the industry by reallocating resources toward the more productive firms (Melitz, 2003).

Later researchers have extended this model, known as the Melitz model, to incorporate trade in intermediate goods, which is a significant portion of intra-industry trade. Kasahara and Lapham (2013) demonstrate that firms face significant entry costs to importing as well as exporting. As a result, only the most productive firms will self-select into importing intermediate goods, and they reap productivity gains as a result. Thus, importing intermediate goods has similar intra-industry effects as exporting: It reallocates resources, profits, and market share away from less productive firms and toward the most productive firms. I summarize key differences between classic and new trade theories and the logics of inter- versus intra-industry trade in Table 2.6.

Far from being harmonious, then, intra-industry trade has winners and losers. To find these winners and losers, we must look within industries at the individual firm level, something the older trade models did not do (and were unable to do without firm-level data, which has only become available in recent years). There are significant adjustment costs associated with intra-industry trade as less productive firms suffer losses of profit and market share, with important implications for trade politics. First, intra-industry reallocations toward exporters mean significant short-term losses for the large number of workers in domestically oriented firms. Second, intra-industry trade contributes to higher overall wages, but also higher wage inequality (Beaulieu et al., 2011; Redding, 2011). Larger firms tend to pay higher wages, as do exporting firms. Thus, trade-generated reallocation of resources to the most productive firms in an industry raises wages, but only in these leading firms. By contrast, liberalization lowers wages at domestic-oriented firms or firms which are "marginal globalizers" (Amiti and Davis, 2012). However, others argue that the reduced prices for consumer goods may be enough to raise the real wage of workers in less productive, non-exporting firms as well (Bernard et al., 2007b).

An Example: Trade liberalization between Canada, Mexico, and the United States

Trefler (2004)'s study of the effects of the Canadian–US Free Trade Agreement (CUSFTA) provides strong empirical evidence in support of theoretical claims about the firm-level effects of intra-industry trade. His findings are even more interesting when considered alongside effects of subsequent trade liberalization between the US and Mexico under NAFTA. Canada and the US implemented reciprocal tariff reductions in manufacturing industries in 1989, under CUSFTA. Debate about the FTA was heated, especially in Canada, and the conflict was between domestic-oriented firms and their workers, who expected short-term losses, and export-oriented firms that expected to reap short- and long-term gains. These expectations were borne out in reality. Trefler finds that Canadian manufacturing industries that lowered tariffs under the FTA suffered 100,000 short-term job losses. This represented 5 percent of manufacturing employment. In the most impacted import-competing sectors, up to 12 percent of jobs were lost. However, the FTA led to major productivity gains for Canadian manufacturing. In the most export-oriented sectors, labor productivity rose by 14 percent at the plant level in the seven years following the implementation of the FTA. In the most import-competing sectors (many of which are also export-oriented), labor productivity at the plant level rose by 15 percent. At least half of these productivity gains, Trefler argues, were due to intra-industry resource reallocation as low-productivity firms exited or contracted their employment. Over time, there have been no long-run job losses in Canadian manufacturing resulting from CUSFTA. Canadian manufacturing has expanded by 6 percent as a whole and real wages rose 3 percent in the next seven years, both at the industry and plant level. Trefler's results, demonstrating the way that trade liberalization between two countries with high levels of intra-industry trade results in both overall welfare gains combined with short-term losses for less productive firms and workers, are consistent with the expectations of the new trade models based on monopolistic competition and heterogeneous firms.

US manufacturing industries, which generally enjoyed higher productivity than their Canadian counterparts pre-CUSFTA due to the fact that they produced for a much larger domestic market, were across the board supportive of trade liberalization with Canada. However, in less differentiated products that use natural resources intensively, US industries were more opposed to liberalization. US timber and lumber producers were the most active lobbyists against CUSFTA (Chase, 2009).

Comparing the effects of trade liberalization with Mexico is instructive. As Chase (2009) argues, although intra-firm trade between US firms and their affiliates in both Canada and Mexico was significant, the firm restructuring induced by NAFTA was different in Canada than in Mexico. In Canada, US affiliate firms rationalized production and specialized in a narrower range of export-oriented products in order to capture economies of scale. In Mexico, firms also specialized, not to capture economies of scale, but to take advantage of the labor cost differences between the US and Mexico. Mexican *maquiladoras* specialized in labor-intensive manufacturing processes with few economies of scale, in order to exploit the much lower Mexican wages. Trade between the US and Mexico was primarily endowments-based, while between Canada and the US, trade occurred to take advantage of scale economies. These patterns of specialization had different effects on workers. The restructuring of Canadian firms to produce higher volumes of fewer product lines had short-term plant-level effects on workers, but no long-term job losses, but Mexican specialization in low-wage, labor-intensive processes has had significant negative effects on low-skilled US workers in labor-intensive industries, such as apparel and leather goods. The US has lost over four million manufacturing jobs since 1994, and while it is very difficult to estimate the proportion of those jobs that were lost specifically as a result of trade liberalization under NAFTA, the Economic Policy Institute estimates that by 2010, approximately 682,900 US jobs had been lost due to trade with Mexico (Scott, 2011).[12]

As might be expected, most of the US lobbying against NAFTA came from labor-intensive employers and unions representing their workers, as well as agriculture (Chase, 2009, p. 212). They feared losses in profits and market share to Mexican firms with much lower labor costs and their fears seem to have been realized. For example, US apparel industry exports to Mexico were almost $1.18 billion in 1994; in 2019, US apparel exports to Mexico were valued at $916 million. During this time, Mexican apparel exports to

---

[12] It is highly debated among economists (as well as politicians) how much of the decline of US manufacturing is directly attributable to NAFTA and trade with Mexico, as it is extremely difficult to isolate the effects of this trade from the other domestic and international variables that affect employment.

the US nearly doubled from \$1.8 billion in 1994 to \$3.3 billion in 2019.[13] Thus, trade that was fairly balanced on the eve of NAFTA, when US apparel industries enjoyed trade protection, has now become much more inter-industry post-liberalization, in line with Stolper-Samuelson predictions about the effects of trade on scarce factors. Though the industry had been in decline prior to NAFTA, employment has dropped precipitously every year since 1994. Employment in the US apparel sector plummeted from approximately 832,000 jobs in 1994 to 106,000 in 2019.[14]

In short, the effects of trade between countries with similar endowments are significantly different from trade between countries with different endowment profiles. In terms of trade with the US, specialization in Canada to capture increasing returns to scale had a net positive effect on Canadian manufacturing industries, despite trade's short-term costs for less productive firms and their workers. US manufacturing industries were largely supportive or "indifferent" about the passage of CUSFTA, while they were deeply divided over the extension of the FTA to Mexico through NAFTA (Chase, 2009), concerned about the industry-level effects of large differences in labor costs across the two countries.

2.6 CONCLUSION

To conclude, this chapter has provided an overview of intra-industry trade in the postwar trade regime. Economists have developed increasingly sophisticated theoretical models to explain this "new" trade that has grown in importance in the postwar period, not only among high-income economies but increasingly among countries at other levels of development as well. Though it is outside the scope of this study, the rise of intra-industry trade in differentiated products has important implications for the future of developing countries and their involvement in international trade. The World Bank contends that "scale economies in production and transport will make it more difficult, not easier, for developing countries to enter these highly competitive markets" (World Bank, 2009, p. 172). In this book, however, I am interested in the domestic political effects of intra-industry trade in the countries most subject to it, the advanced industrialized democracies. Having established intra-industry trade's theoretical basis and its expected distributional effects, by reference to the economics literature on the subject, I now present a model of the political economy of intra-industry trade.

---

[13] Data from United States Census Bureau's US export and import merchandise trade statistics.
[14] Data from US Bureau of Labor Statistics.

The Domestic Politics of Intra-Industry Trade: A Theoretical Model

Why are some trade agreements so much more controversial than others? Why do firms sometimes mobilize for collective action over trade policy but other times lobby alone? What explains this variation in the domestic politics of trade? In this chapter, I argue that shifting the nature of trade away from endowments-based trade to intra-industry trade changes the structure of preferences over trade policy and the way that actors mobilize politically in order to influence trade policy. Intra-industry trade reallocates resources *within* industries, rather than *across* industries, undermining consensus within industries over trade policy and changing the calculus for actors considering whether to mobilize politically and lobby over trade. If collective action is more difficult to achieve, individual firms are more likely to lobby alone. However, not all firms are equally likely to lobby. As the lobbying landscape changes, policymakers are faced with different incentives, and trade policy outcomes change as well. While political economists over the last decade have increasingly begun to take the rise of IIT seriously, neoclassical assumptions still dominate the political economy literature on international trade. This chapter draws on the economics of IIT and new–new trade theories in particular to present the first systematic theory of the effect of intra-industry trade on the domestic politics of trade. The primary focus of this book is on lobbying by firms and industry associations, though IIT changes the preferences and political strategies of national labor unions as well, as I discuss later in this chapter, as well as in Chapter 7.

Throughout the book, I analyze trade in manufactured goods rather than services, consistent with most of the trade politics literature. An empirical challenge related to analyzing trade in services is that cross-national, disaggregated data on trade in services is very limited. Theoretically, the economics of trade in services differs from that of goods trade in some key ways, which is likely to produce distinct political dynamics. For example, many service sectors use mostly non-tradeable inputs and are not involved in importing. Second, services often cannot be delivered remotely, meaning that foreign investment in services is much more frequently aimed at providing services in that location (e.g., transportation or insurance services) than is foreign direct investment in tradeable goods, which is often export-oriented. Third, developed economies are already highly open to service imports, so trade agreements do not have the same potential to reduce barriers to trade, increase import competition and reallocate an industry's profits.[1]

I present my theory of the domestic politics of IIT in three steps, focusing sequentially on preferences over trade, lobbying behavior, and finally, trade policy outcomes.

3.1 INTRA-INDUSTRY TRADE AND TRADE PREFERENCES

Understanding societal trade preferences is the first step in understanding the politics of trade. Based on the economic rationale and effects of intra-industry trade, presented in Chapter 2, we can generate expectations about how intra-industry trade affects preferences over trade openness. To do so, I begin with the following assumptions. First, I assume that firm owners prefer policies that maximize their firm's profits, and industry associations prefer policies that maximize the profits of their member firms. Second, I assume that liberalization is reciprocal. I assume that tariff rates, regulatory barriers to trade and other nontariff measures (NTMs) are negotiated in the context of bilateral or multilateral trade agreements, in which a reduction of trade barriers in country *a* is contingent upon a reduction of trade barriers in country *b*. Thus, in forming their preferences over trade, firms must weigh their expected gains from sales in foreign markets or from cheaper imported inputs to the losses they will incur from increased import competition at home. Finally, I assume that products are differentiated and trading countries are reasonably balanced in terms of competitiveness. These assumptions allow me to generate some specific expectations about the way that IIT affects societal trade preferences.

Classes and Industries

First, in a world of intra-industry trade among similar countries, trade preferences are formed at the firm level, not at the class or industry level. This is a stark departure from the predictions of the Stolper-Samuelson and Ricardo-Viner theorems, which assume inter-industry trade and predict that benefits from trade will accrue to entire factor classes or industries, depending on factor mobility. Rogowski draws on Stolper-Samuelson to argue that owners

---

[1] Political economy analyses of trade in services are sparse. For two thorough treatments, see Baccini et al. (2019) and Chase (2008).

of abundant factors in an economy will form a free-trade coalition against owners of scarce factors, who will ally in favor of protection (Rogowski, 1990). Factoral consensus is unlikely in today's advanced democracies as Ricardo-Viner effects are more likely to hold than Stolper-Samuelson effects. Asset specificity, or low factor mobility, is a characteristic of industries with high barriers to entry, such as pharmaceuticals or other technologically advanced manufacturing that requires industry-specific machinery or intensive research and development (Frieden, 1992, p. 22; Santarelli, 1991). These are features typical of the capital-intensive, high-tech manufacturing in which developed economies specialize.

Because IIT between similar countries does not reallocate resources across factors, broad, factor-owning classes such as labor unions are not likely to hold unified trade preferences in countries with high levels of intra-industry trade. Rather, the adjustment effects of IIT are borne by individual firms, and this undermines consensus not just among capital owners but among workers as well. Recent work applying NNTT to individual preferences over trade suggests that people's trade preferences differ depending on their skill level (the factoral level) but also according to their exposure to globalization at the *firm* level (Walter, 2017).

Moving from factor classes to sectors, as trade becomes increasingly intra-industry, industries will also be less likely to hold unified preferences. In this way my model departs from Ricardo-Viner as well, which expects that trade preferences are formed at the industry level when factor mobility is low, with comparative advantage industries preferring openness while comparative disadvantage industries prefer protection.[2] Trade liberalization in IIT industries may benefit industries as a whole, raising output and productivity, but because IIT occurs most frequently between countries with similar endowments, adjustment costs fall on individual firms rather than entire industries. Thus, depending on each firm's anticipated profits or losses from trade liberalization, firms within the same industry have different preferences over trade.

Ricardo-Viner also predicts that workers have industry-specific skills that tie their preferences to the fate of their industry. In the R-V framework, workers and firm owners across an industry will either jointly benefit from trade or suffer short-term and possibly significant losses. In my model, however, workers' fortunes are closely tied to the fortunes of their particular *employer* rather than their industry as a whole. In short, because IIT leads to an intra-industry reallocation of resources away from small firms and toward the large internationalized firms, trade liberalization creates winners and losers within industries. This means that trade preferences are formed at the firm level, not at the industry or factor level.

---

[2] Hiscox demonstrated this empirically (Hiscox, 2002b).

Internationalized Firms

We can make more precise claims about intra-industry trade's effects on preferences when we look within industries at firms. Specifically, exporting and importing firms in industries subject to IIT are likely to be winners from trade liberalization, while domestic-oriented firms are likely to be trade losers. When trade policy is made in the context of bilateral or multilateral free trade agreements, exporting firms will prefer liberalization and regulatory harmonization as a means of increasing their access to foreign markets and reducing their exporting costs (Betz, 2017; Gilligan, 1997a; Osgood, 2016, 2017; Plouffe, 2017). For most exporters, the increased import competition they face post-liberalization will be outweighed by the benefits they can achieve with lower trade costs in export markets. Thus, reciprocity-based trade policymaking is a key scope condition.[3] If trade liberalization was undertaken unilaterally, exporting firms would not benefit from increased access to foreign markets and would have less reason to support liberalization. Exporting firms are also likely to oppose unilaterally proposed measures of protection, such as anti-dumping safeguards, for fear of foreign retaliation.[4] Importing firms, however, benefit from lower-cost access to imports even if liberalization is not reciprocal. We know that firms in IIT industries are more likely to import intermediate goods than firms in low-IIT industries (Bernard et al., 2007a). This is because the industries most subject to IIT are industries with highly differentiated products and increasing returns to scale. While large firms across the board are more likely to be importers than smaller firms, large firms in IIT industries are the most likely to import, giving these firms an additional reason to prefer lower tariffs both domestically and in export markets. Domestic tariff cuts may help them reduce input costs, regardless of whether cuts are unilateral or reciprocal.

Though there may be certain conditions under which exporters and/or importers do not support trade liberalization, the economics of intra-industry trade, as discussed in Chapter 2, suggest that globally engaged firms in IIT industries are likely to support openness, as these industries tend to enjoy increasing returns to scale, products are differentiated, exporters are likely to import inputs, and trading partners often have similar endowments and levels of development. When products are sufficiently differentiated, some consumers will be willing to pay slightly higher prices for their preferred product variety, so firms with higher production costs can remain competitive both in export markets and domestically (this is the case for luxury goods, such as watches or luxury sedans).

---

[3] Osgood (2016) further refines the conditions for intra-industry division over trade policy, arguing that division is most severe when the countries party to trade liberalization are relatively equal in size and competitiveness.

[4] Jensen et al. (2015) find that this is true of firms engaged in foreign direct investment.

This discussion has focused on exporting and importing, but today's preferential trade agreements (PTAs) go well beyond market access issues. An industry's largest, exporting firms may also be engaged globally through foreign direct investment (FDI). A recent analysis finds that between 1997 and 2017, only 1% of US firms participated in foreign direct investment, but these firms account for 65% of US goods exports and 60% of US goods imports (Kamal et al., 2022). Firms participating in global supply chains will not only benefit from reduced tariffs and NTMs but also from the regulatory harmonization and investment protections that are included in these agreements.

Domestic-Oriented Firms

While internationalized firms generally stand to gain from trade liberalization in IIT industries, domestic-oriented firms expect trade losses. The threat of import competition to small- and medium-sized firms is not only due to the greater number of product varieties available to consumers. These imports are likely to be highly competitive and lower-priced, as only large, productive firms are able to enter foreign markets (Bernard et al., 2007a). Domestic-oriented firms might prefer trade openness if they source inputs from abroad, but these firms are not likely to import, as importing involves considerable entry costs. Like exporting, it is a rare firm behavior and typically only the biggest, most productive firms import intermediate goods (Kasahara and Lapham, 2013). Thus, non-exporting, non-importing firms are likely to prefer protection from foreign competitors.

Even in industries with high product differentiation, where goods are not perfectly substitutable, domestic-oriented firms can benefit from trade barriers protecting them from foreign varieties. There will be no foreign producer selling exactly the same product as any domestic producer, so protection against foreign varieties will benefit all domestic producers producing similar varieties. As exporting is a rare activity even in export sectors, there will be a significant number of these small- and medium-sized firms with preferences for protection. However, domestic-oriented firms suffer *less* from import competition in high-IIT industries than in low-IIT industries because of product differentiation. Some small firms will continue to find a market for their particular product varieties, even if these varieties are more expensive than imported varieties. Others will be able to adjust, adapting their product varieties to differentiate them from those of their competitors and maintain market share. At the same time, in the short term, import competition will exert pressure on non-exporters to contract wages and/or employment. These short-term pressures mean that both workers and owners in domestic-oriented firms may have a preference for trade protection.

Would we also expect internationalized and domestic-oriented firms to hold competing preferences when trade is more endowments-based? Classic trade

TABLE 3.1 *Inter- versus intra-industry trade and trade preferences*

	Protectionist preferences	Free trade preferences
Inter-industry trade	Scarce factors Import-competing industries	Abundant factors Exporting industries
Intra-industry trade	Domestic-oriented firms (management and workers)	Exporting firms (management and workers)

theory is explicit in expecting industries (or factor classes) to be united in their preferences. Though the Stolper-Samuelson and Ricardo-Viner models don't address firm heterogeneity, the firm-centric approach of NNTT would lead us to expect that in comparative advantage industries exporters will strongly prefer liberalization and domestic-oriented firms will be indifferent. Because of comparative advantage, no firm within the industry will be significantly threatened by foreign imports, which would be higher priced. On the other hand, in comparative disadvantage industries, the classic trade theories predict industry (or factoral) unity around protection.

The present model, which is based on NNTT and problematizes the political implications of intra-industry trade, represents an alternative to the Ricardo-Viner and Stolper-Samuelson models. When trade is primarily inter-industry in nature and occurs on the basis of comparative advantage, the R-V or S-S model should predominate, depending on factor mobility. When trade is primarily intra-industry in nature and occurs on the basis of increasing returns and differentiated products, the present model should apply. Table 3.1 presents the likely structure of trade preferences when trade is primarily inter- versus intra-industry in its composition.

3.2 A GENERAL MODEL OF DEMOCRATIC TRADE POLITICS

Given these preferences when trade is intra-industry, when and how will societal actors mobilize to influence trade policy? Although preferences over trade depend on a cost-benefit analysis of trade-related gains and losses, not all losing individuals or groups will undertake costly political action to demand protection. In this section, I present a general model of trade politics in democracies before theorizing the ways in which intra-industry trade influences the politics of trade.

Lobbying over Trade

After preferences are determined, actors have to decide (1) whether to mobilize politically to advance their preferences, and (2) whether to engage in political activity alone or collectively with other actors. In democracies, societal actors typically seek to influence policy through voting, campaign contributions, and lobbying. In this analysis, I focus on lobbying. In doing so, I follow other analysts who argue that lobbying is the most theoretically appropriate form of political activity to analyze in studies of trade politics, as it is the most instrumental, communicates the most information about policy preferences, and business groups devote far more resources to lobbying than to campaign finance (Hansen and Mitchell, 2000; Drutman, 2015). In the literature on lobbying in the US, lobbying activities, such as meeting with policymakers, testifying at Congressional hearings, and drafting legislation are considered theoretically distinct from campaign contributions. Richter et al. (2009) elaborate this distinction and find evidence that firms do reap gains from lobbying activities. Developed economies are home to well-developed lobbying infrastructures that include organized coalitions such as industry associations, labor unions, and consumer advocacy organizations.

Coalitions in politics are more than just actors with shared interests and preferences. A coalition is a group of actors that is organized politically with the intent to influence policy. Industry coalitions typically take the form of a membership-based organization or association, such as the American Furniture Manufacturer's Association or the (US) National Tooling and Machining Association. Within each association, firms cooperate with each other to contribute membership dues and financially support association activities and capacity, which may include the maintenance of a physical presence and a permanent staff. These organizations advocate for their members' interests on many issues, including but not limited to trade policy. In addition to the above groups, like-minded actors can form more temporary, ad hoc coalitions to influence the direction of particular pieces of trade legislation. These ad hoc coalitions may include diverse actors consisting of firms, labor groups, and consumer or public interest groups that share the same preferences over some aspects of particular trade agreements. The goal of political activity is to convince policymakers to adopt their preferred policies.

Like most rational choice political models, I assume elected officials are primarily interested in securing reelection and that they compete to attract campaign contributions and provide societal groups with the policies they demand in exchange for financial and electoral support.[5] I do not assume that parties are unitary actors; in line with many trade policy analysts, I assume that individual legislators cater to constituency interests and the demands of

---

[5] Grossman and Helpman (1994)'s "protection for sale" framework provided an explicit theoretical basis for this assumption, modeling policymakers as interest-maximizers seeking contributions from industry lobbyists to fund their election campaigns. In exchange, policymakers provide industries with trade protection. This contribution was supported empirically by several subsequent studies (Gawande and Bandyopadhyay, 2000; Goldberg and Maggi, 1999), though its own assumption that lobbies seek protection conflicts with more recent findings from the firm heterogeneity literature indicating that certain firms prefer, and lobby for, liberalization.

narrow special-interest groups, departing from party lines when they believe this best serves their electoral prospects (Hankla, 2006; McGillivray, 2004). I assume that bureaucratic agents, like elected legislators, are susceptible to special interest lobbying.[6] Bureaucrats need information, and they depend on private special interest groups to provide them with this information. Though it is too simplistic to assume that government officials are purely conduits for societal interests (see Winslett (2021), for example), this book is focused on societal interest-based lobbying rather than the role of policymakers in mediating between societal demands and resulting policy outcomes.

The Costs of Political Activity

Once organized, coalitions must repeatedly decide when to mobilize to influence policy. Though many of the considerable collective action costs are overcome when a coalition is formed in the first place, undertaking political action on pieces of trade legislation is still a very costly endeavor. Labor unions, industry associations, and public interest organizations must finance and carry out research on the impact of proposed legislation on their members, use this research to file reports with government agencies involved in the policy process, appear in policy hearings, as well as seek to meet individually with policymakers at every stage of the policy process. Much of this activity is contracted to private lobbying firms. Lobbying interest groups and firms may incur additional collective action costs if they seek to form ad hoc alliances with other organizations that have a stake in the outcome of the policy in question.

Lobbying costs vary depending on the structure of the policymaking process and the costs of collective action. Political science research shows that as the number of veto-wielding policymakers increases, lobbying becomes more costly (Henisz and Mansfield, 2006; O'Reilly, 2005). In the US, there are three main stages of trade policymaking and lobbying occurs at each stage of the process. First, Congress must decide whether to delegate trade negotiation authority to the president. Interest groups lobby Congress heavily over this decision, based on whether they believe they will achieve a more favorable policy outcome if Congress or the executive retains authority over negotiations. Next, interest groups lobby the agencies involved in negotiating the specific terms of each trade agreement, such as the US Trade Representative and the International Trade Commission. At this stage, interest groups lobby for specific tariff rates and other specific terms to be included in the trade agreement.

---

[6] There is evidence from the US context that both legislators and bureaucrats are susceptible to lobbying. Firm, industry, and labor representatives attend bureaucratic hearings, as do legislators, who argue for protection for specific industries. For just a few examples from this literature, see Boehmke et al. (2013); Drope and Hansen (2004); Hankla (2006); McKay (2011).

Finally, Congress must approve or reject negotiated trade treaties, and this provides an additional opportunity for special interest groups to influence the final outcome. In the EU, the lobbying situation is complicated by the fact that both national and EU-level representatives are involved in trade policymaking, and lobbying must be targeted at both levels of governance.[7] The institutional costs of lobbying vary across national contexts, and I do not build an institutional theory here. My approach is to make the simplifying assumption that these costs exist. In deciding whether or not to lobby, actors must consider the likelihood that their action or contribution will affect policymaker decisions on adopting the policy.

I build another type of cost into my model: The collective action costs of political activity. There are costs associated with organizing and subsequent costs associated with mobilizing to influence proposed legislation. Collective action is possible when members of a group share interests and preferences. The ease with which groups are able to act collectively, however, varies according to a host of factors. One factor is the size of the group: The costs or benefits of a policy are diffused when they fall on large groups, but as the size of the group affected by the policy shrinks, the costs or benefits are more concentrated on the members of that small group. The implication of this is that members of smaller groups are better able to overcome collective action problems to lobby for their preferred outcome because the stakes are higher for the members of smaller groups (Olson, 1965; Schattschneider, 1935). By stakes, I mean the utility of the outcome as well as the probability that a contribution by a group member will be pivotal to the policy outcome. Pareto described how this applies to trade politics quite succinctly: "A protectionist measure provides large benefits to a small number of people, and causes a very great number of consumers a slight loss. This circumstance makes it easier to put a protectionist measure in place" (Pareto, 1927, p. 379).

A second factor complicating collective action is free-riding. Free-riding introduces a strategic element into an actor's decision to undertake political action: The decision to lobby depends on the probability that other actors with shared preferences will lobby as well (or instead). Actors will free-ride on the political contributions of other actors if they believe that they will benefit from the efforts of others. In other words, if the benefits of a policy are nonexcludable and take on the qualities of a public good, actors are more likely to free-ride (Olson, 1965). Smaller groups are more successful at incentivizing their members to contribute to political action (though this does not mean they will necessarily win political battles) through monitoring member involvement and providing selective incentives. The implication of this for trade policy is that narrow, industry-based groups with fewer member firms are more likely

---

[7] Although trade policy is made at the European level, national delegations seeking to protect their own industries and workers wield considerable influence in Brussels over the terms of trade agreements and levels of protection.

to form and mobilize than broad class coalitions, ceteris paribus. It also suggests that exporters, which are few, will have an easier time mobilizing than domestic-oriented firms, which are many. Lobbying over trade will be less costly for narrow industry groups than for national coalitions of consumers or class-based actors.

However, the decision to engage in collective action is also complicated by whether trade policy is conceived of as a public or a private good. When intra-industry trade is high, product differentiation also tends to be high and there are many different varieties of a particular product available to consumers. Gilligan (1997b) argues that individual firms then have an incentive to lobby *alone* for protection against particular foreign varieties that are most similar to their own product. Trade policy essentially becomes a private good. Bombardini and Trebbi (2012) also model trade policy as a private good, finding that when product differentiation is high, firms tend to lobby alone for product-specific protection, rather than collectively for industry-wide protection.

The present analysis departs from these studies in an important way. Both studies expect IIT or product differentiation to raise protectionist lobbying. Unlike both studies, I argue that intra-industry trade incentivizes not only protectionist lobbying, but also pro-trade lobbying by internationalized firms (multinationals seeking increased access for goods produced by foreign affiliates, importers seeking lower-cost inputs, and exporters lobbying strategically for liberalization in order to secure reciprocal liberalization in export markets). This focus on the heterogeneous political implications of trade is consistent with the more recent focus in the trade literature on exporter lobbying (Gilligan, 1997a; Kim, 2017; Milner, 1988; Osgood, 2021; Osgood et al., 2017). In short, in my model, actors decide to undertake political action when they believe that the benefits they will receive from influencing policy outcomes in their favor will outweigh the costs of political activity. Lobbying costs are not trivial, even when political organization has already been established through the formation of a coalition. When deciding whether to expend resources on political action, actors weigh their stakes in the issue and the likelihood that they will influence policymaker decisions against the costs of collective action. In the context of trade policy, the "stakes" are direct income effects of changes to tariff rates and other forms of protection. The greater the income effects on actor i of a change in protection t, the greater the incentive for i to lobby for or against changes to t.

3.3 THE POLITICAL ECONOMY OF INTRA-INDUSTRY TRADE

In this section, I elaborate the causal logic underpinning the lobbying decisions of industry associations, internationalized firms, and domestic-oriented firms as intra-industry trade increases. As I have shown, in industries where trade is primarily inter-industry and based on comparative advantage, we can expect the classic industry or class-based coalitions to form as predicted by Stolper-Samuelson or Ricardo-Viner models. However, because IIT has different distributional effects upon firms, workers, and industries, I argue that it changes the ability of groups to overcome collective action problems and organize politically to influence trade policy. I develop this argument below.

Industry Associations

As discussed above, intra-industry trade undermines industry consensus over trade and generates competing trade preferences among firms within the same industry. Thus, I predict that lobbying by associations and other industry-based groups to be lower in industries with higher IIT, relative to lobbying by individual firms. Because of competing trade preferences among firms in the same industry, collective action is more difficult. Firms may revoke membership or contributions if trade associations take an active lobbying stance for a trade position that is counter to their interests. The result of this, in terms of trade policy lobbying, is that trade associations may take weaker positions on policy to avoid losing members. They may also stop lobbying for particular trade positions altogether, or they may decrease the amount of resources they spend on lobbying over trade legislation. To take an empirical example, this has been the response of the European Roundtable of Industrialists (ERT), a leading advocacy organization for EU manufacturing firms, to heterogeneous trade policy preferences among its members. While maintaining a general free trade policy stance, ERT does not lobby the EU over specific trade policy legislation.[8] In the US, the National Association of Manufacturers (NAM) lost hundreds of members in the mid 2000s, mostly small- and medium-sized firms, due to conflict within the association over how to address Chinese currency manipulation and the resultant flood of Chinese imports into US markets, an issue that split domestic-oriented and multinational firms (Liss, 2021).[9]

The US ball bearing industry provides another example of these lobbying dynamics. In 2002 and 2003, the industry engaged in strong collective action to lobby for protection from Chinese imports. The president of the American Bearings Manufacturing Association (ABMA) along with executives from six US bearings producers testified before the US International Trade Commission in support of their petition for anti-dumping duties to be imposed on bearings from China. In 2002, US bilateral IIT with China was very low (IIT=0.18), meaning that the US industry faced heavy import competition from China and engaged in fairly little exporting to China. The industry came to Washington presenting a united front in its appeal for protection, led by its association. (USITC ultimately denied the petition.) Ten years later, political involvement in

---

[8] Interview with a representative of the European Roundtable of Industrialists, Brussels, 2012.

[9] After resigning from NAM, these firms went on to form the Coalition for a Prosperous America, which is now the largest association of domestic-oriented manufacturers and espouses a self-described "strategic trade" approach (Liss, 2021).

the TTIP negotiations looked very different. Ball bearings trade between the EU and US was intra-industry in nature in 2012 (IIT=0.61), and MFN tariffs on bearing products ranged from 9.9% to 2.4% at this time. From 1989 to 2012, anti-dumping duties on bearings were in place for four EU countries (France, Germany, Italy, and the UK) and only one member of the industry responded to a USTR request for comments. Timken, a large but primarily domestic-oriented firm that favored "the longest possible tariff phase-out period" for roller bearing products, submitted lengthy and detailed comments to USTR in support of continued protection. Timken also lobbied for preferential rules of origin and the right to continue to use trade remedies under TTIP. In its comments, Timken described itself as a firm whose "primary production and sales market is the United States" in an industry "composed of a large number of smaller producers." Timken emphasized that "producers in the European Union are among the largest bearing producers in the world," allowing them to enjoy economies of scale and sell their products for lower prices than US firms. Timken argued that "low-priced imports not only act to reduce overall prices, they also reduce volume, so that the domestic producer who has lost sales finds it harder to recover its costs."[10] Meanwhile, the CEO of another large bearings producer, Schaeffler, dined with President Obama at a pro-TTIP event in Germany.[11] Notably, ABMA, the industry association representing both Schaeffler USA and Timken, remained silent throughout the TTIP negotiations.

Firm heterogeneity in trade preferences can fall along two different lines within industries, both of which hinder collective action via associations. As in the above example, the primary cleavage is between internationalized firms and domestic-oriented firms. This may cause associations to scale back lobbying, in order not to alienate their domestic-oriented members, but there is an alternative scenario. Large, powerful firms may dominate their associations, and the association may take strong lobbying positions in favor of liberalization as a result. The National Association of Manufacturers (NAM) revealed in a 2006 interview with *CNN Money* that around two-thirds of the association's 13,000 member firms were small- and medium-sized enterprises, yet decision-making operates according to a "one-dollar, one-vote" system that, NAM acknowledged, skews votes toward the preferences of the "biggest donors." At this time, only a quarter of the seats on NAM's board were held by representatives from SMEs (Fromartz, 2006).[12] This incentivizes domestic-oriented firms with opposing interests to lobby alone or through ad hoc coalitions in order to counter the association's stance. Yet there is a second possible cleavage within industries that can complicate associational activity. Even among large, globally engaged firms, not all firms will be affected in

[10] Comments of the Timken Company, submitted to USTR docket USTR-2013-0019.

[11] *Politico*, April 25, 2016. See www.politico.eu/article/politico-pros-morning-trade-merkel-we-should-hurry-up-with-ttip-obama-defends-isds/.

[12] In 2022, according to NAM's website, 90 percent of the association's 14,000 members were small- and medium-sized firms.

TABLE 3.2 *Inter- versus intra-industry trade and the structure of political coalitions*

Structure of trade	Classes	Industries
Inter-industry, high factor mobility (Stolper-Samuelson effect)	Unified	Divided
Inter-industry, low factor mobility (Ricardo-Viner effect)	Divided	Unified
Intra-industry	Divided	Divided

the same way by particular trade agreements. Firms participating in supply chains with the partner country will benefit from lower import and export costs, while firms whose supply chains are located elsewhere will lose competitiveness vis-à-vis these firms. This creates another incentive for large firms to lobby alone on behalf of their own interests. In any of the above scenarios, the result is relatively less collective lobbying through associations and relatively more lobbying by firms going it alone. Table 3.2. summarizes the way that trade composition affects industry and class consensus over trade policy.[13]

Individual Firms

As industry associations become less active in trade policymaking due to competing trade preferences among their members, I argue that individual firms will become increasingly politically active. The next question we must answer is, which firms will engage politically? How does intra-industry trade change firms' cost-benefit calculus when considering whether to lobby?

First, consider the rational behavior of firms under classic, endowments-based trade. In both comparative advantage and disadvantage industries, firm preferences are united, facilitating lobbying by industry associations and creating little incentive for costly action by individual firms. According to the Ricardo-Viner model, in comparative advantage industries all firms within the industry would prefer liberal trade rules and access to foreign markets, whether or not they export. Given that open markets also benefit consumers, as well as workers in competitive industries, societal consensus should coalesce around trade openness. In the absence of protectionist lobbying from a comparative advantage industry, there will be little need for free-trading firms to engage in costly political activity as policymakers are likely to provide liberal trade rules in this situation. In comparative disadvantage industries, on the other hand, firms will be united around protectionist preferences. The costs of openness

[13] It should be noted that this discussion assumes a world of low factor mobility. While factor mobility is irrelevant when IIT is high (Alt et al., 1996), my expectation that lobbying will be industry-based when IIT is low implicitly assumes that Ricardo-Viner effects hold. Of course, if factor mobility were high, Stolper-Samuelson effects would dominate and we would observe lobbying coalitions to be broadly class- or factor-based. I have focused the discussion on industry-based lobbying because conventional wisdom holds that factor mobility is low in advanced industrial economies (Hiscox, 2001, 2002a).

are concentrated on these industries as a whole, making it easier for them to overcome collective action problems and lobby via an industry association. Given shared preferences and concentrated costs, comparative disadvantage industries are the best equipped to engage in collective action, delegating political activity to industry-wide associations and achieving their desired level of protection. When firms fail to overcome collective action problems and form organized coalitions, they are more likely to achieve only a sub-optimal level of protection.

I argue that the calculus determining whether to engage in costly political action is different for firms in industries subject to intra-industry trade, and that this is a key factor in understanding the rise of individual firm lobbying in developed economies in the postwar period. It also helps make sense of why some trade agreements are so much more controversial than others, and why some agreements are able to achieve deeper liberalization than others. First, because domestic-oriented firms may support protection, globally engaged firms within the industry now also have an interest in lobbying for openness to counteract the protectionist pressures coming from within their very industry. Although few small firms lobby, globally engaged firms may need to increase their lobbying to make up for division within industry associations that reduces the amount of lobbying that associations can pursue. They may also need to lobby alone to counter pressure not from domestic-oriented firms but from other globally competitive firms that are not integrated in global supply chains with a particular trading partner.

Second, Pareto's key insight was that protection confers large benefits on a small group, facilitating collective action. Within industries, however, exporters and importers become an even smaller group, as exporting and importing are rare firm activities (Bernard et al., 2007a; Melitz and Redding, 2014).[14] The costs of protection are concentrated on this small group of internationalized firms, and the benefits of liberalization are concentrated on them as well. This gives them an incentive to lobby alone for liberalization. This incentive to lobby alone does not exist in either comparative disadvantage or comparative advantage industries, where industries are united, facilitating collective action through industry associations. Because intra-industry trade of differentiated products confers firm-specific, rather than industry-wide benefits, the gains from trade are concentrated on individual firms, raising the relative likelihood of firm-level political activity. One implication of this is that the effect of IIT on firm-level lobbying should be strongest in net-importing industries that face heavy import competition. In these industries, industry associations are more likely to lobby for protection. Exporting firms in these sectors will have an interest in breaking from the industry position and lobbying individually for liberalization.

---

[14] One cross-national study found that the median number of exporting firms per product is less than three in most cases (Cebeci et al., 2012).

On the other hand, domestic-oriented, import-competing firms tend to be smaller firms with few resources to devote to lobbying. Domestic-oriented firms generally benefit from protection and stand to face significant losses when trade barriers are reduced. If industry associations scale back their lobbying activity because of conflicting preferences held by their member firms, domestic-oriented firms have a strong incentive to represent themselves politically. However, having a strong incentive to lobby is not the same as having the resources to lobby, and small firms are least equipped. If these firms do muster the resources to lobby, they will be far outspent by free-trading firms from within their industry. This, of course, is the rationale behind sharing these costs through collective action via an industry association. In the absence of strong lobbying from their industry association, and without the resources to undertake costly political activity alone, domestic-oriented firms are unlikely to lobby over trade. Those that do are likely to form ad hoc coalitions to share lobbying costs through collective action. These coalitions are likely to be cross-sectoral, bringing together firms from a range of industries affected by a particular piece of trade legislation. This was the response of many firms in the US during negotiations over the Trans-Pacific Partnership. These firms formed cross-sectoral coalitions such as the Alliance for American Manufacturing and the Coalition for a Prosperous America that advocated protectionist policies.

Why don't free-trading firms form ad hoc coalitions to share the cost of political action? They often do, particularly when counter-lobbying from protectionist groups or public interest groups is intense. It is costly to form new organizations for collective action, even among small groups. Olson (1982, p.38) emphasized the "special start-up costs" involved in creating a new organization or "pattern of cooperation." Yet given that only a small minority of firms are globally engaged, and they are the industry leaders, these firms are much better prepared than the much larger number of domestic-oriented firms to overcome collective action problems and organize ad hoc, pro-trade coalitions to supplement their individual political efforts. Large, globally engaged firms may find it in their interest to lobby through a new ad hoc coalition as well as individually, given the substantial gains from openness, their considerable resources to devote to lobbying, and their organizational advantages relative to domestic-oriented firms.

In this way, intra-industry trade dramatically alters the landscape of societal coalitions organized over trade policy. Rather than coalitional politics among unified classes or industries, as the standard trade theories predict, IIT generates a firm-centric political landscape. As IIT increases, individual firm lobbying will increase relative to association-based lobbying, and globally engaged firms seeking openness will be much more likely to lobby individually than domestic-oriented firms. When domestic-oriented firms lobby, it is more likely to be via an ad hoc, protectionist coalition. It is important to note that the argument that exporters are likely to prefer trade liberalization holds whether an industry faces high or low levels of intra-industry trade. What changes in industries with high IIT is not the preference for liberalization but the incentive to lobby. Faced with competing interests from within their industry, exporters have a greater incentive to lobby for openness than exporters in comparative advantage industries where there is not a protectionist counter-lobby. Firm-specific, concentrated gains from trade also undermine collective action and facilitate firm-level activity.

In sum, I argue here that intra-industry trade changes the costs associated with lobbying and incentivizes firms to lobby alone for their preferred trade policies. In this model, intra-industry trade increases the probability that individual firms will be pivotal to trade policy outcomes by making trade policy more contentious within industries, it reduces the costs of firm-based lobbying relative to coalition-based lobbying and it raises the stakes of trade policy for individual firms in industries characterized by two-way trade. Following the existing literature on intra-industry trade and lobbying, I do not specify a level of IIT (or of prospective IIT following the adoption of a particular trade agreement) at which I expect changes in lobbying to occur (Gilligan, 1997b; Kono, 2009; Thies and Peterson, 2015). The amount of two-way trade that will change a particular firm or industry's political calculus is specific to each firm, industry and trading agreement. Rather, like prior studies, I argue that a higher proportion of IIT raises the likelihood that individual firms will lobby alone for their preferred policies, relative to industry associations.

Workers and Labor Unions

The same logic detailed above applies to workers and labor unions. Consistent with this book's focus on lobbying, I consider labor union lobbying, which affects the political strategies of firms and industry associations, rather than attitudes and voting behaviors of individual workers. As the distributional effects of intra-industry trade fall at the firm level, industry-wide or sector-wide labor unions would face the same difficulties forging consensus among their members that industry associations do. Worker trade preferences are likely to align with their employers. This expectation is a departure from both factoral and sectoral approaches that assume worker preferences align either with their factor class (low- or high-skilled labor, as in O'Rourke (2003), Scheve and Slaughter (2001), and Walter (2017)), sector of employment (Irwin, 1995), as well as the "offshorability" of their occupations (Owen and Johnston, 2017). There is significant wage inequality across firms within the same industry, with multinational and other large firms paying higher wages than smaller, domestic-oriented firms (Bernard et al., 1995; Helpman et al., 2010). The gains from trade that accrue to globally engaged firms exacerbate these wage differentials, especially as their domestic-oriented counterparts are harmed by increasing import competition (Amiti and Davis, 2012).

Additionally, if increased import competition causes the exit of domestic-oriented firms, these workers will not necessarily be re-employed at globally engaged firms that pay higher wages. As resources are allocated away from less productive firms to highly efficient multinational firms– including the affiliates of foreign firms – a "productivity effect" takes hold that reduces the overall demand for labor (Egger and Kreickemeier, 2009). Less productive domestic firms will be forced to exit the industry or reduce production, and the most efficient globally engaged firms may rely on labor-saving technologies, reducing the overall demand for workers. These firms are also likely to employ workers with more specialized skills and are unlikely to hire the less-skilled workers laid off from domestic firms. Owen (2015) cites the example of the US auto industry, which lost 243,000 workers between 2000 and 2006 due to domestic firms' plant closures. Meanwhile, foreign affiliates only employed 63,000 US workers.

A key implication of this argument is that labor unions will be less politically active over trade agreements in which IIT is higher, relative to trade agreements where trade among the partners is based on comparative advantage and is more heavily inter-industry. Standard trade theories would predict labor union support of trade agreements that would liberalize comparative advantage industries and expand exports (and therefore, employment opportunities), and opposition to trade agreements that would liberalize comparative disadvantage industries. Historic patterns in US labor unions' trade policy positions roughly fit this pattern: US labor unions generally maintained a pro-trade stance in the early postwar period, when US manufacturing dominated global markets, but this liberal stance eroded as US industries began to experience intense competition from low-wage manufacturing abroad.

In terms of trade agreements between countries with relatively similar endowments and intra-industry trade, labor unions are likely to be broadly supportive for three key reasons. First, trade liberalization between high-income countries with similar endowments and similar labor costs does not threaten entire industries with extinction, and labor unions may expect job-creating effects of these PTAs. Most trade is likely to occur in high-value, differentiated products where firms specialize and there is a market for a variety of products. Second, high-income countries have similar labor standards (though where there is a difference in standards, we should observe more labor opposition to PTAs in the country with higher standards, if labor unions are concerned about the downward harmonization of standards). Third, workers at large firms are more likely to be unionized than workers at small firms. Large firms are most likely to benefit from intra-industry trade, expanding employment opportunities and benefiting workers at these firms. As I will show in Chapter 7, in the US, labor's response to TTIP was muted and cautiously positive overall.

This may be a reason why US labor union opposition to NAFTA as well as the TPP was intense, while "not entirely hostile" to the TTIP (Young, 2016). In fact there was very little US labor union lobbying at all over TTIP (Madeira, 2018). In the USTR's 2013 request for public comments, only seven labor unions participated: the AFL-CIO, the International Association of Machinists and Aerospace Workers, the Transportation Trades Department of the AFL-CIO, the Teamsters, United Steelworkers, the Maritime Coalition, and the Communications Workers of America. With the exception of procurement policies, which four unions objected to liberalizing, none of the labor union submissions addressed concerns over job losses. Rather, all union statements urged "upward harmonization" of labor standards to EU levels. The Communication Workers of America's statement included the following line: "CWA knows from first-hand experience that workers in Germany have more rights and are treated with more respect than workers in the U.S. – even when they work for the same corporation."[15]

Trade Policy Outcomes

Another implication of my model is that at the industry level, tariffs will decrease as IIT increases. As discussed in Chapter 2, the first scholarly analyses of intra-industry trade linked it to easier trade liberalization, a finding confirmed by more recent studies (Manger, 2014, 2015; Thies and Peterson, 2015). Other scholars, however, associate rising IIT with more demands for protection (Gilligan, 1997b) and higher tariffs (Kono, 2009).

My model suggests that industries with higher IIT are easier to liberalize not because there is no objection to liberalization from within the industry, but because protectionist and free-trading actors are not matched in their ability to lobby and provide campaign contributions. Free-trading firms politically overwhelm domestic-oriented, protectionist firms from the same industry and also are advantaged in efforts to form cross-sectoral coalitions in support of their interests. Thus, I expect that as IIT increases in a given industry, tariffs will decrease, and this will hold whether the industry is net-exporting or net-importing. In a net-importing industry, an increase in IIT represents an increase in exports. The few highly efficient firms successful on export markets will lobby for tariff reductions in the context of reciprocity. In a net-exporting industry, an increase in IIT represents an increase in imports. Again, globally engaged firms are likely to accept greater import competition as a tradeoff for maintaining access to export markets as well as imports produced by their affiliates abroad.

Yet as IIT undermines industry-level lobbying by associations acting on behalf of all firms, large firms are likely to succeed in securing nontariff measures of protection (NTMs) that disproportionately benefit them at the expense of smaller firms in the same industry. Excessive product safety regulations, for example, can serve as veiled protection that reduces import competition in domestic markets, but with a heavy cost on smaller firms that may not be

---

[15] Communication Workers of America Comments on the Transatlantic Trade and Investment Partnership Federal Register (April 1, 2013); Docket USTR-2013-0019.

able to afford compliance. This alternative channel through which rent-seeking policymakers can supply targeted protection facilitates tariff reductions as IIT increases. It also illuminates the way in which changes in the composition of international trade affect not only the structure of societal political organization but also the structure of trade policy outcomes.

Additionally, trade between similar countries trading similar products may not inspire strong opposition from organized labor, another factor that affects firm and industry lobbying strategies and ultimately facilitates liberalization. As discussed, labor unions may expect job-creating effects from expanded trade in manufactured goods with high-income countries, they may be unconcerned about a "race to the bottom" in labor standards, and (at least in a country like the US with low unionization rates) unionized workers may be most likely employed at large firms that stand to gain from trade. When labor does not mount a strong opposition to a potential trade agreement, as was the case in US lobbying over TTIP, the path is eased for policymakers to liberalize trade. Additionally, industry associations that are trying to balance divided preferences among their members may decide not to engage in heavy pro-trade lobbying, leaving the bulk of this work up to large, politically powerful free-trading firms.

3.4 CONCLUSION

In conclusion, the economics of intra-industry trade generate new dynamics in trade politics as traditional coalitions are undermined and a more firm-centric political landscape takes shape. Political economists have provided sparse and conflicting theoretical expectations about the political and policy implications of intra-industry trade, and perhaps even sparser empirical evidence. The theory developed in this chapter predicts that intra-industry trade will divide industries and workers and yields a number of testable implications, discussed above, that reveal an understudied link between the structure of international trade and a number of domestic political outcomes. In this way, I provide a structural account of institutional development: Rising intra-industry trade weakens the political role of industry-based associations, paving the way for both firm-based lobbying and cross-sectoral collective action. In the remainder of this book, I demonstrate that this relationship is independent of policymaking institutions and generalizable across advanced democracies.

In the empirical chapters that follow, I assess the following implications. First, Chapters 4 and 5 test my argument that IIT increases individual firm lobbying relative to lobbying by industry associations in two very different institutional contexts: the US and the EU, respectively. Next, Chapter 6 examines intra-industry trade's impact on levels of protection in a cross-national sample of advanced democracies. Finally, Chapter 7 compares lobbying in the US over two major, mega-regional trade deals that were concurrently negotiated by the US – the Trans Pacific Partnership and the Transatlantic Trade and

Investment Partnership – to examine whether and how the lobbying dynamics discussed in this book apply in the case of a trade deal between two economies with high levels of IIT on the one hand (the EU and the US) and a trade deal whose members engage in trade that is much more endowments-based (the US and members of the TPP). In Chapter 7, I also compare the extent and nature of labor's political involvement in the negotiations of these two trade deals, and I assess the composition of lobbying coalitions (industry-based or cross-sectoral). In Chapter 8, I consider the role of IIT in the populist backlash to globalization. A fascinating implication of the rise in IIT is that if labor union and associational lobbying is undermined while individual corporations are politically empowered, trade and investment agreements are more likely to advance the priorities of multinational firms, which include provisions like investor-state dispute settlement that have proven incredibly controversial.

Cleavage and Coalition in US Trade Politics

In March 1945, *The New York Times* wrote that the American Glassware Association had lodged "what was believed to be the first industry protest" against proposed tariff reductions within legislation aimed at extending the landmark Reciprocal Trade Agreements Act.[1] The association released a statement emphasizing the importance of tariff protection for a high-wage, labor-intensive industry that anticipated heavy losses due to imports from lower-wage countries. Tariffs were reduced, however, and in 1952, the association filed a trade injury petition to the Tariff Commission with support from the industry's leading labor union, the American Flint Glass Workers' Union.[2] President Eisenhower, resolving a split decision by the Commission, found no substantial evidence of injury due to import competition, arguing that the industry's troubles were more likely caused by technological innovation and increasing automation of production processes at industry-leading firms, such as the Libbey Glass Company, based in Toledo, Ohio (Bidwell, 1956). Fast forward to 2013 and the negotiations over TTIP. Libbey filed one of the very few comments submitted to the US Trade Representative that expressed strongly protectionist sentiments, urging the USTR to consider the "import-sensitivity" of glass tableware. Libbey, though a large and internationalized firm, emphasized its domestic orientation, noting that its sales within North America accounted for 74 percent of its total sales. Libbey lamented that "imports have captured over half of the US market." It noted the competitiveness of glassware varieties from Germany, Italy, France, Poland, and Austria and asked for

---

[1] "American Glassware Association Lodges Trade Act Tariff Protest; Charges That 'Handcraft Industries Seem To Have Been Overlooked' and Opposes Cuts in Extension Bill." *New York Times*, March 31, 1945.

[2] United States Tariff Commission. September 1953. Hand-Blown Glassware: Report to the President on Investigation No. 22 Under Section 7 of the Trade Agreements Extension Act of 1951, as Amended. Washington.

the "longest possible tariff phaseout period considered."[3] Libbey also signed a letter sent by a group of eight senators and representatives in December 2013 that urged USTR to maintain trade protections for the glassware industry, and in this effort it was joined by another Ohio glass firm, Anchor Hocking.[4] The only other lobbying from the glassware industry came from Corning Incorporated, a US-based multinational firm that joined a cross-sectoral coalition (Trade Benefits America) to lobby in *support* of trade liberalization.[5] The leading industry associations, well-organized and politically active on a range of other issues important to the industry, were silent.

In many advanced industrial democracies, broad class-based trade coalitions composed of workers or industrialists from a wide range of sectors have given way to narrow industry-based coalitions. Increasingly, even these narrow coalitions have crumbled as firms within the same industry have found themselves at odds over their trade preferences. In these instances, individual firms often shoulder the lobbying burden instead. Understanding the ways in which economic actors mobilize and act collectively to influence trade policy is crucial to our understanding of patterns in trade liberalization and protection. Based on the theory I presented in Chapter 3, in this chapter, I develop and test hypotheses about the way intra-industry trade affects trade coalition formation and mobilization in domestic battles over trade in the US.

It is important to note that I do not focus in this chapter on the *direction* of lobbying. In other words, I do not analyze firm and industry preferences over trade policy. The primary reason for excluding preferences here is that it is not necessary for assessing one of the central predictions of my theory, which is that intra-industry trade leads to a rise in individual lobbying by firms relative to collective lobbying by industry associations. Identifying firm preferences is notoriously difficult to do given that this information is not included on lobbying disclosure reports. Lobbying reports filed under the Lobbying Disclosure Act of 1995 require lobbyists to disclose the issues on which they are lobbying but they do not detail their policy positions. Studies aimed at uncovering firm preferences most often rely on surveys, Congressional testimonies, and public position statements. In Chapter 7, I use some of these data sources to analyze firm and industry preferences over recent US trade agreements. In this chapter, however, I focus on the structure of lobbying coalitions and the extent to which firms lobby collectively or alone over trade policy. This approach allows me to situate this analysis squarely in the tradition of the IPE literature on political cleavages and coalitions that Rogowski pioneered. Rogowski,

---

[3] Comments of Libbey, Inc., submitted to USTR docket USTR-2013-0019.

[4] "Lawmakers Press USTR to Shield U.S. Glassware Industry in TPP, TTIP." *Inside U.S. Trade.* December 20, 2013.

[5] The Trade Benefits America Coalition sent a letter to the Senate Finance Committee on April 21, 2015, urging Congress to reauthorize trade promotion authority legislation to ease passage of TTIP and TPP.

Frieden, Hiscox, and others studied how structural factors such as comparative advantage and factor mobility shape societal cleavages and coalitions when trade is liberalized. This book takes the same approach, problematizing the role of intra-industry trade in the structure of societal coalitions. For these reasons, my first two empirical chapters (Chapters 4 and 5) examine the nature of lobbying over trade and the extent to which firms that lobby over trade do so individually or collectively.

This chapter proceeds as follows. First, I examine the changing dynamics of trade politics in the United States during the postwar period, and I demonstrate the ways that these dynamics diverge from what is predicted by the classic trade models. Second, I derive testable hypotheses to assess the influence of intra-industry trade on the structure of political coalitions aimed at influencing trade policy. In the remainder of the chapter, I test my hypotheses about coalition formation in an empirical analysis of the effects of intra-industry trade on trade lobbying in the US, and I discuss my results and their implications for the politics of international trade. In demonstrating the way that changes in international trade have affected domestic political coalitions, and particularly the role of industry associations, I present a structural argument that explains institutional development in the US.

4.1 TRADE POLITICS IN THE UNITED STATES AND THE RISE OF CORPORATE LOBBYING

Until the inauguration of President Donald Trump, US trade policy became reliably more liberal in the period since World War II, as in the world's other advanced democracies. As shown in Figure 4.1, US tariff levels have plummeted since their height in the late 1800s.[6] While trade liberalization in the US has been a consistent process, lobbying activity in the US aimed at influencing trade policy has varied widely at different points in time. In the longest time-series dataset of US trade policy lobbying, Hiscox (2002a) measured the raw numbers of interests groups that lobbied before the House Trade Commission on major trade legislation between 1884 and 1994 and found significant variation over the course of the twentieth century, with lobbying dropping dramatically after the passage of the Reciprocal Trade Agreements Act in 1934 and then steadily rising again in the following decades (Figure 4.2). A similar decline in trade lobbying followed the passage of the US Trade Expansion Act in 1962, the legislation that paved the way for the opening of the Kennedy Round of multilateral tariff reductions, concluded in 1967.

More recent data from the Center for Responsive Politics shows that in the last 15 years, the number of unique actors that lobbied over trade has been

---

[6] While tariff levels have fallen consistently since the adoption of the Reciprocal Trade Agreements Act in 1934, nontariff measures (NTMs) have increased in importance during this time (Kee et al., 2013; Kinzius et al., 2019). Therefore, it is important not to equate a country's tariff levels with its degree of overall trade protection.

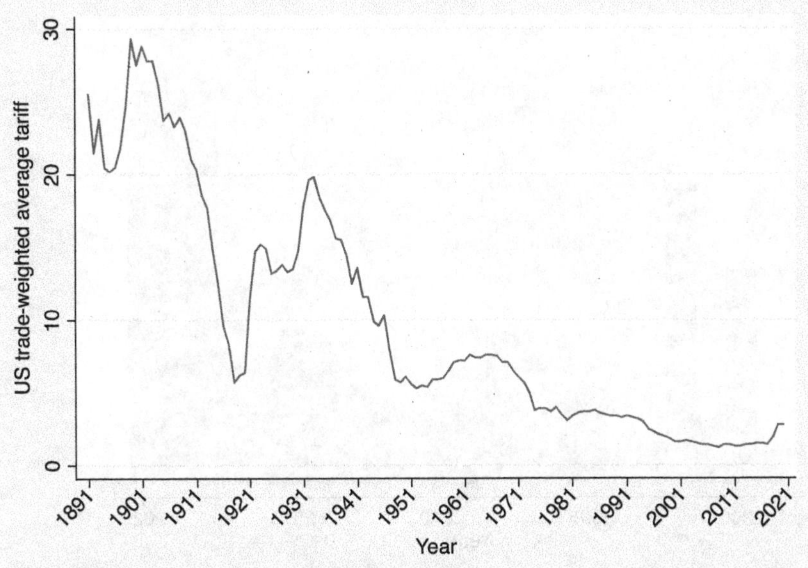

FIGURE 4.1 Trade-weighted average tariff rate, United States, 1891–2019
Data source: USITC.

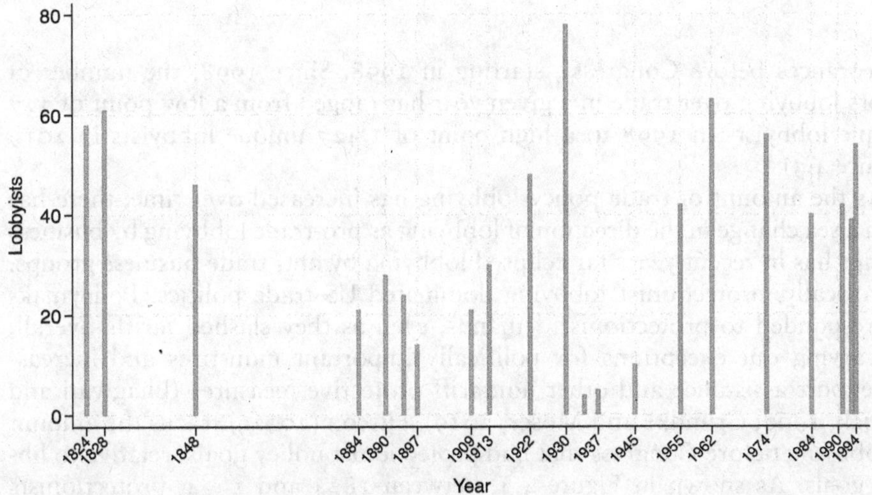

FIGURE 4.2 Number of actors lobbying Congress over trade policy, 1824–1994
Data source: Hiscox (2002).

fairly stable, though increasing slightly over time. These lobbyists include individual firms, industry associations, consumer advocacy groups, labor unions, and lobbying firms hired by these actors. This data includes all lobbying activities before Congress and US government agencies (Hiscox only counts

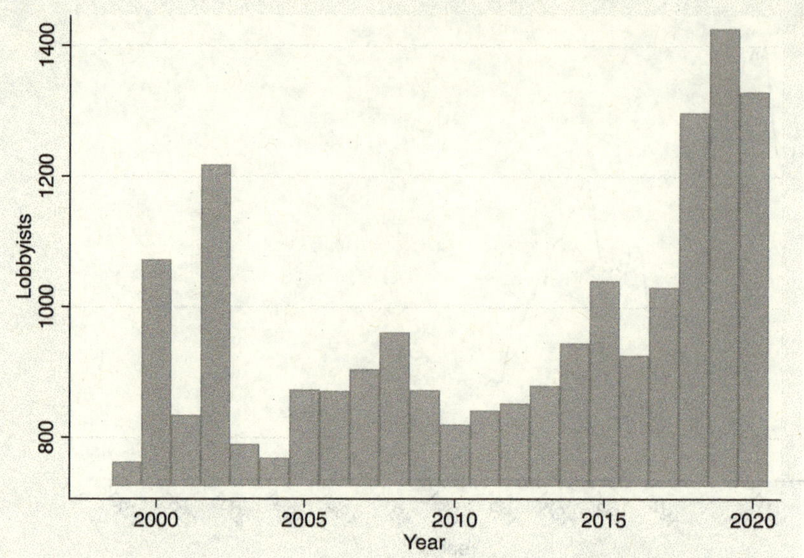

FIGURE 4.3 Number of actors lobbying annually over trade policy
Data source: Center for Responsive Politics and the US Senate Office of Public Records.
Includes lobbying of Congress and US government agencies.

appearances before Congress), starting in 1998. Since 1998, the number of actors lobbying over trade in a given year has ranged from a low point of 727 unique lobbyists in 1998 to a high point of 1,427 unique lobbyists in 2019 (Figure 4.3).

As the amount of trade policy lobbying has increased over time, there has been a sea change in the direction of lobbying as pro-trade lobbying by business groups has in recent years far eclipsed lobbying by anti-trade business groups. Historically, protectionist lobbying dominated US trade politics. Policymakers responded to protectionist demands, even as they slashed tariffs overall, by carving out exceptions for politically important industries and increasing export assistance and other nontariff protective measures (Bhagwati and Patrick, 1990; Grundke and Moser, 2019). Hiscox (2002a) tracks the amount of lobbying before Congress that had protectionist policy goals, relative to liberal goals. As shown in Figure 4.4, between 1824 and 1994, protectionists comprise over half the total lobbying efforts on all major pieces of trade legislation except the infamous tariff of 1828 when free traders from the South lobbied hard – mostly unsuccessfully – against the protection demanded by industrialists and farmers from the Northeast and West. Since 1828 through the 1990s, interest groups seeking protection have been the most politically active voice in trade policymaking, responsible for between approximately 70% and 95% of the lobbying activity on major trade legislation. Verdier

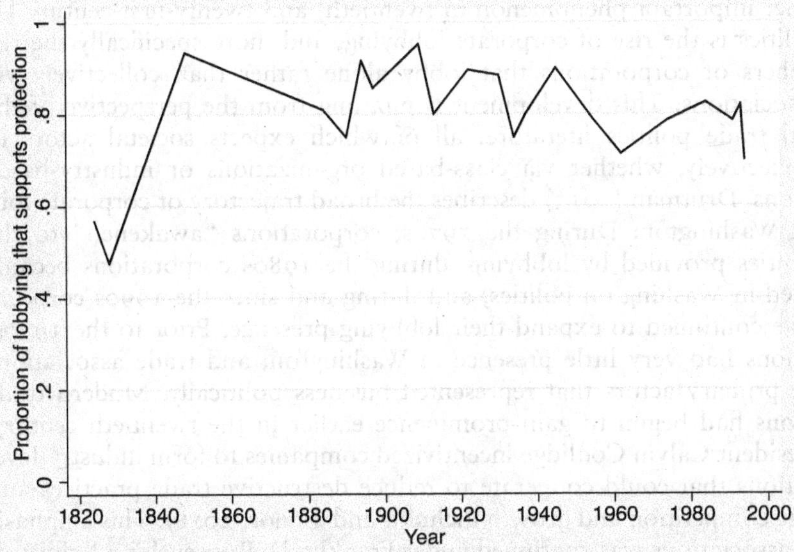

FIGURE 4.4 Percentage of lobbying with protectionist goals
Data source: Hiscox (2002). Based on number of interest groups lobbying before House trade committees on major trade legislation.

(1994)'s data present a similar picture. In his analysis of oral and written testimony at Congressional hearings, he finds that between 1934 and 1987, the percentage of lobbying with a protectionist bent ranged from approximately 50–90 percent, with peaks in 1934, 1955, and 1986.[7] Gilligan (1997b) tracked the number of protectionist complaints brought by US firms to the International Trade Commission, and he found that this number steadily increased over time. More recent studies, however, reveal a profoundly different lobbying landscape in the twenty-first century that aligns with the dynamics first documented by Helen Milner in the 1980s: There has been a demonstrable rise in pro-trade lobbying by large, internationalized firms (Gilligan, 1997a; Kim, 2017; Milner, 1988; Osgood et al., 2017). Among lobbying firms, Blanga-Gubbay et al. (2024) found that over 99 percent of firms that lobbied on recent US free trade agreements were supportive of the agreements, which is consistent with other recent studies of firm lobbying (Osgood, 2021).

---

[7] Though the two datasets present a fairly consistent overall picture of lobbying trends over time, the differences in their findings are likely attributable to differences in their data collection methodologies. Verdier includes testimony before the Senate Finance Committee, for example, while Hiscox only looks at House testimony. Additionally Hiscox's data includes all interest groups while Verdier includes only trade associations and trade unions.

Another important phenomenon in twentieth- and twenty-first-century US trade politics is the rise of corporate lobbying, and more specifically the rising numbers of corporations that lobby alone rather than collectively via trade associations. This development is puzzling from the perspective of the canonical trade politics literature, all of which expects societal actors to lobby collectively, whether via class-based organizations or industry-based associations. Drutman (2015) describes the broad trajectory of corporate lobbying in Washington: During the 1970s, corporations "awakened" to the opportunities provided by lobbying, during the 1980s corporations became entrenched in Washington politics, and during and since the 1990s corporations have continued to expand their lobbying presence. Prior to the 1970s, corporations had very little presence in Washington, and trade associations were the primary actors that represented business politically. Modern trade associations had begun to gain prominence earlier in the twentieth century, when President Calvin Coolidge incentivized companies to form industry-level organizations that could cooperate to reduce destructive trade practices and encourage competition and growth (Schuldt and Taylor, 2018). This emphasis on trade associations was continued under Franklin D. Roosevelt's administration, which viewed trade associations as a way to promote economic stability (Eisner, 2000, p. 5). Eisner refers to this time as the "associational regime." Enjoying a business-friendly environment through the 1950s, individual corporations had little reason to engage in Washington beyond their contributions to and involvement in their trade associations. David Vogel observes, "Through the middle of the 1960s, the political position of business certainly appeared to be a privileged one" (Vogel, 1989, p. 33). Additionally, the early postwar period was a golden era of American prosperity. US producers dominated global markets, as the rest of the industrialized world still reeled from the economic devastation of World War II. Individual businesses faced little competition from foreign firms and had little need for significant assistance from the government (Drutman, 2015, pp. 50–51). Overall, scholarly consensus is that US businesses did very little of their own lobbying during the 1950s–1960s, generally leaving this task to their trade associations (Drutman, 2015; Milbrath, 1976; Vogel, 1989).

This dynamic had completely changed by the beginning of the 1970s, after the tumultuous political movements of the 1960s dramatically expanded the involvement of a wide range of interest groups in Washington, active not only on economic issues but on civil rights, women's rights, environmental protection, consumer safety and beyond. Waterhouse (2014, p. 21) writes that "many prominent business leaders began to feel increasingly isolated from the political power structure." Alongside the growing activism and anti-business attitudes among the general public came a slew of new regulations. There were twenty-five major pieces of regulatory legislation passed between 1974 and 1978 (Waterhouse, 2014, p. 178). Vogel writes that by 1977, "business had been on the political and intellectual defensive for more than a decade" and that the

1970s mark "the nadir of business political influence in the postwar period" (Vogel, 1989, p. 7). Meanwhile overseas, European and Asian countries were industrializing, growing economically, and their firms were becoming globally competitive. Falling transport costs paved the way for imports from oceans away. The combined effect of these dynamics was that firms were now spending more on complying with new regulations even as foreign competition was becoming intense and the US economy was entering a period of serious economic downturn marked by double-digit inflation.

Firms responded to the onslaught of challenges that arose in the 1970s by dramatically expanding their presence in Washington and their involvement in politics (Drutman, 2015; Vogel, 1989; Waterhouse, 2014). Individual firms realized the necessity of investing resources to represent their own interests in Washington beyond participating in and contributing to their trade associations. Although systematic data on business lobbying is not available before the 1980s, a few scholars present some statistical snapshots. Vogel documents the increase of firm-based lobbying in the 1970s and finds that in 1971, only 175 firms had registered lobbyists, but this number increased to 2,445 by 1982 (Vogel, 1989, p. 197). Waterhouse (2014) states that only 130 firms were represented by registered lobbyists in 1961, while 650 firms were represented by lobbyists in 1979. Using the first systematic dataset on business lobbying in the US, I calculated the proportion of individual firm versus trade association lobbying presence over time (Schlozman et al., 2018). The authors of this dataset have coded each actor registered as a client in the Washington Representatives Directory of lobbyists at five time points (1981, 1991, 2001, 2006, and 2011).[8] As shown in Figure 4.5, which measures the number of registered lobbying clients, we see that individual firms have slightly increased their lobbying presence relative to trade associations over this thirty-year period. We don't observe substantial change in the ratio of firm to industry lobbying clients over this time, likely because most medium and large firms had already established a Washington presence prior to the 1980s.[9]

While the above discussion focuses on lobbying *presence*, as indicated by having a DC office or hiring Washington-based lobbyists, in 1995 the Lobbying Disclosure Act was passed, which mandated the disclosure of lobbying expenditures. The Washington Representatives database records expenditures by all lobbying actors for the years 2001 and 2011. We see in Figure 4.6 that the amount of money that individual firms spend on lobbying dwarfs the amount that trade associations spend on lobbying, and that this has been consistent

---

[8] The Washington Representatives Directory was published by Columbia Books and contains all organizations that are "active in Washington politics by virtue of either having an office in the DC area or hiring DC-area consultants or counsel to represent them" (Schlozman et al., 2018).

[9] I included all firms and cooperatives, including foreign ones, in my calculation of individual firm lobbying registrations. I included agricultural associations in my trade association category. Excluding agricultural associations yields an even greater split between firm- and association-based lobbying.

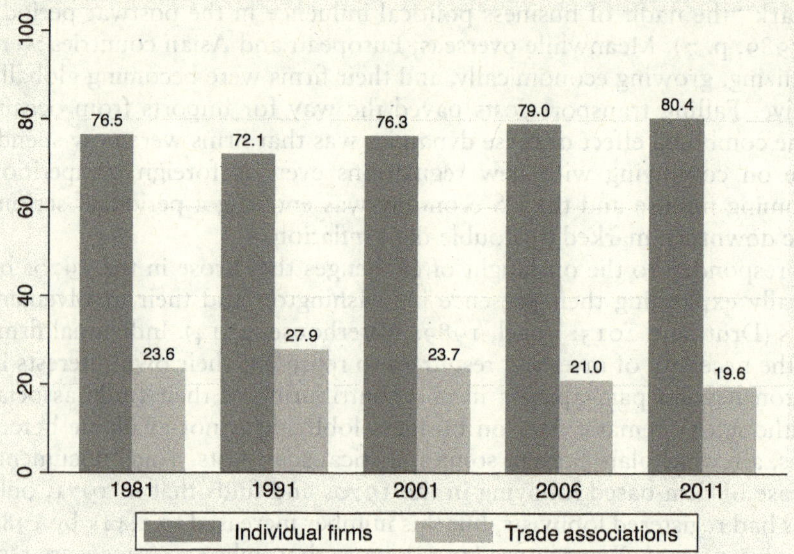

FIGURE 4.5 Individual firm versus trade association lobbying clients
Data source: Author's calculations based on Washington Representatives database of
registered lobbying clients (Schlozman et al., 2018).

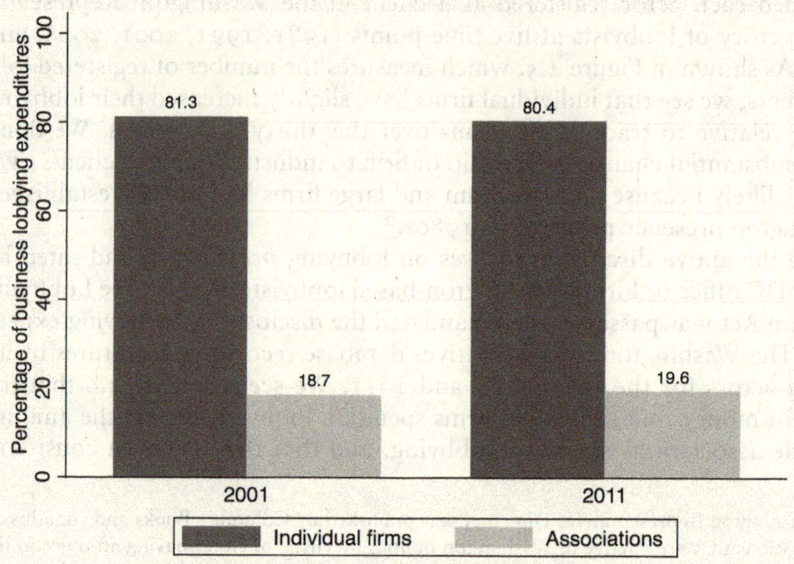

FIGURE 4.6 Individual firm versus trade association lobbying expenditures
Data source: Author's calculations based on Washington Representatives database of
lobbying expenditures (Schlozman et al., 2018).

over this ten-year time period. It is important to point out that this data include lobbying expenditures on all issues, not just trade policy.

In sum, individual firms now maintain a permanent and well-resourced presence in Washington, as do trade associations. Looking specifically at trade policy lobbying, we can characterize this time period as one in which economic actors have remained consistently politically active, and perhaps increasingly active, even as US tariff levels have reached historically low levels. Additionally, recent data suggests that business lobbying in support of protection has declined dramatically, relative to pro-trade lobbying. Finally, perhaps the most interesting development in US trade politics has been the rise of the individual firm as a political actor. Individual firm lobbying activity has increased relative to lobbying activity by industry-wide associations. The frequency with which individual firms lobby today is not an outcome that has been documented in historical studies of US trade politics, which described broad societal coalitions lobbying jointly for shared policy goals, and it is not one that the classic, endowments-based trade theories predicted.

4.2 INTRA-INDUSTRY TRADE AND TRADE POLICY COALITIONS IN THE US

The above discussion presents a picture of a lobbying landscape in the US that has increasingly become dominated by individual firms rather than industry-based associations. During this same time, a major development in the structure of the global economy was the rise of intra-industry trade. As discussed in Chapter 2, intra-industry trade has risen in the US during the postwar period, as it has in almost all of the advanced industrialized economies. Figure 4.7 shows the rise in IIT as a proportion of total US trade, reaching approximately 60 percent at the start of the new millennium. Figure 4.8 is a density plot showing how IIT has changed over time in the US at the industry level. We see that in 1962, most industries were characterized by low levels of IIT but that by 2018, over half of US SITC four-digit industries have IIT levels that reach over 50 percent of the industry's total trade.

As discussed in Chapter 2, developed economies around the world experienced a marked increase in IIT during the postwar period, especially in their trade with each other. An example of these processes at work can be found in the changing structure of the automobile industry in North America in the latter half of the twentieth century. Prior to the Canada–US Auto Pact of 1965, trade in automobiles between the two countries faced a 17.5 percent tariff, and the Canadian industry suffered from major inefficiencies. For example, in 1961, forty-nine different vehicle models were produced in Canada (by affiliates of US automakers) with inefficiently short production runs that drove up retail prices (Thomas, 1997). Prior to the adoption of the Pact, the automobile trade between the two countries was highly inter-industry: In 1964, US automotive exports to Canada (both parts and finished vehicles) were

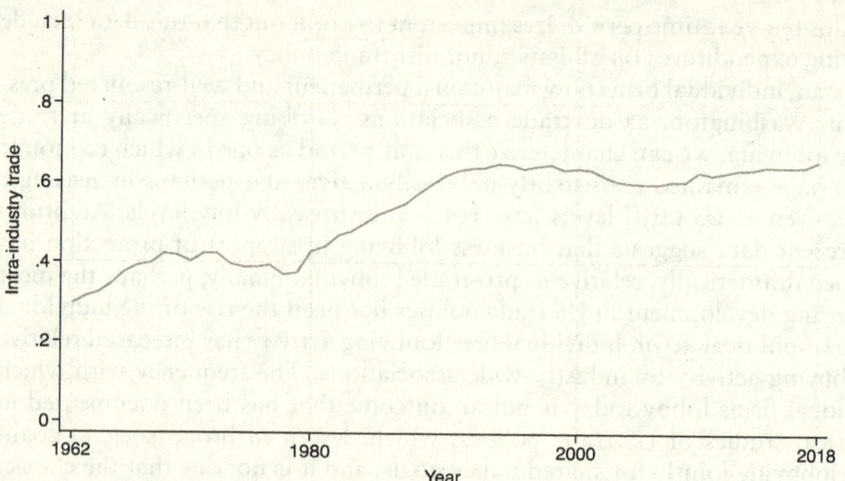

FIGURE 4.7 Intra-industry trade as a proportion of total US trade, 1962–2018
Data source: Author's calculations based on trade flows data from the Atlas of Economic Complexity.

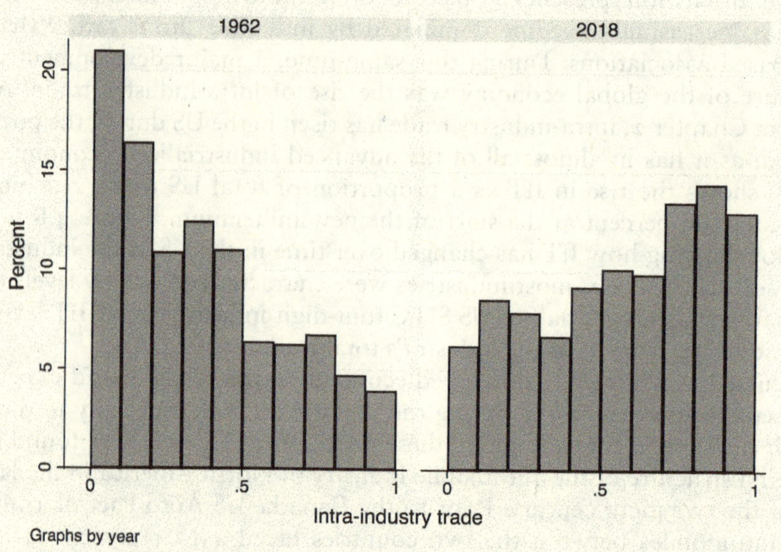

FIGURE 4.8 Distribution of IIT, US SITC four-digit industries, 1962 and 2018
Data source: Atlas of Economic Complexity.

$575 million and imports from Canada totaled only $76 million. As transport costs between the two countries fell with innovations in rail cars, and firms successfully lobbied for tariff liberalization through the Auto Pact, Canadian producers were able to rationalize their operations and substantially increase production, including exports to the US. Intra-industry trade in automobiles rose dramatically between the two countries, and a similar process unfolded in many industries across North America. Intra-industry trade between the US and European countries also rose significantly as Europe recovered from World War II and its manufacturing firms became globally competitive. American consumers developed a taste for German cars and Italian clothing, and manufacturers on both sides of the Atlantic specialized in varieties of high-tech chemicals, pharmaceuticals, mechanical instruments, and machine tools (among other manufactures), seeking foreign markets and foreign suppliers. Not all firms benefited from international trade, however. In the case of the Canada–US Auto Pact, for example, smaller parts-makers on both sides of the border held preferences that directly opposed those of large multinational competitors. These smaller firms expected losses as trade was liberalized, lobbying for continued protection as larger multinationals lobbied in support of tariff reductions (Thomas, 1997).

In this chapter, I test my argument developed in Chapter 3 that as intra-industry trade increases, it leads to a breakdown in industry consensus over trade and incentivizes individual firms to lobby. I argued that intra-industry trade increases the probability that individual firms will be pivotal to trade policy outcomes by making trade policy more contentious within industries, reduces the costs of firm-based lobbying relative to coalition-based lobbying, and raises the stakes of trade policy for individual firms in industries facing IIT. With competing preferences among firms in the same industry, and substantial firm-level gains or losses at stake, firms have an incentive to take political action to counter opposing voices lobbying for trade policies that run counter to their interests.

The implication of this argument is that as intra-industry trade increases, I expect lobbying by associations and other industry-based groups to be lower, relative to lobbying by individual firms. Because of competing trade preferences among firms in the same industry, collective action is more difficult. Firms may revoke membership or contributions if trade associations take an active lobbying stance for a trade position that is counter to their interests. To avoid losing members, associations may take weaker stances on policy. They may also stop lobbying for particular trade positions altogether or they may decrease the amount of resources they spend on lobbying over trade legislation. As industry associations become less active in trade policymaking due to competing trade preferences among their members, some individual firms will become politically active, lobbying alone for their preferred policies. Thus, I expect that as IIT increases, individual firm lobbying will increase relative to association-based lobbying. As an example, many small businesses join the

National Federation of Independent Businesses (NFIB) because they feel that they are poorly represented in their industry-based associations, which are often dominated by large firms holding different preferences over trade and other issues.[10] Yet the NFIB is not active in lobbying over trade policy due to competing interests among its members firms. NFIB surveys its members regarding their preferences over a range of issues, and if there is no consensus above a certain threshold, NFIB does not take a position on that issue. Trade policy is one of these issues where members are not unified in their preferences, constraining NFIB's ability to lobby on trade.[11] I therefore hypothesize the following:

H1: Individual firm lobbying over trade, relative to associational lobbying, will be higher in industries with higher intra-industry trade.

Another implication of my argument is that the effects of rising IIT on the political organization of industries will be strongest in comparative disadvantage industries. In these industries, firms face heavy import competition and are primarily domestic-oriented, with few profitable export opportunities. IIT is low, and firms are united around protectionist preferences. Industry associations are likely to take an active political stance in support of continued trade protection. Yet as some firms are able to find foreign markets for their product varieties, they are likely to support reciprocal trade liberalization to lower the cost of exporting (and importing). In this scenario, these exporting firms have an interest in breaking from the industry position and lobbying individually for liberalization. They are also likely to pressure their industry associations to cease protectionist lobbying. Industry associations are likely to scale back their political activity in order to avoid alienating members with conflicting trade preferences. The result is a greater amount of individual firm lobbying relative to associational lobbying, as IIT increases in comparative disadvantage industries.[12]

In comparative advantage, net-exporting industries, by contrast, an increase in two-way trade means an increase in imports. Heavier import competition may generate a protectionist response only from small, non-exporting firms that don't rely on reciprocal access to foreign markets. If these firms find it difficult to mobilize the resources to lobby for protection or sway the position of their industry groups, we may not observe changes in patterns of political organization, despite competing preferences. This suggests that the effect of IIT on political organization is conditional on the export orientation of an industry and yields my second hypothesis:

---

[10] Author's interview with NFIB staff, April 21, 2021.
[11] Ibid.
[12] When a net-importing industry increases its exports, trade flows become more balanced. In other words, IIT increases. I demonstrate this mathematically in Appendix B.1.

H2: The effect of IIT on firm-based lobbying will be strongest in net-importing, comparative disadvantage industries.

Finally, I expect that lobbying expenditures by industry associations will decrease as IIT increases. As follows from the above discussion, in high-IIT industries, intra-industry division over trade policy preferences will be most acute, and associations will reduce their political activity in order to avoid alienating members.

H3: Lobbying expenditures by industry associations will decrease as IIT increases.

4.3 ALTERNATIVE EXPLANATIONS

Firm- and industry-level factors also influence firm choices about whether to lobby together or alone over trade policy. Industry size and structure play a role in whether industry associations are politically active or not: Less concentrated industries characterized by a large number of firms should find it more difficult to engage in collective action. Many studies have investigated this relationship. Some find that firms in concentrated industries often lobby through coalitions, because industries with fewer firms face lower collective action costs and are most effective at mobilizing member firms to take joint and sustained political action (De Bièvre and Eckhardt, 2011; Drope and Hansen, 2009). Other studies find the opposite, however, (Bombardini and Trebbi, 2012; Bernhagen and Mitchell, 2009), and in general, results of studies attempting to link industry concentration with the mode of lobbying (firm-based or industry-based) are quite mixed. This is likely because although concentrated industries with fewer firms face fewer collective action problems and may be more likely to engage in political action than large industries, these industries may also be dominated by large firms that are able to shoulder the costs of lobbying alone. The extent of product differentiation can also affect firm preferences over trade, undermining collective action (Bombardini and Trebbi, 2012; Kim, 2017; Osgood, 2017).

Within industries, larger firms are more likely to lobby individually than smaller firms because lobbying is costly and larger firms are more likely to have resources available for political activity (Bombardini, 2008; Bernhagen and Mitchell, 2009; Drope and Hansen, 2006; Hansen and Mitchell, 2000). Smaller firms are more likely to channel their political activity (if any) through associations, pooling their resources with other firms in their industry and delegating responsibility to the association (Kerr et al., 2013). Firms that participate in global value chains – whether through importing intermediate inputs or through intra-firm trade – should also hold different preferences than domestic-oriented firms, making collective action difficult. Though firms in industries with high IIT also source foreign inputs and trade with affiliates, these activities are not exclusive to high-IIT industries. Large, competitive firms in all industries are likely to have global linkages, which could undermine industry consensus over trade regardless of intra-industry trade. As industry-leading firms reduce their input costs through trade liberalization, this further disadvantages firms that do not have the capacity to internationalize. Variation in industry concentration, product differentiation, firm size, and integration in global value chains are important alternative explanations for variation in associational/firm-based lobbying that the analysis in this chapter will directly address. I will show that IIT has an independent effect on firm choices about mode of lobbying, controlling for the firm and industry characteristics that also influence their decision-making about whether and how to lobby.

Additionally, political and policymaking institutions affect firm choices about whether to lobby together or alone over trade policy. Institutions incentivize as well as disincentivize political action by different types of interest groups. Much of the institutionalist literature on lobbying homes in on the degree to which various political and policymaking institutions are responsive to particularistic interests. Institutions that are responsive to narrow, particularistic interest groups (as narrow as individual firms) incentivize lobbying by individual firms. Other institutions may be better insulated from particularistic lobbying and societal actors have an incentive to form broad coalitions to demonstrate the breadth of societal support for their preferred policies. The literature demonstrates that institutional differences in electoral rules (Betz, 2017; Grossman and Helpman, 2005; Kono, 2009; Rogowski, 1987), political parties (Hankla, 2006; McGillivray, 2004), location of trade-policymaking authority in the executive or legislature (Lohmann and O'Halloran, 1994), and the ease of accessing the policymaking process (Ehrlich, 2007; Henisz and Mansfield, 2006; O'Reilly, 2005) all affect decisions about whether and how to lobby. Institutions certainly play a major role in structuring societal incentives to mobilize (or not) to influence trade policy. My aim in this book is to show how the rising importance of intra-industry trade in global trade patterns has changed the domestic politics of trade in the countries most affected by it, *independent of political institutions*. I do this by analyzing the effects of IIT on mode of lobbying in the European Union as well as in the United States, two economies with similarly high levels of IIT but very different institutional contexts. We turn to the European Union in Chapter 5.

4.4 DATA AND METHODOLOGY

I test my three hypotheses above using data on trade policy lobbying in the US. I use a data sample consisting of all 459 four-digit US manufacturing industries, minus missing data. The industries are part of the 2000 and 3000 major groups of manufacturing sectors and encompass the entire range of manufactured products, from food products to chemicals to apparel to machinery.

I created this dataset by merging data on lobbying expenditures collected by Bombardini and Trebbi (2012) with trade data and other firm and industry data that comprise my independent variables. Bombardini and Trebbi's data document lobbying expenditures by firms and associations from a wide range of US industries that lobbied over trade policy. This data is sourced from the Center of Responsive Politics and the US Senate Office of Public Records and it consists of lobbying spending targeted at Congress and US government agencies.[13] Data from 1999 to 2001 were pooled to maximize coverage. Each observation is coded to indicate whether the lobbying client was an individual firm or a trade association and matched to a four-digit level industry according to the Standard Industrial Classification (SIC) system. Data are also aggregated to obtain an industry-level measure. While a time- series analysis would allow us to observe how changes in IIT affect a particular industry's lobbying dynamics over time, I rely on a cross-sectional analysis instead for a few reasons. First, lobbying expenditure data are not available before 1998, and not every industry lobbies over the trade issue every single year, meaning that there are limited data points available for each industry over this time period, reducing the utility of a time-series analysis. Second, lobbying disclosure reports do not include standard industry identifiers, so each lobbying actor must be manually matched to an industry. With over 1,000 lobbying reports filed annually in the trade policy issue area, manually coding a long time-series represents a monumental task. A cross-sectional analysis pooling three years of data, however, allows us to maximize industry coverage and compare differences in lobbying patterns *across* industries with widely varying levels of IIT.[14] In the remainder of this section, I describe my dependent and independent variables as well as data sources.

Dependent Variable

The dependent variable in this analysis, *Firm Lobbying Proportion*, is measured as the proportion of an industry's lobbying expenditures that are made by individual firms relative to expenditures by industry associations. This measure was obtained from Bombardini and Trebbi (2012), who coded lobbying actors in the trade policy issue area to indicate whether they are individual firms or industry associations. *Firm Lobbying Proportion* is a bounded continuous variable ranging from 0 to 1. A score of 0 indicates that associations are responsible for all lobbying expenditures in an industry, while a score of 1 indicates that individual firms are responsible for all lobbying expenditures

---

[13] Before the passage of the Lobbying Disclosure Act in 1995, studies of trade politics often used campaign contribution data to measure political activities, which is problematic because it is not possible to know whether contributions were made in order to influence trade policy or other issues entirely.

[14] Chapter 6 of this book, however, does use time-series analysis to analyze how IIT is related to trade policy outcomes at the industry level.

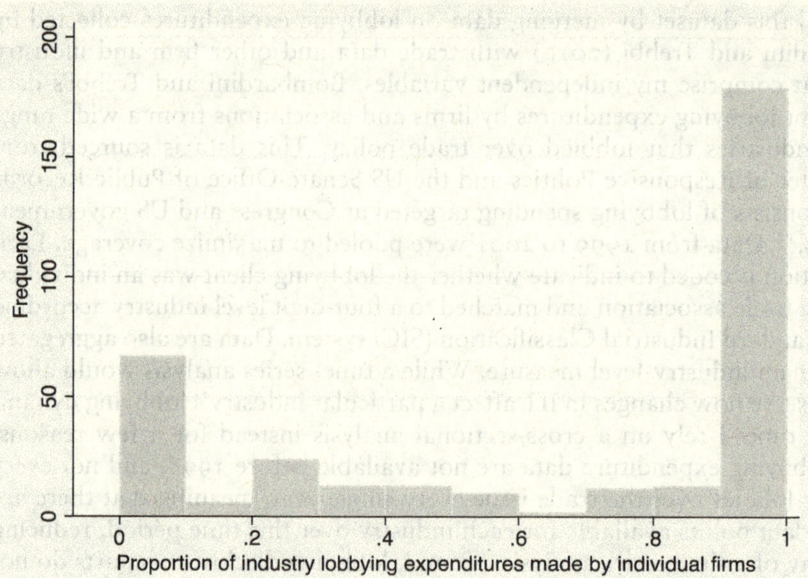

FIGURE 4.9 Trade lobbying by individual firms versus coalitions in US manufacturing industries, 1999–2001
Data source: Bombardini and Trebbi (2012).

in an industry. It is important to note that lobbying disclosure data do not tell us what is being lobbied. I leverage it here because it gives us a picture of how industries are politically organized to influence trade policy. A higher score on the dependent variable indicates greater individual firm lobbying relative to industry associational activity, within a given industry.

A closer look at the lobbying data reveals some interesting empirical observations. Most interestingly for the arguments advanced in this chapter, there is great variation in the ways in which US industries organize politically. In some industries, individual firms contribute nearly all of the lobbying expenditures. In other industries, lobbying is done nearly exclusively by trade associations. The distribution of this dependent variable is strongly bimodal.[15] Figure 4.9 is a frequency histogram showing the number of industries with various proportions of individual firm lobbying versus trade association lobbying. We see that it is common for individual firms to contribute nearly all of an industry's lobbying expenditures, and it is also common for individual firms to contribute nearly none of the lobbying expenditures. Figure 4.9 shows that in 179 industries (or nearly 53% of the 339 manufacturing industries that lobbied over trade policy in the years 1999–2001), over 90% of lobbying expenditures are

---

[15] In this sample, the mean proportion of industry lobbying undertaken by individual firms is 0.59.

made by individual firms. In sixty-seven manufacturing industries (approximately 20% of industries that lobbied), industry associations are responsible for more than 90% of lobbying expenditures.

Independent Variable

The main independent variable in this study is *Intra-Industry Trade*. I employ the most commonly used measure of intra-industry trade, developed by Grubel and Lloyd (1975) and described more fully in Chapter 2. This measure approaches one as trade becomes more balanced, or more heavily IIT, and it reaches zero when there is no two-way trade in the given industry. A low score on the IIT measure indicates that a sector is either a strong exporting sector with few imports or a heavily import-competing sector with few exports. Because the lobbying data in this analysis is coded according to the SIC system, here I use import and export data from the year 1999 classified using this system from Schott (2008).[16]

Control Variables

I include several control variables to test for leading alternative explanations for variation in the structure of political organization, as discussed above. I include a measure of industry concentration to test the argument that lobbying through trade associations will occur in more concentrated industries with fewer collection action problems to overcome. *Industry Concentration* is from Bombardini and Trebbi (2012) and is measured as the four-firm concentration ratio: The percentage of industrial shipments that are produced by the top four firms in an industry. I control for the level of product differentiation using Broda and Weinstein (2006)'s measure of *Elasticity of Substitutability*. Though industries with high product differentiation (low elasticity of substitutability) are also likely to experience high IIT, these two variables are uncorrelated in this sample (corr=0.015).[17] The variable *Average Firm Size* measures the average firm size in each industry, controlling for the fact that large firms are more likely to lobby alone than small firms. Thus, in industries with a large average firm size, individual firm lobbying activity may be higher relative to associational activity. I calculate this variable by dividing each industry's total shipments by the number of establishments. The variable *Industry Size* evaluates the argument that larger industries with more resources may

---

[16] The process of converting Comtrade data to the SIC classification system results in less precise measurements, as in many instances multiple SITC four-digit categories map onto a single SIC four-digit category. The underlying source of the Schott data is the US Census Bureau.

[17] The authors describe this measure in detail in Broda and Weinstein (2006). This measure captures the extent to which consumers can easily substitute one good for another similar good. Goods that are easily substitutable are likely to be more homogeneous goods, while highly differentiated varieties are less easily substituted for each other.

have more active industry associations. I measure industry size using shipment data. These variables are constructed using data from the 1997 US Economic Census, available from Fort and Klimek (2018).

I also include trade-related variables to control for the effects of integration into global value chains. I use a measure of industry use of *Imported Intermediates* in 1999 obtained from Schott (2004), divided by total industry imports to obtain the portion of each industry's imports that consists of intermediate goods. To control for intra-firm trade, I use data from 2002 (the earliest year available) on related-party imports and exports from the US Census Bureau Related-Party Trade Database. I create an index of total *Related-Party Trade* for each industry by summing related-party imports and exports, then divide that number by total trade to measure the portion of each industry's trade that consists of trade with affiliates.[18]

Finally, I control for existing levels of tariff protection using data from UNCTAD TRAINS. In industries that already have low tariffs, overall lobbying levels may be low. The variable *Tariff* is constructed using trade-weighted Most Favored Nation tariff averages at the SIC four-digit level in the year 1999. In all models, I include SIC-1 level fixed-effects to control for unmeasured factors that may differ across the two groups of manufacturing sectors included in this analysis. Sectors in the 2000-group include agricultural and food manufacturing, mills, tobacco products, apparel, textiles, paper products, and chemicals, while sectors in the 3000-group include plastics, footwear, metal products, machinery, electronics, laboratory instruments, vehicles, and others. I report descriptive statistics for all variables in Appendix Table B.1.[19]

4.5 EMPIRICAL ANALYSIS AND RESULTS

To test my argument that an increase in intra-industry trade leads to more active lobbying by individual firms relative to industry associations, I estimate the following model using Tobit regression:

$$\textit{Firm Lobby Proportion}_i = \alpha + \beta IIT_i + \beta X_i + e_i, \qquad (4.1)$$

---

[18] The Census Bureau data are coded according to the NAICS 2002 industry classification system. I manually matched the NAICS data to the SIC87 data employed in this chapter using the concordance provided by the US Census and available at www.census.gov/naics.

[19] One potentially important control variable that is missing from this analysis is the extent of labor's political activity. When labor unions are highly mobilized and active over a particular trade issue, this is likely to affect lobbying choices by firms and industry associations. Yet because labor unions typically represent workers in a wide variety of industries, they cannot be matched to the four-digit industries used in this analysis. Lobbying by the United Steel workers, for example, could potentially be matched to many industries, and lobbying disclosure reports do not specify the industries of concern. I consider the role of labor union lobbying in the case study in Chapter 7.

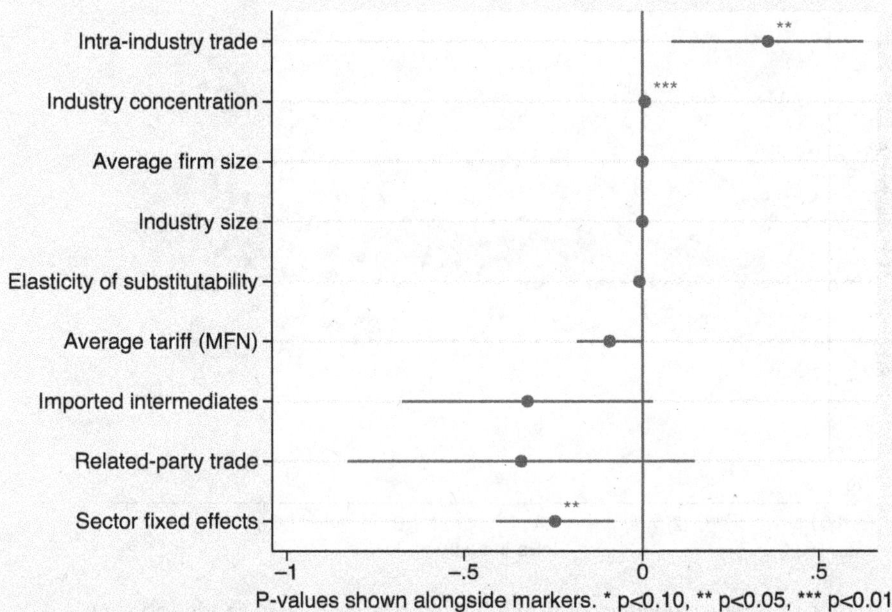

FIGURE 4.10 The effect of IIT on firm lobbying relative to association lobbying: Main model

where *Firm Lobby Proportion* is the proportion of industry i's lobbying expenditures undertaken by individual firms, *IIT* is industry i's level of intra-industry trade and X includes the control variables described above. I estimate this model using Tobit because the dependent variable is measured as a proportion of one with non-normal distribution and censoring occurring toward both zero and one (see Figure 4.9). Therefore, I treat the proportion as a continuous variable censored at 0 and 1, employing a two-limit Tobit model.[20]

Coefficient estimates of the fully specified regression are displayed graphically in Figures 4.10 and 4.11. A full regression table including various model specifications is presented in Appendix Table B.2. The results show that intra-industry trade is positively and significantly related to more active lobbying over trade policy by individual firms, relative to trade associations (*H1*). A one-unit increase in IIT results in a .34 unit increase in the proportion of firm lobbying relative to association lobbying, and the size of this effect is substantial relative to the other variables in the model. We can see that as IIT increases, political activity by individual firms becomes more likely, while collective political activity at the industry level becomes less likely. Firms in industries with

---

[20] Long (1997) and others argue that dependent variables measured as a proportion or a percentage out of 100 can be treated as a censored variable. Tobit models are used to analyze dependent variables that cannot take values above or below certain limits (Roncek, 1992).

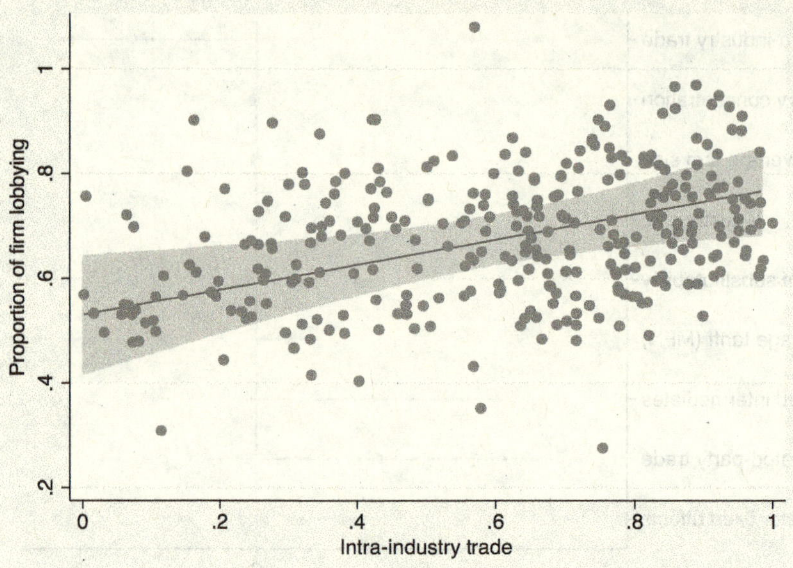

FIGURE 4.11 Predicted values of firm lobbying relative to association lobbying

high levels of IIT contribute a substantial proportion of the industry's lobbying expenditures, relative to associations. In industries with low levels of IIT, individual firms lobby less intensively relative to industry associations.

This result holds even when controlling for leading alternative explanations that are expected to influence the way firms and industries mobilize politically. Industry concentration is also positive and significantly related to firm-based lobbying, although the size of the effect is very small. When an industry's production is more concentrated into the hands of the four leading firms within the industry, these firms are slightly more likely to lobby alone than firms in less concentrated sectors.[21]

To check the robustness of the results of the primary model in Figure 4.10 I tested for the effect of outliers, and results hold when high-leverage observations are removed. Second, I repeated the analysis using probit and logit

---

[21] As concentration decreases and an industry's production is more dispersed among many firms, these firms are more likely to engage politically via an industry-based association. This finding seems to challenge the Olsonian expectation that industries with fewer firms, or fewer big firms, have an easier time organizing to jointly influence policy. However, Olson's logic rests on an assumption of shared preferences. In an industry with heterogeneous trade preferences, trade associations are reluctant to take a strong lobbying stance. Firms that want to influence policy are faced with two options: (1) lobby alone, or (2) form a new, smaller coalition with like-minded firms. Olson also argues that new collective action organizations are extremely costly to create. Thus big, influential firms at the forefront of highly concentrated industries may calculate that resources are best spent lobbying directly than building ad hoc coalitions.

estimation techniques.[22] Results are similar using both these estimators. Third, I included Busch and Reinhardt (1999)'s measures of political and geographic concentration to control for other determinants of industry-level lobbying strength. The results are similar and all of these alternative specifications are presented in Appendix Tables B.3, B.4, and B.5.

To increase confidence in the independent effect of IIT on political organization, I repeated my analysis using discretized elasticity measures (capturing low, medium, and high levels of substitutability, which correspond to high, medium, and low levels of product differentiation, respectively), and my results hold (see Appendix Table B.6). Product differentiation is also significant in each of these models. While product differentiation is one factor that affects how industries and firms lobby over trade, the results presented here demonstrate that IIT has an independent effect on lobbying regardless of the level of product differentiation. The two phenomena are in fact not correlated in this sample. At all levels of product differentiation, two-way trade incentivizes lobbying by individual firms for their preferred trade policies.

4.6 COMPARATIVE ADVANTAGE AND DISADVANTAGE INDUSTRIES

Hypothesis 2 predicted that the effect of IIT on the structure of industry lobbying will be conditional on whether that industry is primarily export-oriented or import-competing. I expect that increasing IIT will have the strongest effect on firm-based lobbying in net-importing (comparative disadvantage) industries. In the next model, I interact IIT and a dummy variable that proxies revealed comparative advantage, in order to assess the relationship between IIT and political organization at different levels of import competition. To create the dummy variable, I define an industry as net-exporting (RCA dummy=1) if its export – import ratio is greater than 1, and import-competing if its export – import ratio is less than 1 (RCA dummy=0). Regression results of this interaction are displayed in Appendix Table B.7 and illustrated graphically in Figure 4.12. I centered the IIT variable at its mean so that the coefficient of the interaction term is more directly interpretable.[23] We see that among net-importing industries, the effect of IIT on political organization is significant, positive, and substantively meaningful: A one-unit increase in IIT leads to a 0.55 unit increase in firm-based lobbying relative to associational lobbying. The effect of IIT on firm-based lobbying among net-exporting industries $(\beta_1 + \beta_3)$ is negative (-.33) and not significant. We also see that at mean levels of IIT, firm-based lobbying is higher in comparative advantage industries than in comparative disadvantage industries (.22), and this difference is statistically significant.

---

[22] To estimate probit and logit models, I converted the dependent variable to a dichotomous variable with values of 0 if firm lobby proportion is less than or equal to 0.2 and 1 if it is greater than or equal to 0.8. The number of observations drops to 208.

[23] In the plots displayed in Figure 4.12, however, I used the untransformed IIT variable to ease the interpretation of the graphical results.

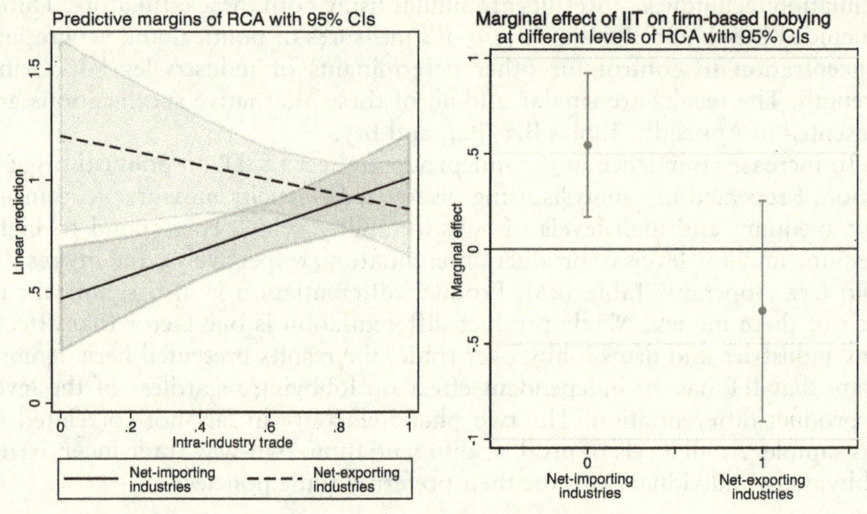

FIGURE 4.12 Effects of IIT on firm-based lobbying in net-exporting vs. net-importing industries

Taken together, the results of the interaction show that increasing IIT is associated with increased firm-level lobbying in comparative disadvantage industries, but it does not have a statistically significant effect on lobbying in comparative advantage industries.

This is strong support for *H2* and more generally for the theory presented in this book, which argues that IIT generates competing intra-industry preferences, hamstringing the political activity of industry associations in precisely the industries where associations are likely to be most active: Net-importing, comparative disadvantage industries. Recall that in net-importing sectors, an increase in IIT represents an increase in exports relative to imports. Thus, we likely see more firm-level lobbying in net-importing sectors as IIT increases because industry associations have a more difficult time taking positions on trade policy that satisfy the diverse needs of their members. This means they are less likely to lobby while large firms are more likely to lobby alone for more liberal trade policies. In strong exporting industries, an increase in IIT represents an increase in imports relative to exports. This may generate support for trade protection only from small, non-exporting firms that don't rely on reciprocal access to foreign markets. If these firms find it difficult to mobilize the resources to lobby or sway the position of their industry groups, we may not observe changes in patterns of political organization. The results of these models show that IIT may not have a uniformly positive effect on firm-level lobbying in all industries. If the effect of IIT on lobbying is to erode industry consensus and generate greater lobbying efforts by individual firms, the effect appears to be weakest when large exporting firms and industry associations are aligned in their trade preferences (comparative advantage industries). Small, domestic-oriented firms are the least equipped to lobby effectively against powerful exporters and industry associations. Thus, the effects of IIT on lobbying are weakest in net-exporting industries.

4.7 IIT AND AMOUNT OF LOBBYING EXPENDITURES

In the previous analyses, I examined the relationship between intra-industry trade and the *proportion* of industry lobbying made by individual firms relative to industry associations. We see that as IIT increases, individual firms are more active lobbying relative to associations. In this section, in order to evaluate H_3, I examine the relationship between IIT and total domestic industry lobbying expenditures, total domestic firm lobbying expenditures, and total domestic industry association lobbying expenditures. The data source for expenditures data is the Bombardini and Trebbi (2012) data described earlier. Though this analysis can only analyze changing lobbying expenditures among industries that lobbied, a large majority of industries lobby over trade policy. Over the ten-year period from 1998 to 2008, Bombardini and Trebbi (2012) found that 84 percent of sectors lobbied in this issue area. In the following analyses, I include the same covariates described in Section 4.4. Each of these three dependent variables is continuous, so I estimate OLS models with robust standard-errors. Each dependent variable is square root-transformed to reduce skew.

Results of these analyses are shown in Figure 4.13 and full regression tables are presented in Appendix Table B.8. First, I examine the relationship between IIT and an industry's total domestic lobbying expenditures, and we see that IIT has a negative and significant effect on spending. IIT has a negative but insignificant relationship with overall lobbying expenditures by individual firms, and a negative and significant relationship with overall lobbying expenditures by industry associations. Substantively, a one-unit increase in IIT results in a .34 unit decline in industry association expenditures. This means that if an industry's trade shifted from being completely inter-industry to having perfectly balanced imports and exports (IIT=1), we would expect that industry's association to cut its lobbying expenditures by approximately one-third. These results hold even as we control for other leading factors that contribute to lobbying expenditures. Average firm size is not significant in these models, likely due to moderately high levels of multicollinearity with industry size. Average firm size is positively and significantly related to firm spending in two of the models when industry size is excluded (see Appendix Table B.9).

This is an important set of findings that helps to further clarify the effect of two-way trade on the political behavior of firms and industry associations. Interestingly, while the models presented in Sections 4.5 and 4.6 demonstrated

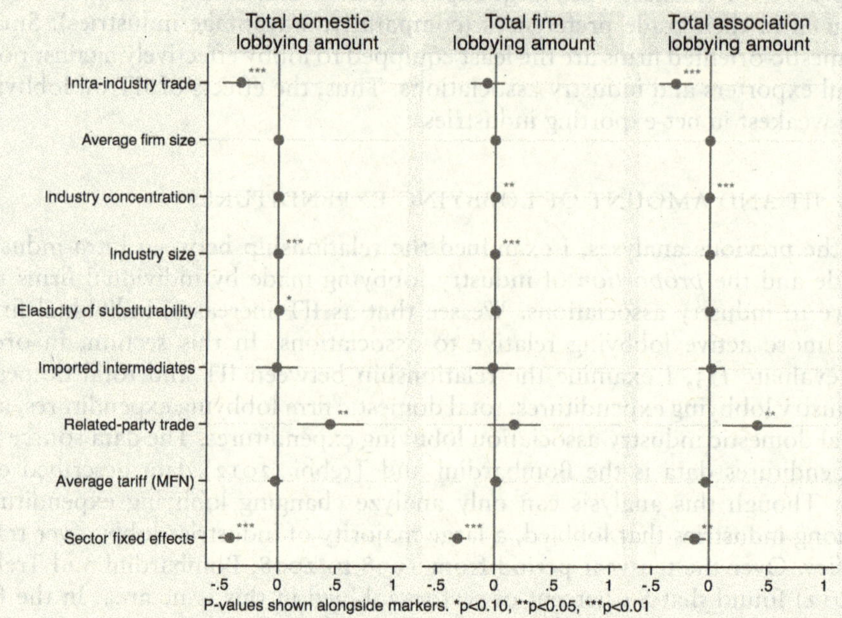

FIGURE 4.13 IIT and lobbying expenditures

that IIT has a strong positive effect on firms' *share* of overall industry lobbying relative to industry associations, the analyses in Figure 4.13 show us that increasing IIT leads to a decrease in the overall *amount* of industry lobbying, and particularly the amount of lobbying expenditures made by industry associations. This further confirms one of the central arguments made in this book, which is that IIT erodes consensus within industries and makes collective action at the industry level more difficult to achieve. The findings here show that the effect of IIT on political organization is primarily driven by the decline in lobbying by associations. Overall lobbying expenditures fall as associations reduce their lobbying due to the heterogeneity of member preferences, but we do not see an increase in firm spending: The relationship between IIT and the amount of individual firm expenditures is not significant. Instead, we see that increases in firm spending are driven by industry concentration, industry size, and revealed comparative advantage (and average firm size, when we model it separately from industry size, as in Appendix Table B.9). These findings suggest two things about firm lobbying. First, that the small subset of very large, internationalized firms lobby alone for firm-specific trade policy preferences regardless of levels of IIT (this is also supported by the findings in Figure 4.12, which showed that IIT did not have an effect on firms' share of lobbying in industries with revealed comparative advantage).

Second, anti-trade firms do not systematically substitute for declining associational lobbying through increased lobbying of their own. If so, we would expect to see a positive and significant effect of IIT on firm-level lobbying expenditures, which we do not. These findings are consistent with other recent work that emphasizes how little lobbying is carried out by anti-trade firms (Blanga-Gubbay et al., 2024; Osgood, 2021).

4.8 CONCLUSION

The results of my analyses provide support for my arguments about the relationship between intra-industry trade and the structure of domestic political coalitions organized to influence trade policy in the United States. In brief, I argued that the firm-level adjustment costs of trade liberalization in industries with high IIT lead to a breakdown in industry consensus over trade policy, limiting the extent to which industry associations can lobby for a particular trade position. This claim is supported in my analyses: Controlling for a host of factors, I consistently found that industry-based associations are less active relative to individual firms in industries with higher IIT. Additionally, I found that industry associations are less active overall as IIT increases. The dampening effect of IIT on industry-level collective action is stronger in import-competing sectors than in strong exporting sectors, and IIT appears to disincentivize association-based lobbying more than it incentivizes new firm-based lobbying. In other words, the very large, internationalized firms that benefit from free trade already actively lobby for their own interests, and IIT does not appear to incentivize much lobbying by smaller firms that are more limited in political resources and ill-equipped to match the political influence of industry-leading, pro-trade firms. As IIT has grown over the past few decades to account for an increasingly large share of total US trade, this may be one way to understand the rise of corporate lobbying in US trade politics. Large, globalized firms lobby intensively for their interests (across issue areas) while industry associations are less able to manage the competing preferences of internationally engaged and domestically oriented firms, scaling back their lobbying activity.

While the trade politics literature has recently emphasized the influence of industry- and firm-level characteristics on the structure of political organization, my study demonstrates the continued importance of international factors. My results confirm that firm and industry characteristics such as industry concentration, industry size, firm size, and product differentiation affect the way that firms and industries organize themselves politically, but I also show that political organization is affected by the nature of an industry's trade exposure. When trade creates opportunities for exporters at the same time that it results in greater import competition, industry-wide consensus is undermined, and this fracturing of trade policy preferences makes industry- level lobbying more difficult, no matter the size of the industry, the size of the average firm in the industry, or the extent of product differentiation. However, the effect of

IIT on lobbying in this study was strongest in industries facing heavy import competition, and it was weakest in strong exporting sectors. This suggests that large, exporting firms may lobby for freer trade as a counterweight to more protectionist industry associations, given the concentrated benefits they reap from trade. However, greater import competition in strong exporting industries (a result of reciprocal liberalization) does not generate additional lobbying by smaller, domestic-oriented firms that are less likely to find it profitable to lobby against the interests of politically powerful firms for greater protection.

Finally, the results of this study have fascinating implications for the rise of progressive opposition to free trade and globalization more broadly. I have documented a pronounced shift away from collective, industry-based lobbying as IIT increases and undermines shared preferences within industries. As industry associations have scaled back lobbying over trade, and small businesses opt out nearly entirely, the result is a lobbying landscape dominated by large corporations lobbying for their own private interests, and the public sees this. Public interest groups decry the heavy corporate involvement in the drafting of recent trade policy legislation, and progressive anti-trade groups explicitly articulate a desire to rein in corporate power over the design of FTAs. Additionally, mobilizing a broad coalition has historically been very important to influencing policymakers in trade policy negotiations. Policymakers are in general more responsive when an entire industry voices its support for a particular policy, or better yet an even broader coalition across industries, or between industry and labor. Though large firms certainly wield significant political influence, it is possible that policymakers are more hesitant to support agreements that have not received clear support from a broader range of societal interest groups. This is especially interesting when considering the failure of an agreement like TTIP. Trade between the US and EU is heavily intra-industry in nature and further liberalization of already low tariffs (as well as the liberalization of trade-related regulatory barriers) would not threaten US industries or pose a significant risk to American jobs. Thus the failure of an agreement like TTIP is puzzling, though perhaps less so considering the important role that coalitions have always played in US trade politics as signaling mechanisms for broad business and societal support. A corporate-dominated lobbying landscape generates fears of hyper-globalization benefiting corporations at the expense of the environment, public health, and workers, and in this way, the decline of associations and the rise of firms may contribute to the progressive backlash against trade.

5

Lobbying over Trade Policy in the European Union

In today's European Union, trade policy has become deeply contentious and hotly contested. Over the last decade, major political battles have erupted within the EU over specific trade agreements (the TTIP, the Comprehensive Economic and Trade Agreement with Canada, and the EU–Mercosur free trade agreement) as well as over recurring hot-button issues in international trade (the liberalization of trade in agriculture, the battle over genetically modified food, and public outcry over imported chlorine-washed chickens, to name a few).[1] Until recently, trade policymaking in Brussels was the domain of technocrats and narrow business and industry representatives, who provide information at the Commission's request about the projected effects of proposed trade rules on their industries. For a long time, analysts remarked on the underrepresentation of interest groups in Brussels. Shaffer (2003, p.70) noted that in stark contrast to the US Trade Representative, an agency that is constantly bombarded with input from industry groups, firms, and consumer advocacy groups, the European Commission found itself in the odd position of reaching out to firms and business groups asking them to weigh in on trade policy issues. Many scholars argued that the underrepresentation of interest groups in Brussels working on trade policy was a result of institutional design, concluding that the delegation of trade policy to the EU level insulated policymakers from narrow, protectionist interests, enabling them to pursue their pro-liberalization mandate in a relatively opaque policy setting (Meunier, 2005; Nicolaidis and Meunier, 2012; Woolcock, 2005).

But more recent studies indicate that as trade policy has become highly politicized, interest groups and lobbying infrastructures have become

[1] The heated public debate over free trade in agricultural products is largely due to concerns that trade liberalization would compromise EU member states' longstanding opposition to genetically modified organisms.

entrenched in Brussels (Coen et al., 2021; Ehrlich and Jones, 2016; Young, 2016). As interest groups, NGOs, foreign firms, industry associations, and consumer groups have set up shop in the European capital over the last decade, scholars have noted how widely the lobbying landscape varies across policy areas, as well as how some types of interest groups enjoy a strong and influential presence while others do not seem to exert much influence. Additionally, there is wide variation in the extent to which individual firms have Europeanized, setting up government affairs offices in Brussels, as opposed to working through a more traditional hierarchy of representation in which firms and domestic-level interest groups are members of national sectoral associations, which in turn are members of Eurofederations (Bernhagen and Mitchell, 2009). In some cases (notably in the battle over TTIP), entirely new types of coalitions have formed, such as transnational alliances of pro-trade firms, which none of our standard trade theories predict (Young, 2016). Furthermore, even during the recent years of highly politicized trade agreements in Europe, some EU trade agreements fly nearly under the radar, arousing little public interest (FTAs with Japan, Korea, Malaysia, and Vietnam, for example) (de Bièvre and Poletti, 2020).

In this chapter, I assess how well the theory developed in this book can explain some of the heterogeneity we observe in the structure of political coalitions organized for the purpose of influencing the EU's trade policy. Specifically, I explain the noted rise of the individual firm as a political actor lobbying alone in Brussels (Bernhagen and Mitchell, 2009; Coen, 2007). I argue that, as in the US case, the changing structure of international trade in developed economies away from inter-industry trade and toward intra-industry trade has undermined the traditional class-based and industry-based coalitions that historically formed for or against trade openness. Because European firms within the same industry may no longer share the same preferences about trade, long-standing industry associations are limited in the degree to which they can put forth strong policy positions, reducing their political influence relative to individual firms. I test this theory with an original dataset of lobbying activity in the European Commission's open consultation process.

The EU represents a hard case for my theory, and the analysis in this chapter makes several important contributions. First, it is the first study to test theoretical claims about intra-industry's effects on domestic politics outside of the US case, an important addition to the literature on the politics of IIT. Scholars have recently observed that there are no studies thus far linking firm heterogeneity in trade gains to the decline of associational lobbying over trade policy in the EU (Dür et al., 2020). This study is the first, and extending the analysis in Chapter 4 to a second country case shows that the effect of IIT on trade politics is a structural phenomenon, not merely an artifact of American politics. In testing a theory developed and tested with success in the US case, this study connects the US and EU literatures on trade politics, advancing our theoretical understanding of the way intra-industry trade affects political activity across developed democracies with diverse institutional contexts. Second, in the EU, the formation of broad coalitions that span industries as well as member states has been of paramount importance for interest groups seeking influence in Brussels. Policymakers in Brussels are charged with making policy that advances pan-European interests, and institutions in Brussels are designed to insulate Eurocrats from special interest, particularistic lobbying. Interest groups in Europe have long realized the need to mobilize broad "peak" associations that bring together a range of interests from across member state lines, in order to demonstrate the breadth of societal support. In this political context, lobbying via association is much more likely than in the US, even among firms with the capacity to lobby alone. We can have more confidence in the effect of IIT on political organization if we observe a rise in firm-based lobbying in the EU, where associational lobbying has long been the norm. Finally, I make an empirical contribution in my construction of a new dataset of trade policy lobbying in the EU.

This chapter proceeds as follows. First, I briefly discuss the nature of trade policy in the EU, and then I survey the literature on the politics of trade in Europe, with a focus on the state of our knowledge about the character of political coalitions and the involvement of industry associations and individual firms in the trade policymaking process. Second, I discuss the role of intra-industry trade in the EU and present my argument about the way that IIT has eroded the ability of European industry associations to lobby jointly over trade policy. Third, I introduce the dataset I use to assess my argument and discuss my quantitative analysis and results.

5.1 EU TRADE POLICY

What are the political dynamics of trade policymaking in the European Union? Trade policy was one of the earliest purely supranational policies, with the Treaty of Rome granting exclusive authority to the European Economic Community (EEC) to decide upon common external tariffs.[2] Hanson (1998) argues that the EEC's commitment to the creation of the single market biased it early on toward liberalization of its external tariff policies as well. The commitment to market liberalization and free trade policies is evident in the EU's low tariff levels today. While the United States has also been at the forefront of the postwar global free trade regime, many scholars argue that EU policymakers are insulated from protectionist pressures in a way that US policymakers are not, as a result of the EU's supranational system and distinctive institutional design (Zimmermann, 2007, p. 247; Woolcock, 2005). Meunier (2005) argues that the Commission is able to pursue a more liberal course in trade policy than would be possible for elected officials at the member state level, who are

---

[2] The EEC was the name given to the regional organization established by the Treaty of Rome in 1957, the precursor to the modern EU. The original EEC member states were Belgium, France, West Germany, Italy, Luxembourg, and the Netherlands.

more susceptible to protectionist demands from their constituencies.[3] Adopting a principal-agent perspective, Dür and Elsig (2011) argue that the long chain of delegation from the EU's principals (the voters) to national parliaments, to national executives, and finally to the European Commission allows the agents in Brussels considerable autonomy to pursue liberal policy goals even in the face of strong protectionist pressures from society. Finally, the size and national diversity of the EU today – currently consisting of twenty-seven member states with industries largely specialized along national lines – makes it exceedingly difficult for a single member state to lobby successfully in the European Council for protection for a particular industry.

Despite the EU's stated commitment to free trade, its institutional biases toward liberal trade policies, and its low tariff levels, there remain many protectionist aspects of EU trade policy and plenty of opportunities for societal groups to influence policy in a trade-restrictive direction, especially given growing public skepticism about the value of free trade (Dür et al., 2020; Young and Peterson, 2006). The EU's anti-dumping policy has become a notorious and important tool with which import-competing sectors secure punitive duties on foreign imports, and the EU imposes anti-dumping duties extensively (Ketterer, 2016).[4] Efforts to reform anti-dumping policy in a more liberal direction have failed, due to lobbying from societal interests that want this protectionist tool at their disposal (De Bièvre and Eckhardt, 2011), and the EU has strengthened its trade defense instruments in recent years. Other analysts (and many of the EU's trading partners) argue that the EU's strict internal market regulations are a tool to restrict market access for foreign imports (Brülhart and Matthews, 2007). Finally, a recent study of NTMs found that the EU is second in the world in terms of the frequency with which it imposes NTMs on imports (the world leader in use of NTMs is the US), and agriculture is the sector in which NTMs are imposed most frequently (Grübler and Reiter, 2021). In short, while the EU maintains a stated commitment to free trade and relatively low tariff barriers in most sectors, there remain significant regulatory barriers to trade and effective instruments with which domestic producers can obtain protection.

5.2 TRADE POLITICS IN THE EUROPEAN UNION

How do firms and industries lobby in Europe over trade policy, and what explains industry-level variation in political organization? As in Chapter 4, I define lobbying as a political activity undertaken by societal actors, targeted

---

[3] Adopting similar assumptions about bureaucratic autonomy, Destler (1992) argues that in the US, members of Congress frequently delegate trade policymaking authority to the executive as a way to skirt protectionist pressures from their districts and ensure that welfare-enhancing liberal trade policies are adopted.

[4] Punitive duty imposed on Chinese solar panels was a recent high-profile anti-dumping case (Curran, 2015).

at relevant policymakers, for the purpose of influencing policy outcomes in a way that furthers their goals. Lobbying actors often provide goods desired by policymakers. In some policymaking contexts, notably the US, these goods often take the form of financial contributions to elected officials' campaign efforts. In the EU, however, the goods coveted by policymakers tend to be informational goods that communicate how proposed policy changes will affect European industries, firms, and member states (Broscheid and Coen, 2007; Coen et al., 2021). There is wide variation in the ways that European firms, labor unions, and other business interests organize for the purpose of influencing trade policy. Lobbying may take the form of direct action by firms, but more commonly it takes the form of collective action by groups of firms organized into industry-based associations or cross-sectoral coalitions. Interest groups must successfully influence national governments as well as European-level institutions (to varying degrees, depending upon the issue area).

Some industries have highly active industry associations at the European level, such as the European Chemicals Industry Council or the European Apparel and Textile Confederation. These Brussels-based peak associations are often called Eurofederations, and their memberships include national industry associations, labor unions, and individual firms. These federations must represent the interests of a very diverse membership, including large firms, small firms, and firms from many different member states. Perhaps not surprisingly, in some industries Eurofederations are weak, underfunded, and individual firms and national associations take a bigger role in trade policymaking. Machinery, for example, is one of the EU's strongest export sectors, but it is fairly disorganized as a sector and its leading firms like Siemens and Bosch typically represent their interests through direct engagement with policymakers. Firm choices about whether to lobby alone or via broader coalitions is of major concern to policymakers and scholars, given that lobbying by particularistic interests can produce inefficient policy outcomes that favor narrow special interests at the expense of broader societal interests (Huneeus and Kim, 2018; Martin and Swank, 2004; Olson, 1982).

In Chapter 4, I discussed the historical trajectory of corporate lobbying in the US, which grew dramatically over the course of the twentieth century as large firms relied less on their industry associations to represent their interests and established their own strong presence in Washington, lobbying on behalf of their own particularistic interests. In Europe, the rise of Brussels-based lobbying came later. The EU gradually expanded its competencies over the European economy, and the single market was established through landmark pieces of legislation such as the Single European Act and the Maastricht Treaty. With these major changes, business interest groups in Europe recognized the importance of establishing a presence in Brussels. By the 1990s, over 300 large firms had established government affairs offices in the European capital and began to develop a distinct "EU style of lobbying" that mixed national and supranational access points as well as direct and associational lobbying (Coen et al., 2021).

Two concurrent developments in Brussels-based lobbying dynamics are important to mention here. The first is the rise of direct lobbying by individual firms, even as EU institutions incentivize lobbying via broad coalitions. Studies of lobbying in the trade policy domain (as well as more general lobbying studies) indicate that individual firms have become increasingly active in EU politics since the 1990s, shouldering the burden of lobbying responsibility themselves instead of delegating it to an industry association or other coalition (Bernhagen and Mitchell, 2009; Coen et al., 2021; Greenwood, 2017). At the same time, the EU only began systematically collecting information about lobbyists in 2014, so longitudinal studies of lobbying are few and scholars are limited in the claims they can make. A recent study finds that individual firms have gradually increased their presence relative to industry associations and NGOs since 2008 and make up 44% of lobbying actors in the 2014–2019 period, compared to 39% for associations and 17% for NGOs (Hanegraaff and Poletti, 2021).[5]

A second key dynamic was the rise of Eurofederations, which were the result of national-level industry associations restructuring themselves into united, European-level associations. The rationale was that by presenting a unified front across national lines, industries could better demonstrate the breadth of the support behind their policy preferences, a point of great importance to Eurocrats tasked with prioritizing pan-European interests over those of individual member states. Eurofederations provide many services to their members, including but not limited to political advocacy in trade policy and other issue areas. A recent survey shows, however, that firms believe that representation in the EU institutions is very often the most important service that these associations provide. The survey asked individual members of "Euro group" associations to rank the importance of various services provided by the association. Ninety-four percent of respondents said that "representing members' interests in Europe" was the most important service provided by the association, and "access to EU advisory committees and working groups" was the most important service to 63% of respondents (Aspinwall and Greenwood, 2013). Given these dynamics, the rise of individual firm lobbying in Brussels is counterintuitive.

5.3 EXISTING EXPLANATIONS OF LOBBYING DYNAMICS IN THE EUROPEAN UNION

Because demonstrating broad societal support is especially important for interest groups in the European Union, with its need to satisfy constituencies of

---

[5] This is largely consistent with Berkhout et al. (2018), who find that individual firms make up around a third of all interest groups that actively lobby EU institutions.

twenty-seven member states, firm-based lobbying in Brussels emerged later than in Washington DC, and it is only fairly recently that the EU lobbying literature has focused specifically on individual firms.[6] For years, scholars have observed that the vast majority of studies of EU lobbying focus on business associations (and civil society organizations) rather than firms, noting many analysts exclude firms from their analyses altogether (Bernhagen and Mitchell, 2009; Hanegraaff and Poletti, 2021).[7] In one important book-length study of EU interest group lobbying, Mahoney (2008) examines why interest groups sometimes form ad hoc advocacy coalitions and other times choose to "forge ahead alone," but her units of analysis are interest *groups*, such as business associations. Individual firms are not considered in her analysis. In a review of the literature, Hanegraaff and Poletti (2021) note that the studies that do focus on lobbying by individual firms tend to examine whether firms lobby directly or do not engage politically at all, ignoring the third possibility that firms may participate in collective political activity through associations and coalitions.

In the multilevel lobbying context of the EU, what explains firms' choices about whether to lobby alone or collectively? Eckhardt (2018) asserts that state-centric explanations have long "dominated" the EU trade policy literature. These studies posit that various aspects of the EU's *sui generis* institutional context shape interest group politics more than interest groups shape EU trade policy. Across issue areas, the EU's pan-European mandate means that interest groups may exert more influence in Brussels through the formation of Euro-level coalitions that transcend national borders and demonstrate the broad support behind their preferences (Bouwen, 2002; Coen et al., 2021). The perceived benefits of lobbying via EU- or national-level industry associations may also be a result of the history of corporatist interest intermediation systems in many member states, which may have also taken hold at the EU level (Greenwood, 2017; Woll, 2006), though other studies find EU policymaking to be quite pluralist, often rewarding large firms lobbying alone (Coen et al., 2021; Eising, 2007). More specific to trade policy, an influential thesis holds that the EEC's founders deliberately delegated authority over trade policy to Brussels to insulate policymakers from protectionist interests (Meunier, 2005; Woolcock, 2005), though many subsequent studies find that trade policy aligns closely with interest group demands (Bernhagen et al., 2015; Dür, 2008; Dür and De Bièvre, 2007).

A prevailing pro-trade orientation in Brussels would plausibly influence political organization. The need to demonstrate broad support across national lines may be especially true for protectionist interests. Free-trading interests may be in a better position politically to forego collective action costs and

---

[6] In an overview of the EU lobbying literature, Bunea and Baumgartner (2014) describe a "new yet fast growing field" and observe that most studies within this field have appeared since 2007.

[7] Two notable exceptions are David Coen, whose research agenda since the 1990s has focused specifically on the role of large firms in EU policymaking, and Pieter Bouwen.

lobby alone, given that their preferences broadly align with the EU's liberal orientation to trade. A caveat here is that the EU is not a unitary actor, and some EU institutions and agencies take more protectionist stances than others (Eckhardt, 2018), another factor likely to influence lobbying strategies. In general, however, free trading interests may be more likely to lobby at the European level, particularly the European Commission, while protectionist actors may find more success at the member state level, hoping national governments will represent their interests in the Council of Ministers (Woll, 2009). Finally, the varying informational needs of the different EU institutions cause individual firms to have preferred access to some EU institutions (the Commission), while European federations and national associations are granted preferred access at other institutions (the Parliament and the Council) (Bouwen, 2002). The growing importance of independent regulatory agencies may privilege individual firms, which are better at providing technical information (Dür and Mateo, 2016; Hanegraaff and Poletti, 2021).[8] Thus, institutional factors may be important to firm decisions to lobby alone or collectively. However, none of these explanations can explain variations in coalition formation across issue areas or across industries within the trade policy issue area.

As the lobbying complex in Brussels has grown in recent decades, an increasing number of societal-centric studies focus on how firm and industry characteristics affect the ways that firms organize politically. The literature on lobbying in the EU confirms some of what researchers have found in the more developed literature on lobbying in the US, which I discussed in Chapter 4. As we would expect, and consistent with my findings in Chapter 4, studies show that firm size is a predictor of direct corporate lobbying at the EU level (Bernhagen and Mitchell, 2009; Bouwen, 2002; Dellis and Sondermann, 2017). Large firms can afford access; small firms cannot and they must exert influence through associations or other coalitions. Also consistent with the US analysis in Chapter 4, Bernhagen and Mitchell (2009) find that firms are most likely to lobby directly and bypass collective action in highly concentrated industries characterized by a small number of firms or a few leading firms. However, De Bièvre and Eckhardt (2011) find that firms in concentrated industries are most likely to lobby collectively through their trade associations, because there are fewer firms to coordinate and mobilize in more concentrated industries. These researchers also found that internationalized firms were more likely to lobby alone.[9] Greenwood (2017) emphasizes the great diversity of

---

[8] The different lobbying dynamics across EU institutions were apparent in my interviews in Brussels, where the Chair of the Trade Committee of the European Parliament emphasized how rare it is for firms to lobby alone at the European level, whereas a former staff member of Directorate-General Trade at the European Commission spoke about how commonly large firms lobby, especially over firm-specific interests.

[9] De Bièvre and Eckhardt (2011) found that policymakers responded to the highly mobilized, protectionist groups lobbying against liberalizing reform of the EU's anti-dumping policy, despite the fact that many large, leading EU firms lobbied alone in favor of this reform.

firm preferences over trade rules and regulatory issues, owing to differences in firm levels of internationalization, exposure to trade competition, and production profiles. Firm heterogeneity in size and available resources means that some firms have more influence over policymakers than others, and this affects firm decisions over whether to lobby directly or whether to lobby collectively through associations or ad hoc coalitions.

A third category of explanation focuses on the nature of the issue being contested and on the ways that the distribution of interests could affect collective action. When there is high political conflict over a policy proposal and many competing interests, this may make individual, direct corporate lobbying a more attractive and less costly type of political action. In her analysis of lobbying over EU environmental policies, Bunea (2014) demonstrates empirically that actors with identical policy preferences are more likely to lobby via coalitions than actors with differing preferences, suggesting that when conflict is higher, actors may be more likely to lobby alone. Dür et al. (2015) find that business groups are indeed more successful in their lobbying efforts when conflict among them is low. High-salience issues may also incentivize lobbying via association (as well as cross-sectoral coalitions) in order to demonstrate breadth of support (Beyers and De Bruycker, 2018).

This survey of the literature on interest group lobbying in the EU demonstrates how young this field is, especially compared to the US literature, how recently systematic lobbying data have become available, and how much remains to be learned about the determinants of lobbying behavior and political organizational structures. Scholars have identified a wide range of factors influencing firm decisions about whether to lobby directly or through an industry-based association, as well as whether the coalitions that do form are broad and cross-sectoral or narrow and industry-based. The existing literature shows that the shape of political coalitions varies across policy areas as well as across policymaking institutions. The literature on trade politics specifically suggests that large firms are more likely to lobby alone at the EU level than small firms are, but this doesn't explain the substantial variation in political organization that we observe across industries. As this chapter will show, in battles over trade policy, large firms in certain industries are much more likely to lobby via industry associations than large firms in other industries. By adopting an approach that focuses on the structural role of international trade in organizing domestic trade politics, my contribution not only makes sense of this variation, but it is generalizable across liberal democracies and testable in a comparative research design.

5.4 THE RISE OF INTRA-INDUSTRY TRADE IN THE EUROPEAN UNION

As discussed in Chapter 2, in all of the OECD economies, trade has become increasingly intra-industry rather than inter-industry, but economists first began to notice this phenomenon in the context of trade among members of the EEC during the early years of European economic integration. In the early 1960s, after the EEC was established by the Treaty of Rome (1957), there was considerable anxiety among member states that the new customs union would cause EEC members to specialize along industry lines (Greenaway and Milner, 1986). According to the logic of comparative advantage and conventional wisdom on the effects of customs unions, policymakers and societal actors alike expected France and Italy to specialize in agricultural goods while West Germany specialized in industrial production. Viner (1950) predicted that the decline of comparative disadvantage industries would lead to rising political opposition to European integration. Yet economists began to uncover a different pattern: The reduction of tariffs on intra-EEC trade led primarily to intra-industry specialization rather than inter-industry specialization (Balassa, 1966). In other words, producers in EC member states began to specialize in certain product lines, and a large-scale demise of comparative disadvantage industries did not materialize. The process of intra-industry specialization was most pronounced in member states with more developed manufacturing sectors. In his seminal study of the rise of IIT in Europe, Balassa (1966) noted that there were no examples of declining industries within the EEC as a result of the customs union, nor was there resulting unemployment, and he argued that this was likely because the EEC members were at similar stages of industrial development (with the exception of Italy). Balassa (1966) suggested that the EEC's experience would bode well for efforts to reduce tariffs among industrialized countries as part of the Kennedy Round of General Agreement on Tariffs and Trade (GATT) negotiations. In sum, the effect of economic integration in postwar Western Europe was trade-creating, rather than trade-diverting, and this trade was primarily intra-industry in nature (Greenaway and Milner, 1986).

As the EEC progressed toward creation of a single European market while also enlarging to include more member states, trade liberalization within the bloc continued to be surprisingly non-disruptive. Economists widely concluded that the ease with which Europe was able to liberalize within the bloc was due to the pattern of intra-industry specialization and rising IIT among member states. There were certainly adjustment costs to economic integration in Europe, but these were less severe than many analysts had expected. Brülhart and Hine (1999, p.3) argue that distributional implications became clearer in the 1970s and 1980s, as growth slowed, but that the expansion of redistributive Structural Funds effectively offset adjustment costs by compensating trade's losers. Stagnating IIT among EEC members in the 1980s was a worrisome sign to economists that adjustment costs were becoming more severe and a rise in protectionism was a likely possibility.

As trade liberalized within Europe, tariffs also fell substantially among industrial economies worldwide. Today, well over 60 percent of the EU's external trade is intra-industry trade, and it has risen steadily since the 1970s (see Figure 5.1). This trade primarily occurs with other high-income countries.

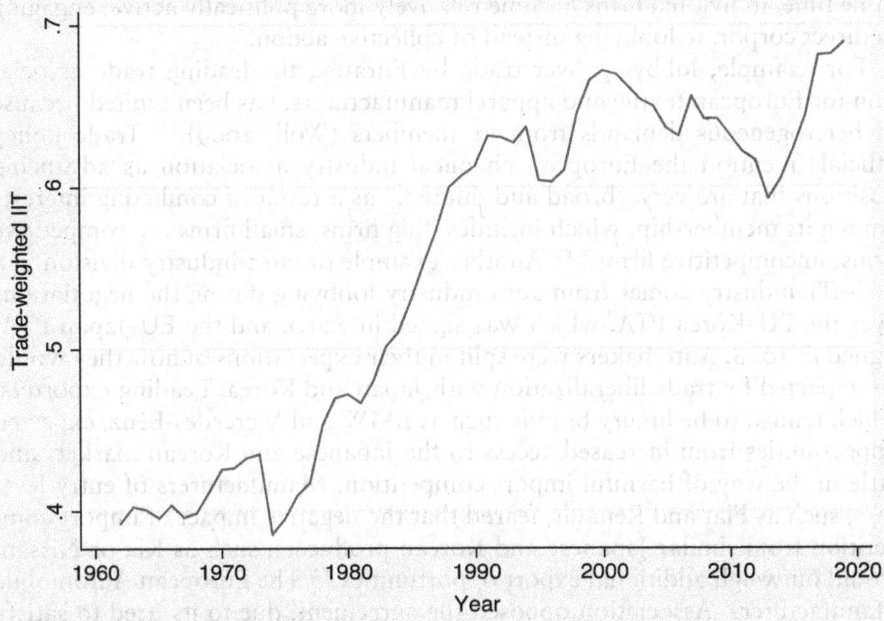

FIGURE 5.1 IIT as a proportion of total external trade, European Union, 1962–2019
Data source: Author's calculations based on Comtrade trade flows data.

5.5 INTRA-INDUSTRY TRADE AND POLITICAL COALITIONS IN THE EU

In this chapter, I argue that this fundamental change in the structure of international trade can explain variation in EU trade politics at the industry level. In EU industries subject to a high degree of intra-industry trade, we would expect associations to be less active relative to individual firms than in industries with lower levels of intra-industry trade.

As elaborated in Chapter 3, I argue that IIT undermines industry preferences over trade policy. This heterogeneity in firm preferences has the effect of weakening industry consensus over trade, making it more difficult for firms and labor unions to overcome collective action problems for the purpose of influencing trade policy via coalition. Industry-wide trade associations find it more difficult to secure broad support from their member firms on trade policy positions. Firms may revoke membership or contributions if trade associations take an active lobbying stance for a trade position that is counter to their interests. The result of this, in terms of trade policy lobbying, is that trade associations take weaker stances on policy to avoid losing members. They may also stop lobbying for particular trade positions altogether, or they may decrease the amount of resources they spend on lobbying over trade legislation. At the same time, individual firms become relatively more politically active, engaging in direct corporate lobbying instead of collective action.

For example, lobbying over trade by Euratex, the leading trade association for European textile and apparel manufacturers, has been limited because of heterogeneous demands from its members (Woll, 2009).[10] Trade policy officials mention the European chemical industry association as advancing positions that are very "broad and diluted," as a result of conflicting interests among its membership, which includes "big firms, small firms ... competitive firms, uncompetitive firms."[11] Another example of intra-industry division in a high-IIT industry comes from auto industry lobbying during the negotiations over the EU–Korea PTA, which was signed in 2010, and the EU–Japan PTA, signed in 2018. Automakers were split in their expectations of how they would be impacted by trade liberalization with Japan and Korea. Leading exporters, which tended to be luxury brands such as BMW and Mercedes-Benz, expected opportunities from increased access to the Japanese and Korean markets and little in the way of harmful import competition. Manufacturers of entry-level cars, such as Fiat and Renault, feared that the negative impact of import competition from similar Japanese and Korean producers, such as Kia or Nissan, would outweigh additional export opportunities.[12] The European Automobile Manufacturers' Association opposed the agreement, due to its need to satisfy the largest segment of the industry (and its membership), which are affordable consumer car producers.[13] As a result, automakers representing luxury brands mounted their own lobbying campaign in support of the agreement, lobbying individually.

A few years later, in negotiations over TTIP, Dür et al. (2019) note how unified business lobbying groups were in support of the agreement, with the exception of a few coalitions of small- and medium-sized businesses. These coalitions were most active in Germany, Austria, the Netherlands, and the UK. A group of anti-TTIP businesses from Austria explains their position on their website: "Over 90% of the Austrian economy does not participate in transatlantic trade, and a weakening of the European trade area in favor of trade with the USA would have serious negative effects on the backbone of the Austrian economy."[14] These examples highlight intra-industry differences in trade preferences that can split industry associations, generate new cross-sectoral coalitions that may take positions that differ from those of their members' industry associations, and generate increased lobbying by individual firms.

---

[10] EU trade policy officials also frequently made this claim about the textile sector during my interviews with them in Brussels, 2012.

[11] Interview with representative of DG Trade, European Commission, Brussels, 2012.

[12] Interview with representative of the European Roundtable of Industrialists, Brussels, 2012.

[13] Interview with member of the European Parliament, Brussels, 2012.

[14] Author's translation from the original German on the group's website, accessed on June 15, 2021 at www.facebook.com/kmusgegenttip/about/.

In Section 5.6, I assess my argument that these intra-industry divisions will be most pronounced in industries with higher intra-industry trade. As IIT increases, I expect that it becomes more difficult for industry-wide associations to build consensus among members about optimal levels of protection. I expect that this will decrease the relative frequency of association-based lobbying and incentivize direct lobbying by individual firms. Conversely, in industries with lower levels of intra-industry trade, I expect that firms will hold more unified preferences and will engage more often in collective political action via industry associations. Thus, in this chapter, I test the following hypothesis:

H1: Individual firm lobbying over trade, relative to associational lobbying, will be higher in industries with higher intra-industry trade.

5.6 DATA AND METHODOLOGY

In this section, I examine political activity by industry associations and individual firms in debates over major EU trade legislation. I conduct a quantitative analysis to empirically assess my hypothesis that in industries with higher intra-industry trade, firms will be more likely to lobby over trade policy than associations. I test this hypothesis on an original dataset of firm-level lobbying data. I constructed this dataset using lobbying data from policy position documents submitted to the European Commission as part of four open societal consultations on trade policy conducted over the period of 2010–2012, a period of time when the EU was negotiating trade deals with major trading partners such as Japan, the Mercosur bloc, and the United States (see Table 5.1).[15] Open consultations are an instrument that the Commission uses to gather stakeholder and broader public input about proposed policy changes. In the early policy formulation stage, the Commission announces open calls online for policy statements from stakeholders and the public, and it provides online questionnaires that interest groups or individuals can answer and submit. The Commission then analyzes the responses it receives, publishes a report and also publishes the individual responses to the questionnaire. Participants have the right to choose whether or not their response is made public. Five-hundred ninety-five societal actors who participated in the four consultation events agreed to make their responses public (out of 813 total participants). Of these, 170 are firms, 325 are industry associations, and the rest are other types of actors such as labor organizations, private citizens, government institutions, academic institutions, consumer groups, and other NGOs. Because the focus of my analysis is how business interests organize themselves politically, I only included firms and industry associations in my analysis.

The descriptive statistics below include the 495 firms and industry associations that lobbied at least once during the four different consultation periods

---

[15] The results of the Mercosur societal consultation were not made public.

TABLE 5.1 *EU trade policymaking events: Responses made public*

Consultation	Year	Firms	Associations	Other	Total
Consultation on Future Trade Policy	2010	20	175	82	277
EU–Japan Trade and Economic Relations	2010	5	31	3	39
EU–US Trade and Economic Relations	2012	14	46	10	70
Modernisation of Trade Defence Instruments	2012	131	73	5	209
Totals		170	325	100	595

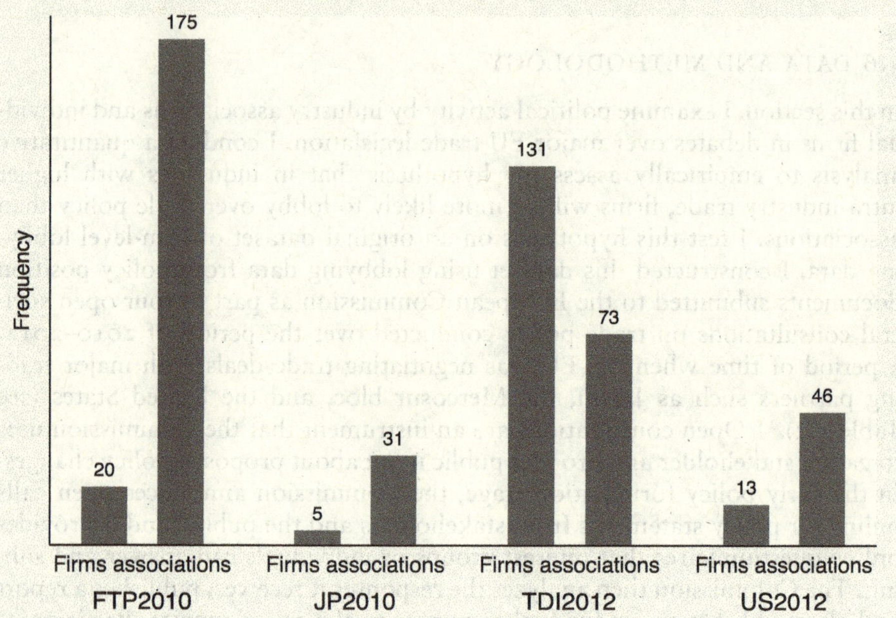

FIGURE 5.2 Publicly available contributions from firms and associations in trade consultations

(and made their contributions public). These actors include European firms, foreign and multinational firms, peak and cross-sectoral associations, and narrower industry associations, ranging from raw material and agricultural goods to high-tech manufacturing and services. The four consultations constituting the dataset vary in terms of the actor types represented, the sectors represented, and the proportion of firms to industry associations (see Figure 5.2).

For the following analysis, I exclude actors representing service industries because of the difficulty in acquiring international trade data for services. I also exclude actors representing cross-sectoral and peak organizations that could not be matched to specific industries (e.g., chambers of agriculture, EuroCommerce, BUSINESSEurope, FoodDrinkEurope, Danish Farmers Association, etc.). I also exclude non-EU actors.[16] My final sample includes 133 unique firms and 92 unique industry associations.

I assign each lobbying actor an industry identifier. I manually matched each actor with a four-digit code (or codes) using the Harmonized System (HS) of goods identifiers, 2017 version.[17] Information about each actor's industry was self-reported on the consultation responses themselves, or when this was missing or vague, I collected it from firm and industry association websites. Many industry associations, such as Eurometaux, the umbrella association representing the non-ferrous metals industries, represent broad coalitions of producers from a number of metals-producing industries. Other actors, such as the firm Morad, which produces motorcycle wheels (a product with a 6-digit code), represent only one specific and disaggregated product category. When firms produced products falling into multiple product categories, or when associations represented firms spanning a range of industries or product categories, I created an observation representing each four-digit industry or product category covered by that firm or association. This approach results in a sample in which the unit of analysis is the industry-consultation. Each industry for which lobbying occurred is coded according to whether the lobbying actor representing it was a firm. There may be multiple firms or associations lobbying on behalf of an industry, so an industry may be represented several times. Coding in this way results in 843 industry-consultation level observations.[18] This strategy, while more accurately depicting the full range of industries represented in the lobbying data, also creates dependence among the observations. This dependence occurs across industries within each consultation. I discuss how I addressed this problem in the analysis and results section.

In the final sample, we see that IIT ranges from very low to very high levels, with many actors representing sectors with quite balanced trade (fairly equal values of exports and imports) as well as heavily imbalanced trade (Figure 5.3). IIT also varies across the four consultations. The EU's trade with Japan, for example, is much more heavily inter-industry than EU trade with the US (Figure 5.4).

I focus on this stage and venue of the trade policymaking process because it has several advantages. First, societal consultations are the second most popular lobbying venue in the EU, second only to private meetings with

---

[16] There are eleven foreign firms and six foreign associations in the full dataset, which I exclude from the analyses in this chapter for theoretical as well as methodological reasons.

[17] As discussed in Chapter 2, the four-digit HS code (also known as the "heading" level of that system) best captures the classification level that contains varieties of goods that consumers would consider to be similar. For example, passenger cars are classified at the four-digit level (HS code 8703), while disaggregating cars further to the six-digit level yields separate categories for electric cars and cars with different engine sizes. Conceptually, the four-digit level better captures the "automobile industry" and the varieties of similar products its firms offer.

[18] This is similar to the approach taken in Osgood (2018).

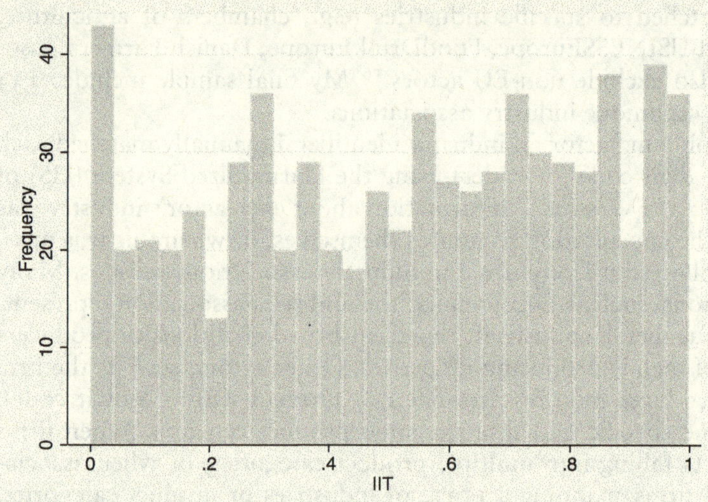

FIGURE 5.3 Distribution of IIT in represented industries

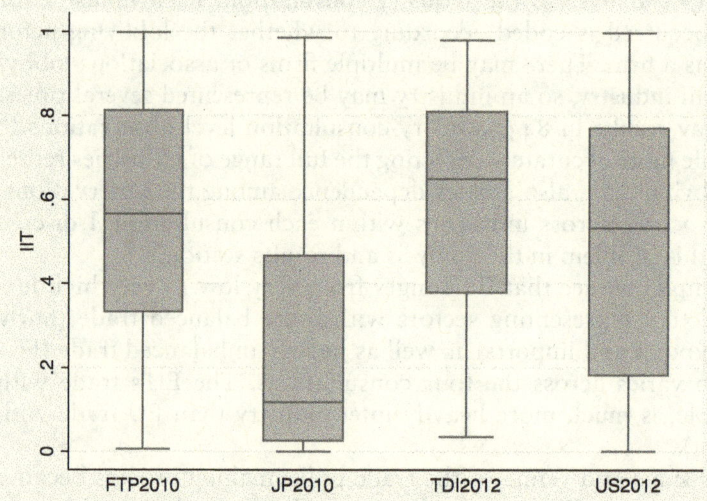

FIGURE 5.4 Distribution of IIT by consultation

policymakers (Mahoney, 2008, p. 132). There is obviously no systematic data about private meetings. Second, consultations occur at an early stage of the policymaking process, encouraging greater societal involvement. A third major advantage of this data is that it provides information on lobbying over trade policy specifically, compared to other sources of data such as the Transparency Register that list registered lobbyists but cannot distinguish which policy areas are of greatest interest to firms and other organizations. Another problem with using the Transparency Register as a data source is that it is purely optional and it is highly criticized for the fact that many large firms that lobby heavily have not entered themselves in the register.

Still, there are some drawbacks to using the open consultation data. One drawback is that it is not terribly costly to lobby in this way. There are certainly costs involved in answering an in-depth questionnaire with ninety-five questions about how an array of technical aspects of trade policy will affect one's business or the members of one's coalition, and it becomes still more costly to answer in a sophisticated way that is persuasive and provides valuable information to policymakers. But at the same time, this is probably not as costly as other forms of lobbying, such as meeting with policymakers, hosting events, testifying at hearings, preparing technical reports, or drafting legislation. As a result, it is possible that individual firms are overrepresented in the survey responses and that at other stages of the policymaking process involving more concerted and sustained government relations efforts, firms are more likely to rely on associations and coalitions to represent their interests. Financial data is very limited in the EU because money spent representing one's interests in Brussels is not disclosed as it is in the US, so this is not a possible data source. Finally, approximately a quarter of respondents do not allow their responses to be published. It is typically large firms that choose to keep their responses private, an issue that results in associations, and smaller firms, being overrepresented in the sample.

Dependent Variable

The dependent variable in this study is the type of lobbying actor. In this study, I am interested in whether firms or industry associations are more politically active depending on their industry's level of intra-industry trade. As an indicator of my dependent variable, *Actor Type*, I assign each lobbying actor a code from 1 to 6 indicating that actor's type: Individual firm, industry association, labor organization, nongovernmental organization, consumer association, or other.[19] Only firms and industry associations are included in the present analysis. Thus, the dependent variable is dichotomous, taking a value of 0 when a lobbying actor is an industry association and 1 when a lobbying actor is a firm.

Independent Variable

The main independent variable in this study is *Intra-Industry Trade*. I employ the same measure of IIT that I described in detail in Chapter 2, developed by Grubel and Lloyd (1975). This measure approaches one as trade becomes more balanced, or more heavily IIT, and it reaches zero when there is no

---

[19] The actors that fell into the "other" category were typically government or academic institutions.

two-way trade in the given industry. To construct the IIT variable for the analyses in this chapter, I used the four-digit HS identifiers to gather industry export and import data from Eurostat's ComExt international trade database. I calculated IIT for each industry using this data. For this measure and other trade-related measures, I use data specific to the relevant partner under discussion in each consultation (dyadic EU–Japan data, dyadic EU–US data, and multilateral data for EU trade with the world). In this way, my measures capture the relevant trading environment for each industry lobbying in each particular consultation.

Control Variables

I control for leading alternative explanations for variation in the structure of lobbying coalitions, discussed throughout this text. First, I control for *Product Differentiation* using Broda and Weinstein's measure of the elasticity of substitutability of goods. The Broda and Weinstein data is coded according to the SITC four-digit classification system; I manually concorded it to the HS system. I also control for *Industry Size* and *Industry Concentration*. I construct the industry size measure using industry sales data available from the OECD's Structural Business Statistics. Without firm-level sales data I cannot construct a true concentration ratio, so I use OECD data on the number of enterprises in each industry as an alternative specification of market structure (Hansen et al., 2005). I create the measure by calculating $1/n$, where n is the number of enterprises in the industry. As the number of firms increases, industry concentration decreases. Both of these measures are available at the individual country level and I sum them to create an EU-level measure. OECD industry data is available in the ISIC Revision 4 nomenclature at the four-digit level; I matched industries manually to the HS system.

Second, I address variation in firm engagement in global supply chains. Firms that source intermediate inputs from abroad, whether from foreign firms or from subsidiaries, have a strong interest in maintaining access to imported inputs. In industries with higher levels of intermediate inputs, I expect to observe more firm-level political activity relative to associational activity. I control for this using industry data on *Imported Inputs* from Eurostat's supply, use, and input – output tables. This data is classified according to the NACE Revision 2 system at the two-digit sector level, which I matched manually to the industries in my sample.

Finally, I control for each industry's existing level of protection. In the EU, where trade policy is marked by a liberal bias, industries that remain heavily protected may be those for which there is strong societal consensus in favor of protection. I would expect that in more protected industries, lobbying is most likely to take place via industry association, as these sectors are likely characterized by greater consensus around the benefits of protection. I control for existing *Tariffs* using data on MFN trade-weighted average tariffs from the year prior to each consultation, from the World Bank's WITS database. Furthermore, given the EU's pro-trade bias, there is little incentive to lobby for protection in industries where tariffs are already relatively low. In these industries, protectionist firms are likely to be outvoiced by powerful industry-leading exporters, so I would expect most lobbying in industries with low tariffs to come from large, internationalized firms registering their continued support of openness. I present summary statistics of all variables in Appendix Table C.1.

5.7 ANALYSIS AND RESULTS

To analyze the relationship between intra-industry trade and the structure of business lobbying, I begin by estimating the likelihood that as an industry's IIT increases, lobbying actors from that industry are more likely to be individual firms. Due to the way that lobbying firms and associations may be mapped onto multiple industries, there is dependence among observations within each policy consultation. To address this, I employ a random effects multilevel model, which accounts for this within-group clustering. I estimate the following model using multilevel logistic regression:

$$Pr(\textit{Firm Lobbying})_i = logit^{-1}(\beta IIT_i + \beta X_i + \alpha_j + \epsilon_{ij}) \tag{5.1}$$

$$\alpha_j \sim N(0, \sigma_\alpha^2),$$

where *Firm Lobbying* is a dichotomous variable that takes a value of 1 when a lobbying actor from industry i is an individual firm and a value of zero when the lobbying actor is an industry association. *IIT* is industry i's level of intra-industry trade, X includes the control variables described above, ϵ is the industry-level error term, and α is a random intercept that is allowed to vary at the policy consultation level (the group level j). Both error terms are assumed to have a mean of zero and the variance of α is estimated from the data. All independent variables are log-transformed.

I report results graphically in Figure 5.5, and full regression tables with various model specifications are present in Appendix Table C.2. Coefficients can be interpreted as changes in the percentage chance that a lobbying actor is a firm, rather than a trade association. The LR test formally assesses the model against a logistic regression model without random effects, and it indicates that it is appropriate to include the random effects. As shown in Figure 5.5, the results of this analysis provide support for the theory developed in this paper. As predicted, we see that IIT is positive and statistically significant, indicating that as intra-industry trade increases, the likelihood of firm-level lobbying relative to all lobbying increases, even when controlling for other factors that may influence the likelihood of firm-level lobbying. We see that two control variables are significant as well in the main model, industry concentration and industry size. I find that firms are more likely to lobby in sectors with higher concentration, meaning that most production is concentrated in the hands of a smaller

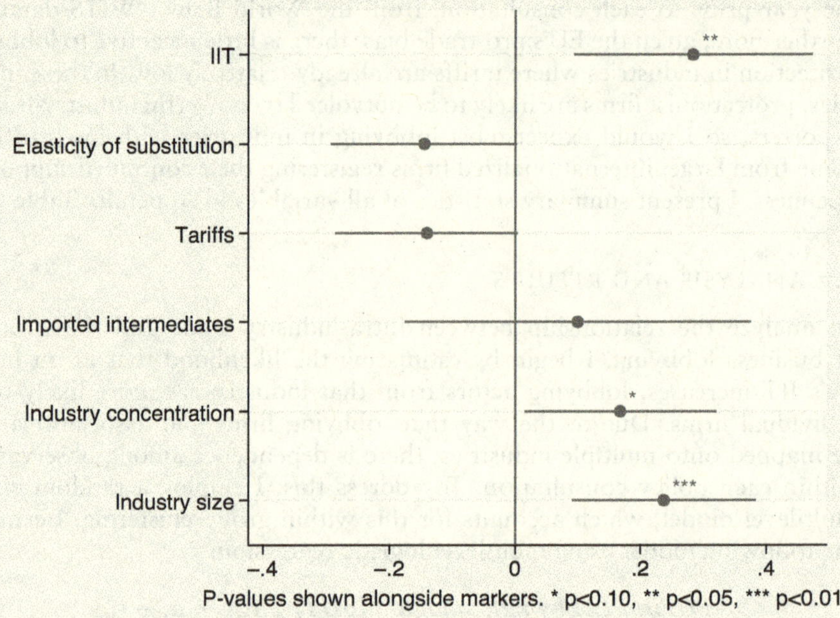

FIGURE 5.5 The effect of IIT on the likelihood of individual firm lobbying: Main model

number of firms. We also see that firms are more likely relative to industry associations to lobby in bigger industries.

In order to further illustrate the effect of IIT on the probabilities that firms rather than associations lobby over trade policy, Figure 5.6 presents the marginal effects of IIT on actor type from the fully specified model. To ease interpretation, I plot marginal effects of the original, untransformed values of IIT. Holding all other variables at their means, we can examine the effect of increased IIT from its minimum to its maximum. When IIT is close to zero and trade is almost entirely inter-industry in nature, the probability of individual firm lobbying is less than 10 percent. As IIT increases, the probability of an industry's lobbying actor being an individual firm increases to approximately 47 percent when trade is entirely intra-industry (IIT=1).

Robustness Checks

The main results reported in Figure 5.5 are also robust to a number of other model specifications. First, although AIC, BIC, and likelihood-ratio tests all indicate that a multilevel model is a better fit compared to standard logistic regression, the results are nevertheless robust to estimation of standard logistic regression with robust standard errors, and the effect of IIT on the

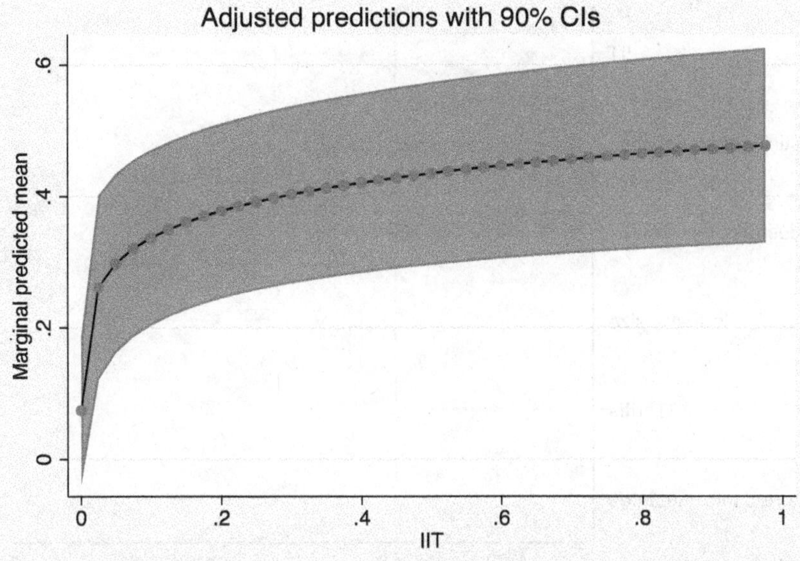

FIGURE 5.6 Marginal effect of IIT on the likelihood of individual firm lobbying

likelihood of firm lobbying reaches a higher level of statistical significance. Second, the results are also robust to clustering the standard errors at the level of the individual actor, an alternative approach to addressing correlations across multi-product firms or associations. These models are available in Appendix Tables C.3 and C.4. Finally, I construct an alternative outcome variable to further ensure that dependencies created by my research design (specifically, assigning multi-product firms or industry associations to multiple four-digit industries) are not driving the results. Here I adopt an approach similar to that taken in Chapter 4, as well as that of Bombardini and Trebbi (2012). I create an industry-level variable that measures the proportion of lobbying actors in a given industry that are firms, relative to industry associations.[20] To construct this variable, for each consultation, I added up the number of firms and number of associations that lobbied from each four-digit industry, and I divided the number of firms by the total number of lobbying actors. This variable is thus a proportion ranging from 0 to 1. This approach results in a sample in which each four-digit industry is represented only once per consultation, rather than multiple times (once for each time an actor from that industry lobbies) as in the main models. Because the dependent variable is a ratio of counts, I estimate these models using a GLM estimator with a logit link and robust standard

[20] In Chapter 4, I measure the proportion of firm *expenditures* relative to association expenditures, whereas in the present analysis, I measure the relative number of firms and associations that lobby in each industry.

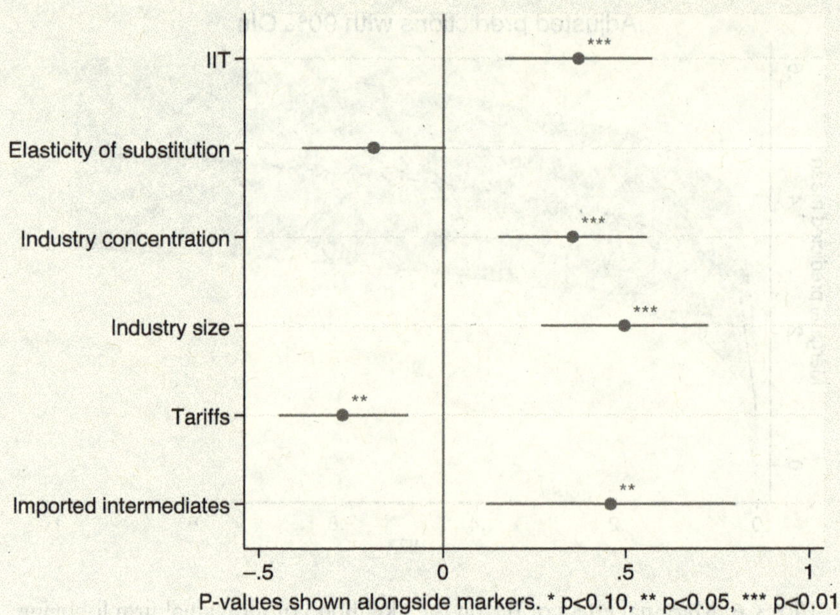

FIGURE 5.7 The effect of IIT on the likelihood of individual firm lobbying: Alternative DV

errors. I present the coefficient estimates in Figure 5.7 and full regression results in Appendix Table C.5. The results show that the positive and statistically significant effect of IIT on firm-level lobbying is robust to this estimation strategy as well.

Comparative Advantage and Disadvantage Industries

In Chapter 4, I showed that in the US, IIT has its strongest effect on political organization in comparative disadvantage industries, which are the industries where collective action (to secure protection) is most likely and increasing IIT undermines that collective action. In this section, I examine the relationship between IIT and comparative advantage in the EU case. As in Chapter 4, I interact my IIT variable with a dummy variable that proxies revealed comparative advantage. This dummy takes the value of one if an industry has a positive export-import ratio (net-exporting) and a value of zero if the industry has a negative export-import ratio (net-importing). I present the results of this analysis in Appendix Table C.6 and visually in Figure 5.8. Here we observe interesting differences from the findings in the US case.

In this analysis, we see that IIT has a positive and significant effect on firm-based lobbying only among net-exporting industries. This is different from what I found in the US case. In the US, the effect of IIT on firm-based

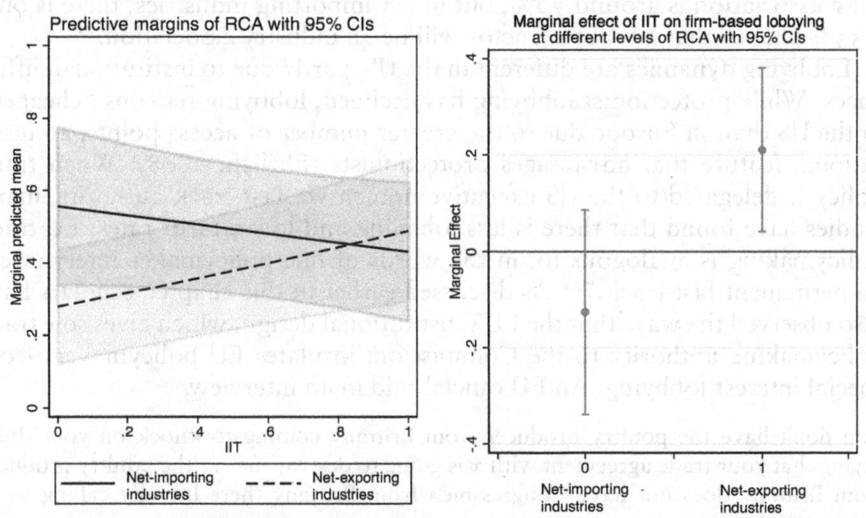

FIGURE 5.8 Effects of IIT on the likelihood of firm lobbying relative to associational lobbying in net-exporting vs. net-importing industries

lobbying was strongest in comparative disadvantage industries. My analyses suggested that associations in comparative disadvantage industries reduced their lobbying amidst a breakdown in industry consensus around the benefits of protection. In contrast, in the EU, we see that the effect of IIT on firm-based lobbying is strongest in strong exporting industries, where increasing IIT has a significant and positive effect. IIT does not have a significant effect on political organization in net-importing industries. The left-hand plot in Figure 5.8 shows that when IIT is very low, lobbying in net-exporting industries is more likely to occur collectively via associations than in net-importing industries, by a difference of nearly 20 percent. As IIT increases, firms in net-exporting industries compete with more imports relative to their exports. The result, visible in Figure 5.8, is that relatively more firms become active relative to associations. This can occur in two ways: As firms choose to represent their own interests politically, or as associations reduce their activity in the face of intra-industry division over preferred trade policy.

My analyses of the EU and US cases show that the effect of IIT in both polities is to make collective action via associations more difficult, but how do we interpret the differences in the findings across the two cases? To make sense of these differences, we must recall the ways that the EU's institutional structure incentivizes interest group activity differently than US institutions do. In the EU, there are very few European business associations that take openly protectionist positions. This well-known feature of EU trade politics is consistent with the findings present in the left-hand plot in Figure 5.8. At low levels of IIT, the probability that a lobbying actor in a strong exporting industry is an association is around 70%, but in net-importing industries, there is only a 55% chance that a lobbying actor will be an industry association.

Lobbying dynamics are different in the US, partly due to institutional differences. While protectionist lobbying has declined, lobbying remains "cheaper" in the US than in Europe due to the greater number of access points, an institutional feature that advantages protectionists (Ehrlich, 2008). When trade policy is delegated to the US executive branch via fast-track authority, many studies have found that there is less lobbying and lower tariff rates. EU trade policymaking is analogous to, in the words of one policymaker interviewed, "a permanent fast-track."[21] As discussed earlier in this chapter, scholars have also observed the ways that the EU's institutional design, which gives sole trade policymaking authority to the Commission, insulates EU policymakers from special interest lobbying. An EU official said in an interview,

You don't have the poultry producer from Brittany coming to knock on your door, saying that your trade agreement with *x* is going to destroy me ... the poultry producer from Brittany does not have Congressmen from Brittany there literally calling us to account.[22]

This insulated institutional structure that grants relatively few access points to special interest groups – and individual firms – in Brussels is one reason why Woll (2009) found that groups seeking protection are more likely to lobby at the national level rather than in Brussels, hoping to persuade their national governments to represent their interest in trade policy negotiations.

In addition to limited access points, the EU's strong normative commitment to open markets and mandate to act in the best interest of the bloc as a whole mean that in order for interest groups to maintain credibility and influence within trade policy negotiations in Brussels they must advocate broadly free-trade positions. An official at BusinessEurope said in an interview, "No one will ever say openly that they are a protectionist. Everyone wants to say openly that they are a liberal ... you don't use that word ever," referring to protectionism.[23] Another reason there is little protectionist activity in traditional lobbying venues is that EU firms and industries rely heavily on anti-dumping petitions as a way to remedy trade damages, and the EU is one of the most active imposers of anti-dumping duties globally. In comparative disadvantage industries, Brussels-based industry associations often take a broadly liberal/neutral stance on trade legislation as a way to maintain influence with policymakers, even as firms within their industries file anti-dumping claims.[24]

---

[21] Interview with staff member of the Trade Strategy unit at Directorate-General Trade, EU, Brussels, 2012.

[22] Ibid.

[23] Interview, staff member of BusinessEurope, Brussels, September 2012.

[24] To file an anti-dumping complaint, petitioners need to represent at least 50 percent of their industry, so anti-dumping claims still (for the majority of industries) require collective action.

Keeping these institutional and political dynamics in mind, this suggests that IIT's divisive effects, which undermine collective action and incentivize firm-level lobbying in both the EU and US, operate differently in the EU. In strong exporting industries, sectoral associations and Eurofederations can take a pro-trade stance, actively representing their member interests in Brussels, aligning themselves with the European Commission's liberal agenda, and maintaining positive relationships with policymakers. As IIT increases, import-competing firms may lobby alone for firm-specific protections (and robust trade defense instruments) that their sectoral organizations are unwilling to advance, given the export orientation of these industries overall, combined with Brussels-based associations' reluctance to advocate protectionist positions. At the same time, associations previously advocating liberal trade policies may reduce or moderate their political activity as some of their members express concern about import competition.[25] The result of these dynamics is more firms going it alone. By contrast, Eurofederations and national industry associations representing import-competing industries face a political challenge in liberal Brussels. In net-importing industries, increasing IIT had no effect on political organization, possibly because these industry associations have long understood the strategic utility of taking generally neutral official positions on trade.

5.8 EXAMPLES OF LOBBYING DYNAMICS IN EUROPEAN INDUSTRIES

The European textile and garment industries provide an example of the way in which highly organized and protectionist industry associations had to adjust their strategies in the face of rising IIT and trade liberalization. From the 1970s to the 1990s, national industries appealed successfully to their governments for high levels of protection, protection which remained in place until the EU agreed to the WTO's Agreement on Textiles and Clothing, which required WTO members to phase out all tariffs by January 2005. During this time, IIT increased dramatically in textiles as competition grew intense from China and other developing countries with low labor costs. The trade balance in textiles had fallen from an export surplus of 764 million ECU in 1986 to a deficit of 4 billion ECU in 1997 (Ugur, 1998). Woll (2009) and other observers of the EU textile sector document the way that the textile associations had to "reorganize" to adjust to the EU's commitment to a liberal trade policy for textiles. In order to maintain productive relationships with EU trade policymakers, EU-level textile associations like COMITEXTIL and Euratex made a strategic choice in the 1990s to stop lobbying for protection and to adopt a cooperative, broadly liberal stance focusing on increasing market access for European exporters (and pushing for the longest tariff phase-out period possible).

---

[25] Contradicting the idea that large firms inevitably dominate their industry associations, an official from BusinessEurope described trade associations as "the voice of medium-sized companies." Interview in Brussels, September 2012.

Yet this strategic shift in lobbying strategy by the European sectoral associations was complicated by intra-industry division among member firms. Firms restructured to specialize in higher value-added products for the luxury or technical market, a process which the Commission was aware would create firm-level winners and losers, as not all firms would be able to adjust (Ugur, 1998). Eckhardt (2013) documents the emergence of an important split within the industry in 2005 as import quotas on Chinese textile and clothing products were removed, after forty years. In the first few months of 2005, Chinese imports in nearly all product categories rose dramatically, as high as 500 percent in some industries. Import-competing firms successfully pressured Euratex and national associations to lobby the Commission for temporary protection in the form of safeguards (short-term quotas) on several clothing products, and the EU and China reached an agreement on safeguards in June 2005. Yet the safeguards created not only winners but losers: Import-dependent EU firms strongly opposed these measures. These firms ranged from retailers to many textile and garment manufacturers that relied on imported inputs from China. According to Eckhardt, a cleavage emerged among firms at each stage of the textile and garments supply chain: producers of raw materials to yarn producers to textile manufacturers to garment manufacturers. Import-competing firms at each stage held trade preferences that were directly at odds with import-dependent firms in the same industry.

A similar cleavage emerged between import-competing firms and export-dependent firms, and many of the latter were also dependent upon imported inputs. The import/export-dependent firms specialized either in luxury varieties of consumer clothing or technical textiles and garments that are technology- and capital-intensive. The globally competitive producers of technical products tended to be located in Northern European countries like Germany and the Netherlands and supported liberal trade policies. More labor-intensive producers of lower-cost varieties tended to locate in Southern and Eastern European countries. France and Italy were home to both labor-intensive producers of lower-cost varieties as well as labor-intensive but high-cost luxury manufacturers. In this way, the members of national industry associations were divided as were European-level federations like Euratex. The 2005 battle over safeguards split the industry and created political chaos. Woll (2009) argues that the increasingly heterogeneous demands from Euratex caused the organization to change its strategy once again and refrain from taking a position in trade policy disputes. Instead, according to Woll, the organization shifted its focus to "pan-European stances to maintain its leadership role at the EU level."

In the lobbying data I collected, some of these dynamics are evident. Euratex submitted comments on three of the four policymaking consultations and took a generally free trade and non-controversial position, emphasizing the importance of market access, while also encouraging the EU to strengthen rules of origin. The positions of its member associations, representing more specific industries within the wider sector, reveal significant differences in preferences. The comments submitted by the European Branded Clothing Alliance (EBCA), which represents mostly large, competitive, importing garment firms took a much stronger pro-liberalization and explicitly anti-protectionist stance (the garment industry has low IIT and imports heavily from global supply chains). The EBCA urged the EU several times to resist "populist" calls for protection and support competitive industries, rather than "artificially subsidising or protecting traditional industries."[26] No individual apparel companies lobbied, consistent with my argument that firm-level activity is rare when IIT is low.

On the other hand, Gdynia Cotton Association, which represents the Polish cotton industry (import-competing, moderate-IIT), struck a more protectionist tone, describing EU trade policy as one in which "the interests of domestic European manufacturers, SMEs, and employees' groups are totally disregarded."[27] The cotton association also accused the Commission of "sacrificing the European industry and broadening the access to the European market for goods from third countries" in exchange for "vague promises pertaining to the service sector." Similarly, CIRFS, the European Man-Made Fibres Association (import-competing, moderate IIT) and Assofibre (its Italian national counterpart) expressed skepticism about the pursuit of further FTAs and specifically criticized protection for the cotton industry, which it views as a direct competitor of man-made fiber firms. Two individual firms from this industry lobbied as well, urging the EU not to weaken trade defense instruments that are important to import-competing firms. Given these conflicting preferences among the various industries within the broader garments and textile sector represented by Euratex, it is not difficult to see why Euratex has decided to take moderate positions.

Other industries provide additional examples of the divergent lobbying dynamics of high- versus low-IIT industries. The fishing net industry is a strong exporting industry with high levels of IIT (0.9 in 2012, when all lobbying occurred in the sample). There was significant firm-level lobbying in this industry. Four individual firms lobbied, all were import-competing producers advocating protectionist positions aimed at strengthening trade defense instruments. There was no counter-lobbying by exporters or importers. Two associations did lobby (Eurocord, and the national association of Portuguese fishing net producers), and they limited their comments to support for maintaining robust trade defense instruments, citing the interests of their import-competing member firms. None advocated for protectionist policies beyond this. Furniture manufacturing is another industry with high IIT (averaging 0.75 in the sample) and significant firm-level lobbying that demonstrated the lack of consensus within the industry. In the 2010 consultation on the future of EU trade policy, two Eurofederations took free trade stances that emphasized increasing reciprocal market access, especially for SMEs. But one

[26] Comments submitted by the European Branded Clothing Alliance in 2010 to the EU's public consultation on Future Trade Policy.

[27] Comments submitted by Gdynia Cotton Association in 2010 to the EU's public consultation on Future Trade Policy.

small Italian furniture producer took a conflicting stance, asking the EU to limit imports, and especially very low-price products that threaten firms that manufacture in Europe. Countering this position, three large importing and exporting firms lobbied (including Ikea) in support of greater liberalization. Ikea specifically criticized EU use of anti-dumping duties, arguing that "AD slows down [the] EU's move to competitiveness."[28]

Finally, the auto parts industries provide examples of collective action predominating when IIT is low. Trade in car parts between the EU and Japan was heavily import-competing in 2010 (bilateral IIT = 0.34). The European Association of Automobile Suppliers (CLEPA) submitted comments to the 2010 consultation on trade with Japan, emphasizing the heavy trade deficit with Japan and urging against an FTA with Japan or any further tariff liberalization. No individual firms lobbied, except for the Czech subsidiary of a Japanese multinational (Showa), which lobbied in favor of an FTA with Japan. In contrast, European-produced car parts enjoy a strong trade surplus with the world as a whole (multilateral IIT in 2010 averaged 0.29), and in the EU's 2010 consultation seeking input on multilateral liberalization, one actor lobbied in support of continued liberalization, and it was an association representing the British automotive supply industry (Society of Motor Manufacturers and Traders).

In sum, this book's arguments about the relationship between intra-industry trade and firm-level lobbying are supported by the analysis of lobbying over four recent trade policymaking events in the European Union. Where IIT is low, industry preferences are likely to coalesce around either a pro-trade or protectionist position, and lobbying activity is more likely to be delegated to industry associations and Eurofederations. Yet when IIT is high, firms are more likely to advocate for their particular trade preferences, due to competing preferences within the industry that make collective action difficult. Due to the particular institutional environment in Brussels that privileges free-trade interests, more industry associations advance liberal positions, relative to the US, where protectionist lobbying is much more common. Thus, in Europe, the effect of IIT's splitting of preferences within industries would be to reduce lobbying among industry associations in competitive industries that were actively advancing free trade positions, and this is exactly what we observe in the above analysis.

5.9 CONCLUSION

The results of this analysis of lobbying over trade policy in the European Union provide additional support for the theory advanced in this book. Chapters 4 and 5, taken together, demonstrate that the relationship between intra-industry

---

[28] Comments submitted by Ikea in 2012 to the EU's public consultation on Modernisation of Trade Defence Instruments.

trade and firm-level lobbying holds across two developed economies with dramatically different policymaking environments. While lobbying in the EU (and in some respects, EU politics more broadly) is often treated as *sui generis* as a result of the EU's unique institutional structure, this analysis shows that lobbying over trade in the EU is subject to some of the same dynamics as in the US. Specifically, my analyses in these two chapters demonstrate that the structure of international trade and the extent to which it is inter- versus intra-industry affects domestic political organization, even when differences in political and policymaking institutions are taken into account.

Second, my investigation of the different lobbying dynamics within import-competing and export-dependent sectors contributes to our understanding of the ways that the structure of international trade interacts with the institutional environment to yield different political dynamics in different political contexts. I have shown that IIT contributes to firm-level lobbying in both the EU and US context, but this dynamic played out differently in the two polities. As discussed earlier in the chapter, EU institutions strongly incentivize collective interest representation within sectoral associations and particularly European-level associations. Additionally, according to Greenwood (2017, p.19), US firms are used to "working outside of groups," whereas European firms more used to corporatist traditions "tend to place a greater emphasis upon collective associations," though this is certainly changing (Coen et al., 2021). Consistent with this, my findings suggested that European sectoral associations are more active than their US counterparts, and particularly those advocating liberal policy stances. In both chapters, I found that rising IIT caused firm-based activity to increase in sectors where industry associations had been most active. In the US, these are typically net-importing, comparative disadvantage industries, while in the EU, these are typically strong exporting industries. In these industries, associations reined in political activity in the face of competing preferences held by member firms, as some firms also began to actively represent themselves politically.

To conclude, in this chapter and the prior chapter on lobbying over trade in the US, I found that intra-industry trade is associated with greater firm-based lobbying and a smaller role, in comparison, for trade associations, even when controlling for leading alternative explanations. The results are robust to various model specifications and alternate dependent variables, and hold across two very different policymaking contexts. By drawing on firm heterogeneity and modern understandings of international trade, my work provides a generalizable explanation for the growth of firm-based lobbying across developed democracies, a phenomenon that classic approaches to studying trade politics have had difficulty explaining. In Chapter 6, I examine the effects of intra-industry trade on trade policy outcomes.

Intra-Industry Trade and Protection in Developed Democracies

6.1 INTRODUCTION

A central and puzzling feature of the postwar global economy, especially in the years since 1980, has been the unilateral liberalization of trade policies in economies all over the world, developed as well as developing. Rodrik et al. (1994, p. 62) described the time as a "rush to free trade" and claim that this liberal shift since the early 80s represents a "genuine revolution in policymaking." In Chapters 4 and 5, I analyzed the relationship between intra-industry trade, trade preferences, and lobbying behavior. I found that higher intra-industry trade is associated with relatively more political activity on the part of individual firms, and relatively less on the part of industry associations, a profound shift in how business mobilizes to influence trade policy. In this chapter, I move to the next step in the analysis and I examine the effects of intra-industry trade on resulting levels of protection. I argue that intra-industry trade has incentivized free-traders to be more active in trade policy lobbying, giving policymakers greater freedom to reduce tariffs, but also to make trade policies that align with the interests of large, powerful firms rather than the interests of industries as a whole.

Whereas in Chapters 4 and 5, I focused primarily on the "demand side" of trade policy, in this chapter, I consider the role of political and policymaking institutions in order to develop and test hypotheses about the effects of trade structure on trade policy outcomes. Most of the political science literature that seeks to explain trade policy outcomes can be categorized as societal-based explanations, statist or international-level explanations, and institutionalist explanations. Societal-based explanations argue that trade policy is endogenous to domestic groups' preferences, expressed through lobbying and campaign contributions. A long-held assumption of this approach was that protectionists lobby more than free-traders, so politicians implement tariffs as a way to satisfy protectionist groups and "purchase" electoral support from key constituencies, and there is robust support for this claim (Conybeare, 1991; Gawande and Bandyopadhyay, 2000; Grossman and Helpman, 1994; Magee et al., 1989; Mayer, 1984). Other scholars extended the model to trade liberalization, demonstrating that policymakers reduce tariffs as a response to lobbying by pro-trade industries and firms (Chase, 2003; Gilligan, 1997a; Milner, 1988). The firm-centric approach that currently dominates the trade literature associates liberal economic policies – which extend far beyond tariffs to trade-related regulatory policies and investment protections – with increased lobbying by multinational corporations and other large, productive, firms engaged in exporting, importing, and FDI (Anderer et al., 2020; Blanchard and Matschke, 2015; Kim, 2017; Manger, 2009). Some firm-centric approaches attribute rising NTMs to lobbying by multinationals. Gulotty (2020) finds that large, competitive firms often lobby in favor of strict product regulations and high standards that smaller, less competitive firms cannot manage, driving smaller firms to exit.

A critique of society-centered models developed in the context of the US political system is that they may not be very generalizable to countries where policymakers are more insulated from lobbying. Scholars of policymaking in the EU argued for many years that lobbying-centric models are less relevant there, due to deliberate institutional design intended to shield Brussels-based policymakers from interest-group lobbying (Meunier, 2005; Woolcock, 2005). However, EU scholars more recently have challenged this assumption, demonstrating that EU trade policy aligns with interest-group demands much more closely than previously thought (Bernhagen et al., 2015; Coen et al., 2021; Dür and Mateo, 2016). Furthermore, all too often, demand-side models generate flawed predictions of trade policy outcomes because their models draw a straight line from domestic interest-group preferences to policy outcomes, overlooking the role of mediating factors such as institutions (Mansfield and Busch, 1995).

Thus, another approach prioritizes the role of the domestic political institutional context.[1] Institutions "filter" or mediate between policy demands and policy outcomes, affecting the political decisions of interest groups and policymakers alike. Leading accounts focus on the role of electoral systems (Kono, 2009; Mansfield and Busch, 1995; Postnikov and Bastiaens, 2020), party institutions (Grossman and Helpman, 2005; Hankla, 2006), location of trade policymaking authority (Lohmann and O'Halloran, 1994), societal access to the policymaking process (Ehrlich, 2007; Ehrlich and Jones, 2016; Henisz and

---

[1] In this analysis, I limit my discussion to democracies and institutional differences within democracies. However, many scholars have studied whether democracy promotes trade liberalization, and they have come to varying conclusions. For arguments that democracy increases openness, see Eichengreen and Leblang (2008); Mansfield et al. (2002); Milner and Kubota (2005); Wintrobe (1998). For arguments that democracy may promote protectionism, see Kono (2006) and Verdier (1998).

Mansfield, 2006), or constituency/district size (Ehrlich, 2009; Hankla, 2006; Kono, 2009). While most of these studies focus on tariffs, several analyses find that levels of NTMs are also related to electoral rules and the degree to which policymakers are responsive to special interest groups (Mansfield and Busch, 1995; Rickard, 2012).

A third major explanatory category focuses on the role of state priorities, ideas held by policymakers, and the role of international institutions. Many scholars find that a prevailing liberal bias among policymakers at the national level was a significant factor in the multilateral trade liberalization of the postwar period (Goldstein, 1988; Krueger, 1997; Meunier, 2005), and that governmental beliefs and priorities continue to play a role in complex negotiations over trade-related regulatory issues (Winslett, 2021). Others point to American hegemony, reciprocity in trade policymaking, and the rise of rules-based international institutions as primary factors behind the multilateral liberalization of trade policies (Betz, 2017; Davis, 2003; Goldstein et al., 2007; Rose, 2005). The best of these analyses also integrate domestic politics into their accounts. Kono (2006), for example, finds that democracy affects the structure of trade protection by giving policymakers an incentive to please voters by reducing tariffs, while also granting protection to special interest groups via NTMs.

Much of this existing scholarship is complementary, rather than competing. In this chapter, I combine insights from several approaches into an argument that can account for both demand- and supply-side factors – preferences, collective action costs, and the role of domestic policymaking institutions. I use the theory presented in Chapter 3 and results of my analyses of trade policy demands in Chapters 4 and 5 to generate new hypotheses about resulting trade policy outcomes. This chapter proceeds as follows. First, I discuss some of the key features of trade policy in the developed economies in the postwar era. Second, I present a model of the ways in which I expect intra-industry trade to affect trade policy outcomes, building on the insights about lobbying that I developed in the previous chapters. Just as scholars disagree about the impact of intra-industry trade on trade lobbying coalitions, there is no consensus in the literature on how it will affect levels of protection. Third, I present my empirical strategy and discuss the ways it can resolve some of the conflicting findings in the existing literature. Finally, I discuss my results and their implications for the study of trade policy.

6.2 TRADE POLICY IN OECD COUNTRIES

Perhaps the most important feature of the international trading system since World War II is the remarkable and dramatic liberalization of national trade policies, the dismantling of tariff barriers to trade, and the proliferation of preferential trade agreements that go far beyond tariff reduction to remove beyond-the-border barriers to trade and investment. What was initially a

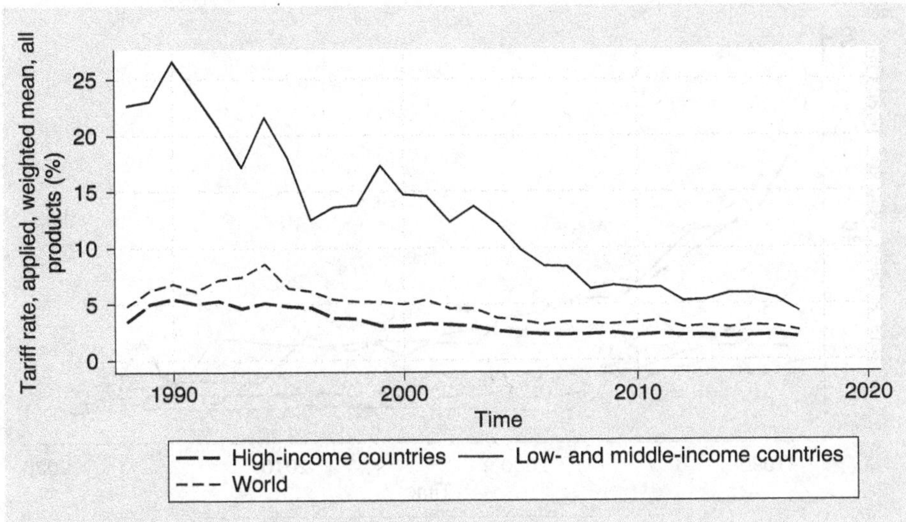

FIGURE 6.1 Average tariff rates over time, 1988–2017
Data source: WITS.

liberal project embarked upon by the United States, Western Europe, Japan, and other advanced democracies has become a truly global endeavor, as developing countries began in the 1980s to unilaterally, and often rapidly, open their economies and join the rules-based international trading regime.

After signing the General Agreement on Tariffs and Trade in 1947, the twenty-three original signatories (mostly developed states and their colonies or former colonies) set about systematically reducing their tariffs through a reciprocal system that granted preferential tariff rates to other GATT members. By the early 1980s, the United States' average tariff was about 4.5%, which was 92% lower than its average tariff in 1947. Japan's, Canada's, and Western European countries' tariffs dropped to similar levels, and developing countries began clamoring to join the wealthy, free-trading club (see Figures 6.1 and 6.2). The result of these multilateral efforts was an enormous increase in world trade: The value of trade doubled between 1960 and 1970 and increased another 85 percent from 1970 to 1973 alone (Grieco, 1990, p. 52).

With tariffs at historically low levels across developed economies, one might assume that societal preferences in these countries overwhelmingly favor free trade. Yet studies of trade politics and policy have found that liberalization has been highly contentious even among the early liberalizers that have seemingly marched steadily toward less and less protection. Protectionist lobbying has not abated (Magee et al., 2019), so we have little reason to expect to observe consistently liberal trade policies across sectors and across countries. This may be one way to understand the rise of nontariff measures. As tariffs fell globally in the postwar period, it was widely accepted that nontariff measures could

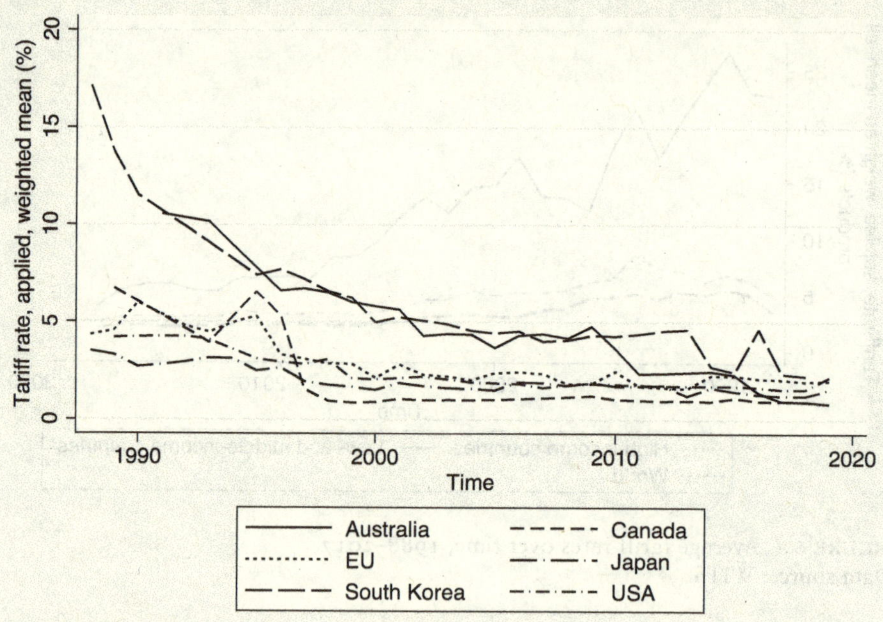

FIGURE 6.2 Average tariff rates on manufactured products over time, 1988–2019
Data source: WITS.

serve a substitionary protectionist effect (de Melo and Nicita, 2018; Kee and Nicita, 2022). These concerns are fuelled by the observation that as tariffs have fallen, overall trade costs remain high (Cadot et al., 2018). Nontariff measures could serve legitimate public policy objectives – they include product safety and environmental regulations – and they were also increasingly recognized as tools with which policymakers could protect domestic firms, industries, and workers from trade competition without running afoul of tariff-based international trade agreements (Kono, 2006; Kuenzel, 2020; Mansfield and Busch, 1995).

Trade economists, as well as policymakers, understood the distortionary effect of nontariff measures by the early 1970s. GATT members initiated a new negotiating round, the Tokyo Round (1973–1979), specifically to address NTMs that may distort trade, such as customs valuation and import licensing procedures, anti-dumping, government procurement, subsidies, and counter-vailing duties. Upon the establishment of the WTO in 1995, all WTO members were required to adopt the Agreement on Technical Barriers to Trade, which strengthened the Tokyo Round's provisions on standards and attempted to distinguish between technical requirements designed to limit trade, as opposed to technical requirements that serve legitimate public objectives. The TBT Agreement covers regulations, technical standards, and testing and certification

TABLE 6.1 *Ad valorem equivalents of estimated multilateral NTMs, averaged over eighty-six countries, 2012–2015*

HS section	Overall AVE estimate (%)
Live animals	20.3
Vegetable products	15.8
Fats and oil	20.0
Processed food	28.7
Chemical products	8.5
Rubber plastics	9.9
Raw hide skins	10.4
Wood	26.8
Paper	7.7
Textile	12.9
Footwear	8.3
Stone cement	8.4
Precious stones	9.5
Base metals	6.4
Machinery and electrical equipment	6.1
Motor vehicles	22.3
Optical medicals	7.7
Miscellaneous	8.6

Data source: Cadot et al. (2018). Single-year estimate based on UNCTAD data collection beginning in 2012.

procedures. In the last two decades, as climate policy has become increasingly connected with trade policy, de Melo and Nicita (2018, p. 3) conclude that today's NTMs "increasingly serve precautionary rather than protectionist motives."

Just how trade-distorting are NTMs? NTMs are difficult to measure, and quantitative studies of their incidence and impact have only become available in the last fifteen years. A new database covering NTMs globally, begun by UNCTAD and several other agencies in 2012, demonstrates that there are substantial nontariff trade-related costs. Table 6.1 shows the overall tariff equivalent (ad valorem equivalent, or AVE) of multilateral NTMs in a sample of eighty-six countries. Cadot et al. (2018) present single-year averages based on data collected since 2012. Using the same underlying UNCTAD data but a different approach to calculating NTMs, Niu et al. (2018) present multilateral NTM data for ninety-seven countries over the time period 1997–2015.[2] In Figure 6.3, I use Niu et al.'s data to show how NTM protection has evolved over time in high-income OECD economies since 2000 (there were too few countries reporting in 1997 for that estimate to be meaningful). We see that in 2015, the average tariff equivalent of NTM protection was at a high of

---

[2] Niu et al. (2018) employ Kee et al. (2009)'s pioneering method for estimating the AVEs of NTMs. Their work extends the time period of available data.

FIGURE 6.3 Average AVEs of NTMs in high-income OECD countries
Data source: Niu et al. (2018).

57 percent. (The large drop in NTMs in the early 2000s is likely due to the
end of the Multi-Fiber Agreement and the resulting removal of quotas on
textile imports from developing to developed countries.) In Figure 6.4, I compare average applied tariff levels with the AVE of NTMs in select high-income
OECD countries in the most recent year available, 2015.

What the data from a variety of sources suggest is that despite multilateral tariff reductions in the past several years, and low tariff levels that in
many cases may seem insignificant, there remain substantial opportunities for
governments to manipulate trade policy, especially via NTMs, in a way that
produces highly protectionist results. Even tariff rates remain quite variable,
and they remain higher in many more cases than one might expect, given the
strong free-trade rhetoric among the developed countries especially.

Several significant puzzles emerge when considering these features of the
global trading regime. Was liberalization as "painless" for firms, workers, and
industries in the developed countries as is often claimed, or does the rise of
restrictive NTMs suggest that protectionist pressures remain highly charged in
these countries? What explains variation in protection at the national level?
And finally, what explains variation in protection at the sectoral level? In
Section 6.3, I develop an argument linking intra-industry trade to some of the
variation we observe in trade policy outcomes across OECD countries.

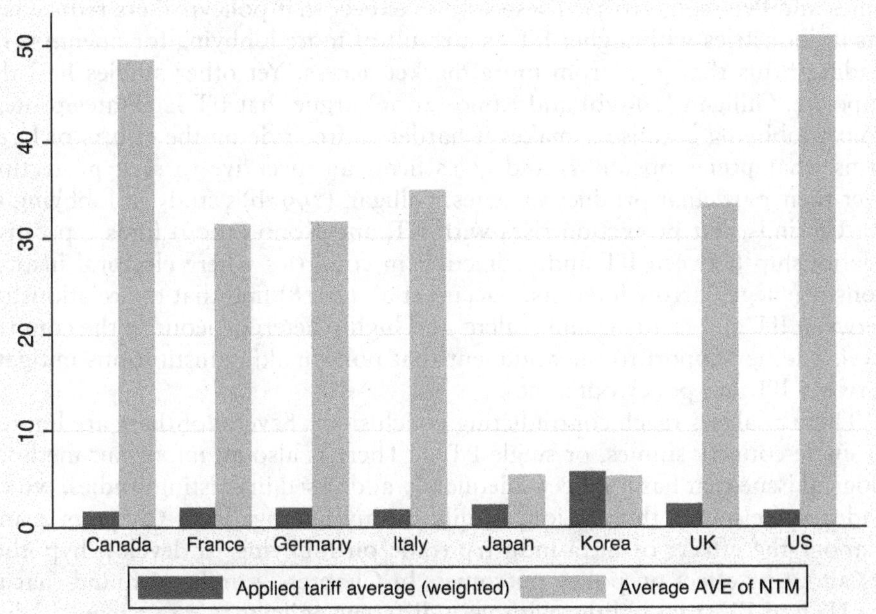

FIGURE 6.4 Overall tariff and NTM restrictiveness in 2015, high-income OECD countries
Data source: WITS and Niu et al. (2018).

6.3 INTRA-INDUSTRY TRADE AND PROTECTION

As I have discussed, intra-industry trade has been credited with easing trade liberalization globally since World War II (Balassa, 1966; Lipson, 1982; Milner, 1999; Verdier, 1998), and it has been used to explain why trade liberalization among some trade partners is less contentious than among others. The frequent assertions that intra-industry trade (a) causes fewer adverse income effects than inter-industry trade, and (b) has paved the way for easy liberalization among capital-rich countries have been too often left untested. These claims prompted the next generation of researchers to search for the losers from intra-industry trade.

In this book, I argue that the "losers" of intra-industry trade are small, non-exporting firms in industries that compete with imports but whose leading firms export as well (Melitz, 2003; Melitz and Trefler, 2012; Trefler, 2004). Given that there are real losers from the liberalization of trade in IIT industries, the claim that the rise in intra-industry trade is responsible for easy liberalization must be probed. The studies that attempt to model the consequences of IIT for trade policy outcomes reach different conclusions. Most studies find that IIT eases trade liberalization by reducing adjustment costs, which are limited to specific firms rather than entire industries (Kim, 2017; Manger, 2014, 2015;

Thies and Peterson, 2015). These studies expect that policymakers reduce tariffs in industries with higher IIT as a result of more lobbying for openness by leading firms that gain from more market access. Yet other studies find the opposite. Gilligan (1997b) and Kono (2009) argue that IIT facilitates protectionist lobbying because it makes it harder to free ride on the efforts of large firms (that prefer openness) and gives firms an incentive to seek protection over their particular product varieties. Gilligan (1997b)'s study of lobbying in the US finds that protection rises with IIT, and Kono (2009) finds a positive relationship between IIT and protection in countries where electoral institutions privilege narrow interests. Baccini et al. (2018) find that the relationship between IIT and tariffs is ambivalent and highly heterogeneous at the country level, adding support to the argument that policymaking institutions mitigate between IIT and policy outcomes.

These analyses reach contradicting conclusions. Several of them are limited to single-country studies, or single PTAs. There is also an important methodological issue that has not been adequately addressed in existing studies, which I address below. In this section, I build on my findings from Chapters 4 and 5 about the effects of intra-industry trade on lobbying to develop hypotheses about its effect on policy outcomes. In Chapters 4 and 5, I found that in the US and EU, two polities with very different policymaking systems, higher intra-industry trade is associated with more firm-level lobbying relative to industry-level lobbying via associations. I argue that this is a result of the heterogeneous nature of trade preferences among firms in industries with high levels of IIT. I also found that total lobbying expenditures in the US decreased as IIT increased, primarily as a result of the dropoff in associational lobbying in the presence of conflicting preferences within industries. What is the policy impact of this new political landscape? How successful will protectionists and free-traders be, respectively, in translating their preferences into policy outcomes?

Tariffs

I expect that the leading, exporting, and importing firms in IIT industries will prefer liberal trade policies, while the smaller, domestic-oriented firms will prefer protectionist policies. Results from Chapters 4 and 5 show that they are more likely to lobby alone for their preferred trade policies than via coalitions or industry associations. Though free-trading, internationalized firms and domestic-oriented, protectionist firms are both politically active, free-trade lobbying overwhelms protectionist lobbying in high-IIT industries. Free-trading firms are far better equipped to engage in political activity than are small firms, whose political resources are scarce, and they are also advantaged in efforts to form ad hoc and/or cross-sectoral coalitions with firms that share their preferences. Additionally, domestic-oriented firms are less threatened in aggregate by trade liberalization of differentiated products than liberalization of trade in homogeneous goods (Helpman, 1981). Though some firms will be driven out of business by competitive foreign varieties, other firms will be able to adjust their product offerings to maintain market share. The result is that the adjustment costs of trade liberalization in differentiated product industries are lower for the industry overall, reducing protectionist demands. Large, efficient, internationalized firms benefit from trade liberalization, and some domestic-oriented firms will lobby for protection but many will not, either due to scarce resources or because they are able to adjust.

Faced with these lobbying dynamics in industries with higher IIT, I expect that trade policymakers are likely to reduce tariffs for three reasons. First, the vast majority of lobbying seeks tariff reductions, as large, internationalized firms with strong preferences for both foreign market access as well as lower import costs on intermediate goods mount aggressive lobbying campaigns in favor of freer trade. This expectation is consistent with the endogenous tariff formation approach, which suggests that tariff levels are set by policymakers in response to interest-group lobbying. Second, these demands from large, politically powerful firms for openness align with the more free-trading preferences typically held by policymakers representing a national (or supra-national) constituency, such as presidents, federal bureaucrats, and EU-level bureaucrats. This convergence of preferences facilitates liberalization.[3] Third, in industries whose firms hold competing preferences, policymakers may be willing to side with the free-trading lobby on tariff rules because they believe they have the ability to compensate domestic-oriented firms with nontariff measures of protection, with *exemptions* from NTMs, or with compensatory measures. Kim and Pelc (2021) show that the US government's trade adjust-ment assistance program, for example, operates as a compensatory, de facto substitute for trade protection.

However, I expect tariffs to be higher in industries whose trade is more heav-ily *inter*-industry and based on factor endowments. Industries with low IIT tend to be those that produce less differentiated, more homogeneous products. In these industries, the adjustment costs to trade liberalization are much higher, compared to industries that produce differentiated products. First, consider how trade liberalization affects comparative disadvantage industries. Trade liberalization harms the industry as a whole, facilitating collective action and strong industry-level lobbying for protection. Because firms in comparative disadvantage industries have the most to lose when trade is liberalized, and

---

[3] This is the presidential liberalism thesis. According to Ikenberry et al. (1988, p.10), the thesis posits that the preferences of national policymakers are "partially, if not wholly distinct from the parochial concerns of either societal groups or particular government institutions, and are tied to conceptions of the 'national interest' or the maximization of some social welfare function." Many studies have supported this thesis, such as Bailey et al. (1997); Grossman and Helpman (2005); Lohmann and O'Halloran (1994); Nielson (2003).

because collective action in support of protection is easiest in these industries given unified preferences, I expect these industries to receive the highest tariff protection.

Other industries with low IIT are comparative advantage industries, with large export volumes and low import competition (such as chemicals, in the US). In these industries, I also expect tariffs to be higher than tariffs in industries with greater intra-industry trade. The logic relies on the insight that trade liberalization in developed economies is typically reciprocal and in recent years is negotiated primarily through PTAs. Two countries with similar endowments and comparative advantage in the production of the same homogeneous goods do not have a strong basis for trade at all, let alone to form a PTA that liberalizes these sectors. Among countries whose trade is primarily inter-industry, an industry that has a comparative advantage in one country may be at a comparative disadvantage in the other. Thus, there will be strong industry-level lobbying for protection coming from at least one country, making reciprocal liberalization difficult. (Contrast these dynamics with IIT industries, where there are loud calls for liberalization from large firms located in each trading partner.) In sum, while I expect tariffs to be lower in comparative advantage industries than comparative disadvantage industries, I expect to observe the lowest tariff levels in differentiated products industries characterized by high levels of intra-industry trade, as *reciprocal* liberalization is easiest in these industries. This yields the following hypothesis:

H1: As intra-industry trade increases, tariffs will be lower.

The question of causality arises here: Do tariffs fall because IIT increases or does IIT increase because tariffs are lower? There are a few reasons why endogeneity is not a major concern, though I address this concern further in the research design. First, recall that intra-industry trade does not measure the volume of trade, but rather the ratio of imports to exports. While tariff liberalization should increase import volume, this does not necessarily result in increased IIT. More imports in an import-competing industry would result in lower IIT, not more, ceteris paribus. Thus, while tariff liberalization will affect IIT, the direction of this effect is indeterminate. Second, virtually all studies of trade policies are affected by this issue. Most of the trade politics literature treats tariffs as endogenous to lobbying, and lobbying as endogenous to the trading environment. Society responds to changes in trade, or anticipated changes in trade, interest groups lobby, and trade policy changes as a result. As tariff liberalization leads to changes in the level of IIT, this new trading environment will affect societal preferences and societal lobbying, which will feed back into trade policy. In this way, the relationship between trade structure and trade protection could perhaps best be characterized as mutually reinforcing, and the question remains whether certain trade structures (inter- versus intra-industry) are associated with more or less tariff protection.

Nontariff Measures of Protection

As discussed above, I expect that leading firms in IIT industries will be strongly in favor of low tariffs, because these firms depend heavily on foreign market access. Additionally, these firms often source inputs from abroad and benefit from low tariffs on imports. At the same time, these firms may have an interest in securing nontariff measures of support in the form of export subsidies, anti-dumping compensation, import licensing, or tax refunds for exporters (to name a few examples of NTMs). Given the competing interests of firms (and workers) in IIT industries, we might also expect that policymakers will compensate the losers of openness with protection of the nontariff variety. NTMs can be applied to support both specific producers as well as an entire industry, so rent-seeking policymakers may find a way to offset the costs of tariff reductions with nontariff protections for industries and firms. In IIT industries, firms and associations may anticipate more success in lobbying for nontariff forms of protection than for tariff protection, so they may target more of their efforts on the policymakers and agents that design and provide protective NTMs.[4]

In the US, the trade policy literature shows that members of Congress are very active in bureaucratic decisions by regulatory agencies such as the International Trade Commission (ITC) and International Trade Authority (ITA) over anti-dumping protections. Members of Congress attend ITC hearings and argue in favor of protection for particular firms and industries, discuss ITC rulings in Congressional committee meetings, and introduce legislation proposing changes in the rules governing the way that the ITC and ITA operate, with the aim of securing greater protection for firms and industries (Caddel, 2014; Drope and Hansen, 2004; Hansen and Prusa, 1996). Even if national-level bureaucrats prefer more liberal trade rules perceived to be in the national interest, evidence indicates that the ITC and ITA are nevertheless responsive to interest-group pressure (Caddel, 2014). The broader American politics literature provides further theoretical and empirical support for the claim that bureaucratic authority over trade policymaking does not ensure autonomy from the influence of special-interest groups (Boehmke et al., 2013; McKay, 2011; Shepsle and Weingast, 1984). Thus, at least in the American political context, it is reasonable to hypothesize that there is a link between Congressional decisions about tariff rates and bureaucratic decisions about nontariff measures, with the one a compromise for the other.[5]

---

[4] There were 545 anti-dumping petitions filed in the US between 1980 and 2009. Half of these were filed by a single firm, and three-quarters of the petitions were filed by three firms or less (Reynolds, 2013).

[5] In the US, Congress votes every three years on whether to delegate trade promotion authority (aka tariff policy) to the president, and Congress is heavily lobbied about this decision, while also heavily lobbied when passing major trade legislation itself. It has usually voted to delegate, though not always. Congress most recently voted to reauthorize presidential trade promotion authority in 2015, for a period that expired in 2021. Ehrlich (2008) shows that in periods when Congress retains trade policy authority, the amount of lobbying is higher.

Turning to the European context, trade authority in the EU is permanently delegated to the bureaucratic European Commission, with the European Parliament retaining the power to approve or reject negotiated trade bills. As I discussed in Chapter 5, scholars of the European Union once commonly argued that models of political competition and lobbying developed in the American politics literature were not applicable in the EU context, but more recent scholarship shows that while an interest-group infrastructure was slow to build in Brussels, special-interest influence is alive and well at the European level. Dür (2008) provides evidence of heavy consultation between business representatives, national governments, and the European Commission during two rounds of WTO negotiations, and in all cases EU negotiators took positions advocated by concentrated business interest groups rather than diffuse, public interest advocacy groups. Other recent work on lobbying in the EU finds that it is now a flourishing fixture of Europolitics and that the European Commission's reliance upon private interest groups for information leaves it susceptible to 'regulatory capture' (de Bièvre and Poletti, 2020; Coen et al., 2021; Greenwood, 2017). In fact, Belloc (2015) finds that EU consultations have a significant positive impact on NTMs.

Despite heavy firm lobbying for lower tariffs in IIT industries, I expect these same firms to seek alternative forms of regulatory protection. Leading exporting firms may be highly efficient, yet competition remains fierce in manufactured goods industries with differentiated products and lots of consumer choice. These industry leaders still must compete with imports, and they have an incentive to seek protection via nontariff channels that are less susceptible to detection by foreign governments or firms. Restrictive nontariff measures are more difficult for foreign governments and producers to identify (though there are certainly high-profile trade disputes involving NTMs being waged in the WTO, the long-running Airbus-Boeing dispute being a prime example). Gulotty (2020) examines regulatory rulemaking in the EU and US and finds that multinational firms heavily lobby to secure regulatory schemes that function as veiled trade protection.

Small firms are least able to bear the costs associated with high standards and strict regulations (Fontagné et al., 2015), and I expect them to oppose restrictive NTMs that make it more difficult for these firms to compete both domestically and in foreign markets. Small firms cannot match the political influence of large, globalized firms, but they can and do participate in lower-cost lobbying venues such as public consultations. They are sometimes successful in their lobbying efforts; Gulotty (2020) shows that small firms often lobby to secure exemptions from new regulatory barriers demanded by large, globalized firms.

Based on this logic, I expect NTMs to increase as IIT increases. Policymakers can satisfy the demands of large, powerful firms for regulatory forms of protection while compensating the domestic losers of new regulations with exemptions and other forms of support. NTMs will be lowest in comparative disadvantage industries with the highest tariffs, and they will also be low in comparative advantage industries with little import competition. They will be highest in IIT industries where industry preferences over protection are divided, collective action is undermined, and the bulk of lobbying is undertaken by large, powerful firms that can benefit from NTMs that keep many foreign firms out of domestic markets. This yields my second hypothesis:

H2: As intra-industry trade increases, nontariff measures will also increase.

6.4 DATA AND METHODOLOGY

To test my hypotheses, I have compiled a cross-national panel dataset including four-digit industry-level data from eleven high-income democracies (as classified by the World Bank during the sample years) over a period from 1995 to 2014.[6] Because trade policy is conducted at the EU level and EU member states share a common external tariff, I include the EU as a single economy and exclude individual EU member states from the analysis. The unit of analysis in this study is the industry-country-year. I measure industries at the four-digit level of aggregation, according to the International Standards Industrial Classification system, Revision 3. I also limit the analysis to trade among high-income countries. I do not use dyadic trade data, which is less useful than multilateral trade data for analyzing the relationship between IIT and domestic politics. Dyadic data would be necessary for an analysis of the role of IIT on relations between states, as in Thies and Peterson (2015), or for an analysis of particular PTAs, as in Baccini et al. (2018). I am interested in the effects of import competition and exporting in general, however, so I use multilateral trade data restricted to trade among high-income countries.

Limiting the analysis by income is important theoretically. IIT between countries with high incomes per capita and similar endowments is likely to take the form of horizontal IIT. Horizontal IIT arises when products are exchanged that are similar in price but differentiated by varieties (Japanese and Scottish whisky, for example). HIIT occurs most frequently between high-income economies (Fontagné et al., 1998). Vertical IIT, on the other hand, is trade of similar goods distinguished by unit value or quality (Italian-made men's suits versus low-cost men's suits made in Vietnam, for example). VIIT is more common between countries with different factor endowments and different income levels, and it can be just as disruptive to the country with higher factor costs as inter-industry trade (Blanes and Martín, 2000). In the medium- term, this type of trade will disappear as producers in the more expensive country are forced to exit. Essentially, in the medium- term, VIIT between two countries with different factor endowments will become inter-industry trade. This is one reason for the heavy interest-group lobbying

---

[6] These economies are Australia, Canada, the European Union, Iceland, Israel, Japan, New Zealand, Norway, South Korea, Switzerland, and the United States.

against trade liberalization between the US and Mexico during the NAFTA negotiations, as well as protectionist lobbying during the negotiations of the Trans-Pacific Partnership. By limiting my sample to high-income economies, I am more likely to isolate trade in similar products driven by consumer preferences for variety and increasing returns to scale.[7]

Dependent and Independent Variables

I have two dependent variables in this study: tariffs and nontariff measures of protection (NTMs). *Tariffs* measures the weighted applied (AHS) tariff rate for industry *i* in country *j*. This data is available for each four-digit ISIC category from the World Bank's WITS database. The measure is an average tariff applied to all goods within the four-digit ISIC category, weighted by the import share of the various goods within the tariff category. Applied tariffs, which incorporate PTAs, are about 30 percent lower, on average, than MFN tariff levels. As shown in Figure 6.1, though tariffs have fallen globally, there is substantial variation in tariff rates over time and across countries. There is also significant variation across industries, as shown in Figure 6.5.

My second dependent variable is *NTMs*. Here I use a measure capturing the multilateral ad valorem equivalent of NTMs at three-year intervals over the period 1997–2015.[8] Niu et al. (2018) use Kee et al. (2009)'s method for estimating tariff equivalents of NTMs, but they use newer underlying data available from UNCTAD's Multi-Agency Support Team that extends coverage of NTMs over time as well as includes broader coverage of measures. While other studies (such as Kono [2009]) use an index of overall trade restrictiveness that encompasses tariffs as well as NTMs, a single, encompassing measure of overall protection cannot examine the question of whether IIT has differing impacts on tariff versus nontariff measures of protection. To assess both of my hypotheses above and examine whether NTMs are playing a substitionary role as tariffs have declined, it is critical to employ two separate dependent variables. I aggregate from the six-digit HS level used by Niu et al. (2018) to the four-digit level, taking mean values when multiple six-digit categories are mapped onto a single four-digit category. Table 6.2 compares tariff to nontariff rates of protection over time. We see that the average tariff equivalent of NTMs

---

[7] In Kono (2009)'s cross-national analysis of intra-industry trade and protection, he did not find that the two were related, except in countries whose political institutions are more responsive to lobbying. In these countries, Kono finds that as IIT increases, protection increases as well. However, Kono includes all available countries in his sample, which means that his analysis includes countries with widely differing factor endowments at very different levels of development. It is likely that he is therefore capturing trade processes that do not conform to the assumptions of intra-industry trade theory, and political dynamics that are similar to those predicted by standard trade theory. This is an important theoretical reason for excluding trade with low- and middle-income countries from the sample.

[8] Niu et al. (2018) adopt intervals in order to "smooth out" year-specific shocks in the continuous variables such as trade volumes that underlay the NTM measure.

TABLE 6.2 *Protection over time in high-income OECD countries: Average tariff and NTM rates*

Year	Observations	Mean rate (%)		
		AVE of NTMs	AHS tariff	MFN tariff
1997	1193	5.05	2.46	3.45
2000	1200	9.15	2.11	3.07
2003	31839	9.67	2.97	4.71
2006	32899	9.52	2.89	4.08
2009	32251	48.66	2.47	3.97
2012	32415	25.98	2.26	3.93
2015	31131	53.21	2.57	3.84

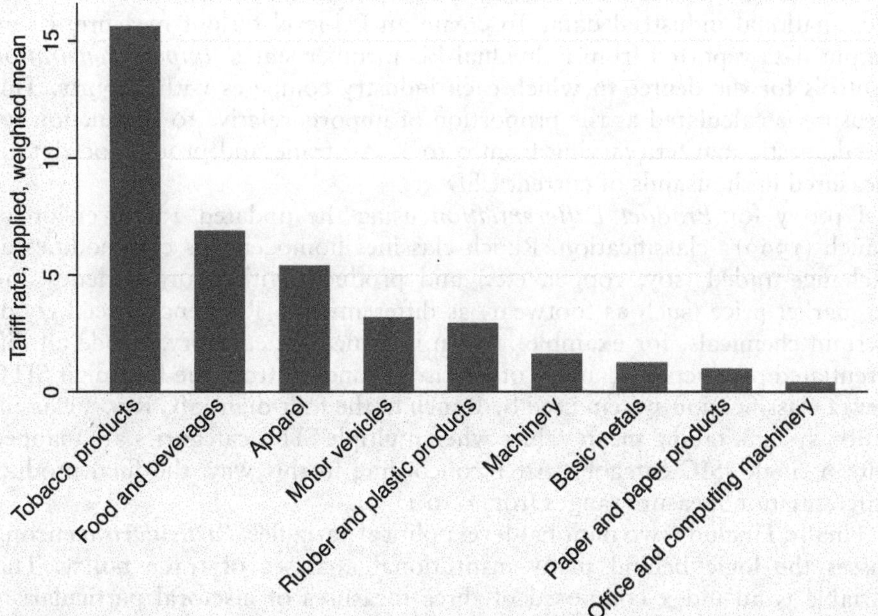

FIGURE 6.5 Weighted average applied tariffs by two-digit ISIC Section, averaged over sample time period
Data source: WITS.

is significantly higher than both MFN and applied tariff rates over the sample period, and it has risen markedly over time, whereas tariff rates during this period have remained low and stable.

My key independent variable is *IIT*, measured using the Grubel-Lloyd index as described in Chapter 2. I construct the IIT measure using export and import data to/from other high-income countries, available from UNIDO's Industrial Statistics Database.

Control Variables

I include several industry-level variables to control for alternative explanations and other factors that influence protection. *Export Dependence* (exports/output) controls for the degree to which an industry is export-oriented. I calculate this measure using export data and industry output data available from UNIDO. This data covers all the high-income democracies in my sample, for all four-digit industries over a time period between 1990 and 2014. Output coverage is spotty, as all countries do not report statistics for every industry in every year. Yet the UNIDO database provides the longest time-series coverage for the broadest set of countries, at a finer level of industry disaggregation than the OECD, which provides the only other source of cross-national industrial data. To create an EU-level output measure, I sum output data reported from individual EU member states. *Import Penetration* controls for the degree to which each industry competes with imports. This measure is calculated as the proportion of imports relative to production for the domestic market, varying from 0 to 1. All trade and production data is measured in thousands of current USD.

I proxy for *Product Differentiation* using the updated 2007 version of Rauch (1999)'s classification. Rauch classifies homogeneous commodities as exchange-traded (soy, copper, etc.) and products with many varieties and no market price (such as footwear) as differentiated. Reference-priced goods (certain chemicals, for example) are an intermediate category. I code all differentiated products as 1 and 0 otherwise. I concord from the four-digit SITC Rev. 2 classification system used by Rauch to the four-digit ISIC Rev. 3 classification system, taking mean values when multiple SITC categories are mapped onto a single ISIC category. After concording in this way, the final product differentiation measure ranges from 0 to 1.

Finally, I include two national-level political variables. *Particularism* encompasses the logic behind many institutional analyses of trade policy. This variable is an index composed of three measures of electoral particularism related to party strength and the degree to which voting is party-based or candidate-based. A higher score indicates a candidate-centric system in which legislators face strong incentives to cater to particularistic interests to cultivate a personal vote. If the standard argument from the trade policy literature is correct, protection will be positively correlated with particularism. However, if IIT incentivizes more active free-trade lobbying, we could observe the opposite effect. This variable was originally developed by Carey and Shugart (1995). Johnson and Wallack (2012) used the measure to compile a cross-national dataset of particularism spanning the years 1978–2005 in 158 countries. For the vast majority of high-income democracies, the particularism variable does not change over this time period; I interpolated values to extend the data to 2014, the last year in my sample. I also control for government ideology, using a measure of the left-right orientation of the executive from the World Bank's Database of Political Institutions. This variable, *Ideology*, ranges from 1 to 3, increasing as the chief executive's party ideology moves from right, to center, to left. I report summary statistics in Appendix Tables D.1 and D.2.

6.5 ANALYSIS AND RESULTS

First, I analyze the relationship between IIT and tariffs. I estimate OLS models, where tariffs are regressed on the independent variables: intra-industry trade, export dependence, import penetration, product differentiation, political particularism, and government ideology. The dependent variable, *Tariffs*, is log-transformed to reduce extreme right skew. Because tariff levels are dependent upon the previous year's tariff levels, we would expect to observe serial autocorrelation within the data, and this is confirmed by a Wooldridge test. I address this by including the dependent variable lagged by one year as a control variable. I also estimate Newey-West standard errors with 3 lags to address remaining autocorrelation and heteroskedasticity.[9] Finally, to partially address concerns about reverse causality, I lag the key independent variable (IIT) by four years. This increases our confidence that IIT is influencing future levels of protection in the ways that I have hypothesized, rather than the other way around.

I report the results of the main model (Model 1) in Figure 6.6. Full regression results are reported in Appendix Table D.3. In the main model, I exclude EU states in order to examine the effect of the two political variables (these are only available at the national level, while EU tariffs are made at the EU level). In Appendix Table D.3, I show the results of an alternate model that includes the EU but excludes the political variables (Model 2). In Figure 6.6, we see that IIT is negatively related to AHS tariffs, and this relationship is statistically significant. Export dependence is also significant and negatively associated with tariff levels. In both model specifications reported in the appendix, we observe that IIT maintains a negative and independent effect on tariff levels. As a robustness check, I employ a mixed-effects estimator on the full sample (Model 3). The Newey method is useful for addressing serial autocorrelation, but it cannot account for clustering within or across groups. The results show that the negative relationship between IIT and tariffs is robust to this specification as well.

While the effect of each of the variables on tariff rates looks small, it is important to note how low tariff rates are during this time period (averaging well under 3 percent). In Model 1, a one-unit increase in IIT (from no two-way trade to fully balanced trade) yields a .032% decrease in the log-transformed tariff rate; this is approximately a 97% decrease in the unlogged tariff rate.

---

[9] The results are robust to including more or fewer lags.

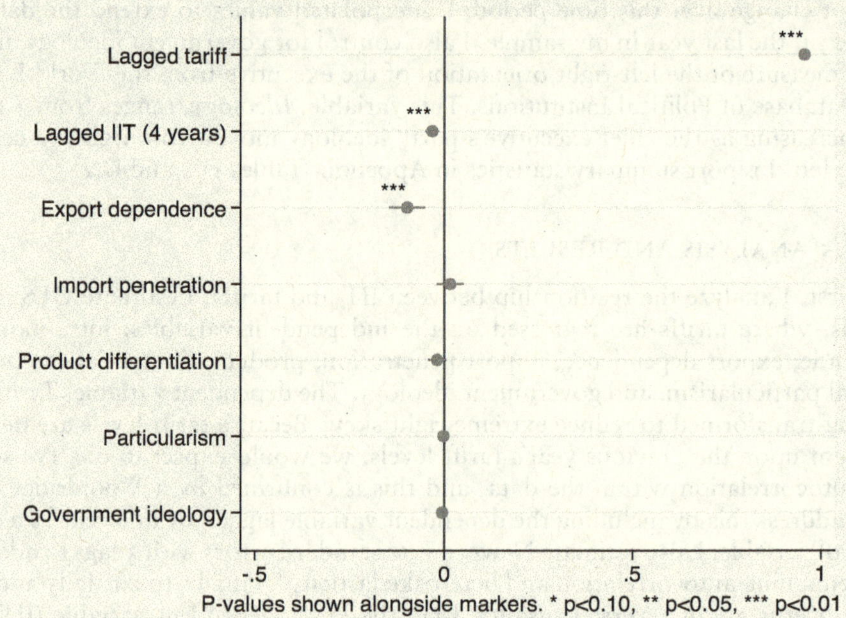

FIGURE 6.6 The effect of IIT on AHS tariffs

This means that a 10% increase in IIT, which is a more realistic change, is associated with a 9.7% lower tariff rate four years later (keeping the lag in mind). In other words, we would expect that if IIT increased by 10%, a tariff of 2.5% would decrease to 2.26%.

I now to turn to the analysis of NTMs. Because the NTM data is classified at the four-digit HS level, for these analyses, I include Comtrade trade data classified according to this system. As in the previous analyses of tariffs, my IIT measure is created using exports and imports to and from high-income economies. Because cross-national industrial output data is not available at the four-digit HS level, I control for imports and exports (to and from high-income countries, log-transformed) to proxy for export dependence and import penetration. EU countries are included separately as NTMs vary at the member state level, while tariffs do not.[10] I also add controls for tariff levels (log-transformed trade-weighted AHS), and the two political variables described above. The dependent variable is continuous (log-transformed) and represents the tariff rate equivalent of NTMs. The three-year interval between each NTM observation is a feature which should reduce serial autocorrelation of the dependent variable, yet Wooldridge tests reveal that autocorrelation remains a problem. To address this, I include the dependent variable lagged by one

---

[10] Existing research on NTMs within the EU also emphasizes variation at the member state level (Ghodsi et al., 2016; Tudela-Marco et al., 2017).

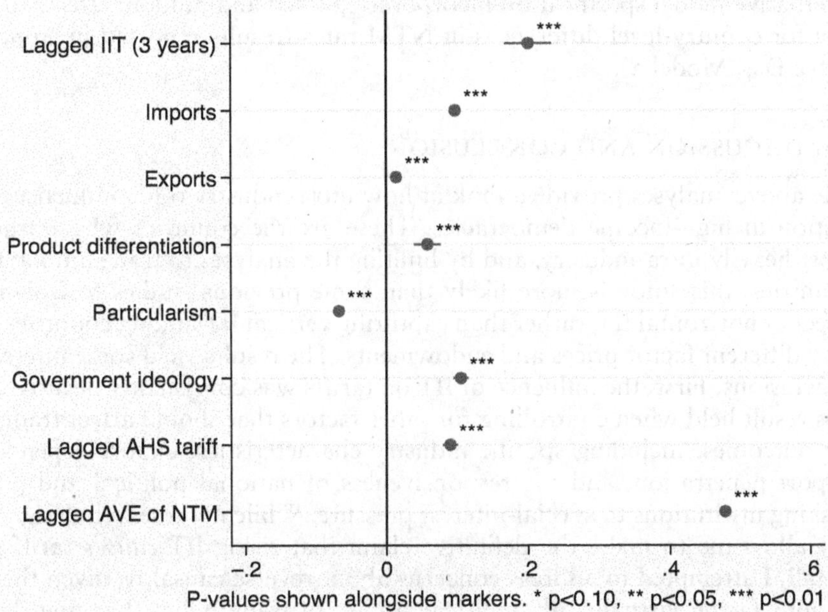

FIGURE 6.7 The effect of IIT on AVE of NTMs

time period (three years) as a control variable. I lag the key independent variable (IIT) by three years and I lag the control for tariff levels as well. Finally, I employ the Newey-West method (with one three-year lag) to address remaining heteroskedasticity and autocorrelation.

I present the results of this analysis in the first column (Model 1) of Appendix Table D.4 and visually in Figure 6.7. We see that consistent with my hypothesis, IIT has a clear positive and significant effect on AVEs of NTMs. The size of this effect is much larger than the size of the effect on tariffs, consistent with the much higher levels of restrictive NTMs in the sample. The coefficient indicates that a one-unit increase in IIT is associated with a 20 percent increase in the log-transformed tariff rate equivalent of NTMs. This represents approximately a 12% increase in the equivalent (unlogged) AVE rate as IIT increases by 10%. The relationship between IIT and nontariff forms of protection holds even when controlling for leading alternative explanations. Imports are positive and significantly correlated with AVEs of NTMs, as are exports and product differentiation. Particularism has a negative and significant effect on NTMs, while the positive coefficient on the government ideology variable indicates that NTMs are higher under left-leaning executives. Higher tariff rates are also associated with higher NTM rates, casting some doubt on the claim that NTMs function as a substitute for tariffs more broadly, though they appear to do so in high-IIT industries. These results are robust to an alternative model specification incorporating fixed and random effects to control for country-level differences in NTM rates (results reported in Appendix Table D.4, Model 2).

6.6 DISCUSSION AND CONCLUSION

The above analyses provide a look at how intra-industry trade influences protection in high-income democracies. These are the countries whose trade is most heavily intra-industry, and by limiting the analyses to trade among these countries, this study is more likely than some previous studies to isolate the effect of horizontal IIT, rather than capturing vertical IIT among countries with very different factor prices and endowments. The results yield some interesting conclusions. First, the influence of IIT on tariffs was consistently negative, and this result held when controlling for other factors that should affect trade policy outcomes, including specific industry characteristics, export dependence, import penetration, and the responsiveness of national political and policy-making institutions to special-interest pressure. While my research design does not allow me to make the definitive claim that rising IIT *causes* tariff rates to fall, I attempted to address concerns about reverse causality, given the limitations facing virtually all empirical studies of trade policy. Lagging the IIT measure, and addressing serial autocorrelation in tariff levels, increases our confidence that changes in IIT facilitate tariff liberalization, rather than the other way around.

The findings in this analysis support the arguments made throughout this book that intra-industry trade among rich countries is unlikely to inspire concerted and well-organized protectionist lobbying, as it benefits leading firms within industries and does not threaten entire industries with extinction. As leading firms find markets for their particular product varieties abroad, they are likely to pressure policymakers to cut tariff levels as a way to negotiate lower reciprocal tariffs in export markets. Similar political dynamics in other advanced economies mean that reciprocal tariff liberalization is easier than it is for industries whose products are more homogeneous and subject to comparative advantage and disadvantage. The losers of IIT are not entire industries but small firms, and they are unlikely to be able to exert the political influence over tariff levels that large firms can.

Second, I hypothesized that we would observe more restrictive NTMs along with rising IIT. This hypothesis was also supported. I found a strong and positive relationship between IIT and the ad valorem tariff rate equivalents of NTMs. This provides some support for the long-standing expectation within the IPE literature that nontariff barriers to trade may play a substituting role for tariffs. However, tariffs were positively associated with NTMs in the sample, suggesting that perhaps the substitutionary effect is limited to IIT industries where business preferences are split and large firms dominate the lobbying process. Even as these firms seek lower tariffs, NTMs can provide a form of regulatory protection that, counterintuitively, may benefit large multi-nationals (Gulotty, 2020). While industry-leading firms can absorb the costs of compliance with regulations, smaller firms often cannot. The result is less competition for large firms and higher prices, while the downsides for consumers are fewer product varieties (and higher prices). My results also support what I have argued throughout this book: namely, that IIT is not costless and the losers are found at the firm level rather than the industry level. While two-way trade in differentiated products provides more consumer variety and provides more opportunities for firms to adjust than when trade is based on comparative advantage, it also provides opportunities for regulatory barriers that disadvantage small firms. The ability for large firms to lobby successfully for product regulations that limit import competition but also competition from smaller, domestic firms is another mechanism through which IIT undermines industry consensus over trade policy, a key argument made in this book.[11]

Third, this chapter advances our understanding of how institutions intermediate between interest group demands and policy outcomes. In my analysis, the degree to which a country's elected officials are receptive to special-interest lobbying was not related to tariff levels. This may reflect the relative ease associated with tariff reductions covering North–North trade. In this sample of trade among wealthy countries, tariff cuts are far less controversial than tariff liberalization in a North–South agreement where factor prices are very different across trading partners. However, I found that NTMs are lower in countries where elected officials have incentives to cater to special-interest lobbying, and this is the opposite of the standard argument from the trade politics literature. This finding also seems to run counter to the logic behind my argument that large firms successfully pressure for NTMs in the presence of two-way trade. One way to make sense of this finding is to recall that elected officials are not always the target of business lobbying over trade policy. Perhaps where elected officials are less responsive to special interest groups, firms and industries focus their political efforts on regulatory agencies, which are often susceptible to lobbying, as I have discussed. This is certainly consistent with the dynamics of trade policymaking in the EU. Tariffs are low in the EU and trade policymakers in Brussels are far more insulated from special interest demands than members of the US Congress, for example. Yet the EU is famous for its aggressive use of anti-dumping and health and safety regulations that either fully restrict or raise the cost of imports.

To conclude, this chapter's findings are consistent with the overall argument in this book that intra-industry trade undermines lobbying by industry associations tasked with representing all firms in an industry, paving the way for

---

[11] Gulotty (2020, pp. 3–5) provides the example of Mattell and Hasbro, two large multinationals that spent millions lobbying in support of stricter US regulations on lead levels in children's toys. The resulting legislation led to significant concentration of the US toy industry, as smaller producers could not afford substantially higher testing costs. Thousands of small Chinese producers exited the industry as well and the profits of multinationals tripled.

large, globalized firms to dominate the lobbying process over both tariffs and NTMs. IIT does not appear to consistently facilitate trade liberalization, as much of the literature has claimed. Rather, it eases the way for *tariff* liberalization while creating more opportunities for regulatory forms of protection via NTMs that benefit the largest firms. This final point challenges the commonly made claim that IIT is generally welfare-enhancing and less disruptive than trade based in comparative advantage, easing the path to trade liberalization. While this may be true for tariffs, my finding that rising IIT is associated with higher NTMs is a significant finding that introduces an additional mechanism through which IIT may benefit leading exporting or multinational firms at the expense of domestic and/or smaller firms. It also highlights a previously unknown channel through which IIT facilitates lobbying by multinationals for trade policies that benefit them at the expense of consumers and smaller firms. In this way, it is worth considering whether the rise of IIT among developed economies has contributed to the growing populist backlash against globalization, which is increasingly perceived as advancing corporate interests at the expense of workers and the broader public.

The Politics of TPP and TTIP in the United States

"TTIP is dead in the water." So rang the headlines on both sides of the Atlantic in August 2016, after Germany's Vice Chancellor and Economic Minister, Sigmar Gabriel, told a German TV station that negotiations on the Transatlantic Trade and Investment Partnership (TTIP) have "failed" and that "nothing is moving forward."[1] After three years and fourteen rounds of negotiating, Gabriel told the media that the United States and the European Union had failed to agree on a single one of the twenty-seven chapters included in the ambitious agreement between the world's two largest economies. Fast forward to November 10, 2016, and the election of Donald J. Trump as President of the United States. Riding to victory after a campaign in which the specter of trade loomed large, during his first week in office Trump withdrew the United States from another massive trade deal that had recently been completed with eleven Pacific Rim nations, the Trans-Pacific Partnership (TPP). Though Trump never mentioned TTIP during his campaign (nor did Hillary Clinton), Angela Merkel stated in a joint press conference with Barack Obama that the TTIP "will not be concluded now" following Trump's victory.[2] When US President Joseph Biden assumed office in January 2021, many analysts predicted that he would revive TTIP negotiations. The US and EU had resumed trade talks late in Donald Trump's term, though primarily as a response to the Trump administration's punitive tariffs on EU aluminum and steel imports, and both partners insisted that the new talks were not part of the TTIP process, which formally closed in 2019 (European Commission, 2018). Under the Biden administration, trade talks with the EU have focused more narrowly

---

[1] *EurActiv.com*, "Germany says TTIP dead in the water," August 29, 2016.
[2] *The Independent*, "Angela Merkel suggests TTIP trade deal won't be concluded under Barack Obama's presidency," November 17, 2016.

on resolving the conflict over aluminum and steel tariffs and cooperating on regulatory issues in digital technologies through a new process called the EU–US Trade and Technology Council, which is in large part motivated by limiting China's influence in internet governance and tech supply chains.

The TPP suffered a much more publicized and dramatic demise. Signed by President Obama in 2016, the mega-agreement became a lightning rod during the 2016 presidential campaign. The three leading candidates all declared their opposition to it, and Hillary Clinton's one-time support of the TPP (she promoted it while serving as Secretary of State) may well have cost her crucial votes in the Rust Belt states of the Upper Midwest whose small towns have been gutted by the decline of US manufacturing. Though President Trump withdrew the US from the pact, important US trading partners such as Japan have publicly expressed hope that the US would rejoin the agreement (now known as the Comprehensive and Progressive Trans-Pacific Partnership, or CPTPP). Instead, the Biden administration is pursuing a narrower digital trade pact with CPTPP members and other states in the region.

While both of these mega-regional trade and investment deals were negotiated concurrently and failed nearly at the same time, the US domestic politics surrounding each agreement were dramatically different. Interestingly, from 2013 to 2015, the most active negotiating period for each agreement, US media coverage of both agreements was sparse in print sources and virtually nonexistent on broadcast and cable television news (Knupfer, 2013; Madeira, 2018; Powell and Harrington, 2015). In the presidential race, however, the TPP became a highly salient and divisive issue while no candidate ever mentioned the TTIP. Yet lack of public interest in a trade agreement is not surprising, from a conventional IPE perspective. What is surprising is the different lobbying dynamics that accompanied the negotiations of the two agreements. Dür and Lechner (2015) analyzed the content of 222 statements submitted to four rounds of US and EU public consultations regarding TTIP in 2012 and 2013. They found that business interests on both sides of the Atlantic overwhelmingly support a "broad and encompassing agreement," noting that there was nearly no protectionist sentiment expressed. Young (2016) reaches the same conclusion in his analysis of USTR consultation data, and he also notes the emergence of transnational business alliances in favor of TTIP, a coalition that none of our standard trade theories would predict. In an analysis of lobbying data over TPP, Ravenhill (2017) found that there was much more division among business groups than there was during TTIP negotiations. While peak business organizations were unanimous in their support of TPP, several high-profile industry associations were strongly opposed to certain aspects of the TPP, ranging from the inclusion of Japan as a member to concerns over rules of origin provisions. Both industries and labor unions were able to mount vigorous lobbying campaigns either for or against TPP, while we hardly observed any US business groups (or labor unions) that lobbied against TTIP.

What explains the different domestic political dynamics surrounding TPP and TTIP? More specifically, why was lobbying more contentious over TPP while lobbying over TTIP was almost entirely in favor of the agreement? And given these very different political dynamics, why did both agreements fail in the US? In this chapter, I present case studies of lobbying in the US over these two pieces of trade legislation. I have demonstrated the relationship between IIT and firm and industry lobbying behavior quantitatively in two different economies; in this chapter, I demonstrate qualitatively how the process of firm- and industry-level lobbying decisions is affected by the structure of international trade. Through these case studies, I show that conflicting preferences within industries and collective action problems are at the heart of the lobbying dynamics I have documented thus far in this book. While the quantitative analyses presented thus far establish the relationship between firm-level political activity and IIT, the process underlying lobbying decisions plays out within industries. Qualitative case studies allow me to assess whether the higher political activity of firms relative to industry associations in industries with higher IIT is a result of a breakdown of industry-level preferences over trade policy, as I have hypothesized. In other words, case studies are a useful complement to quantitative analyses because they better illuminate the causal pathways through which independent variables influence the dependent variable and increase our confidence in the causality of the processes studied (Mahoney, 2007; Sambanis, 2004). This is particularly true when trying to link firm and industry preferences with trade policy outcomes.[3]

The case studies I present in this chapter allow me to assess the causal mechanisms underlying the first two stages of the three-stage theory I presented in Chapter 3. In this chapter, I present further evidence that (1) increasing IIT erodes industry consensus over trade policy, and (2) these heterogeneous preferences undermine the intensity of political activity that industry associations can pursue, paving the way for individual firms to emerge as the primary political actors. There are two leading alternative explanations for the positive relationship between IIT and firm-based lobbying, which the quantitative analyses in Chapters 4 and 5 attempted to dispel and which the case studies in this chapter will further challenge. The first is that the rise of individual firm lobbying is simply driven by firm size or industry concentration into the hands of the leading firms. It is obvious that large firms can afford to lobby alone, while small firms cannot. Thus, perhaps we have observed increasing firm-level lobbying activity as multinationals have expanded globally, increasing their market dominance and the resources they can devote to political activity. The firm heterogeneity literature expects and finds that large, globally engaged firms lobby more than domestic-oriented firms. The analysis I present in this book has thus far demonstrated that there are international economic factors that also affect firm- and industry-level political activity, particularly in making

---

[3] See Winslett (2021) for an excellent example of this approach.

it more difficult for industry associations to take a strong lobbying stance in the face of conflicting preferences among members. This raises the relative activity of firms to associations in industries facing higher IIT, and I will show in this chapter that this provides a key explanation for the very different domestic politics surrounding different trade agreements, such as TPP and TTIP. This also affects trade policy outcomes.

Another alternative explanation is that lobbying patterns are primarily driven by comparative advantage. According to our standard trade models, firms and industries are united around liberalization or protection, depending on the industry's comparative advantage. Perhaps lobbying over TPP was so much more contentious in the US than TTIP because many US industries are at a comparative disadvantage relative to Asian/Pacific economies with lower labor costs. Yet this line of reasoning would predict consensus *within* industries, either in support of or against liberalization within the TPP. I will show that this was indeed the case for comparative advantage/disadvantage industries, but that in industries with higher IIT, consensus eroded and we observe more active firms relative to their industry associations. On the other hand, perhaps there is significant firm-level lobbying in industries at a comparative disadvantage, because firms have more to lose from trade liberalization in comparative disadvantage sectors. Yet in previous chapters, I controlled for comparative advantage to show that the presence of two-way trade within an industry is an independent effect on firm and associational political choices. As two-way trade increases in comparative disadvantage industries, associations had to scale back their political activity to avoid alienating powerful, internationally engaged member firms. In the case studies presented in this chapter, I will tease out these dynamics.

7.1 CASE SELECTION

In this chapter, I select two major recent pieces of US trade legislation and examine business and labor lobbying over each: The Trans-Pacific Partnership (TPP) and Transatlantic Trade and Investment Partnership (TTIP). I select TPP and TTIP for several reasons. First, they were negotiated concurrently and I examine lobbying activity in the years 2013–2014 for both agreements. This serves as a natural control for exogenous factors such as the macroeconomic climate, the trade policy orientation of US policymakers, and industry- and firm-level internal dynamics. The actors within firms and industry associations making decisions about political activity are in all likelihood the same actors across both cases. Second, the TPP and TTIP were the two largest trade agreements that the US has negotiated since NAFTA, in terms of trade volume. This means that US firms and industries had high potential gains and losses from both agreements, relative to trade agreements with smaller partner markets. In 2013, the TPP countries as a group were the largest goods and

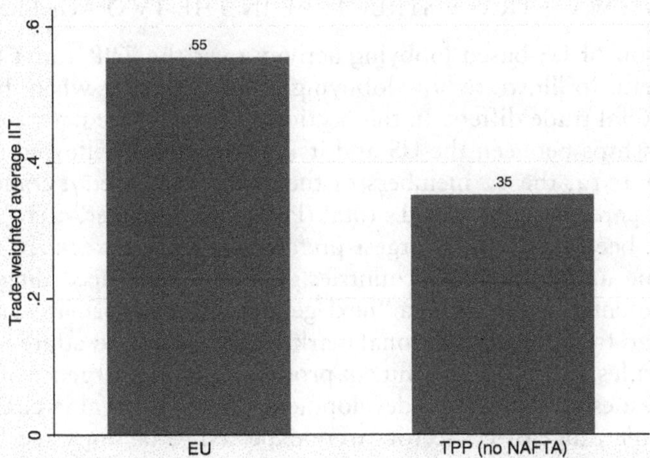

FIGURE 7.1 Multilateral trade-weighted IIT between US and PTA partners, 2013
Data source: Comtrade.

services export market of the US, receiving $613 billion of US goods, representing approximately 42 percent of total US goods exports that year (Comtrade data). The TTIP countries made up the second largest export market for the US after the TPP group, receiving approximately $232 billion of US goods.

There is significant variation on my key independent variable, intra-industry trade, both across and within cases, as I will discuss in depth in Section 7.2. Trade between the US and the EU is more heavily intra-industry than is trade between the US and the TPP states with whom it is not already in a free trade area (Canada and Mexico) (see Figure 7.1). Within each trade agreement, however, we observe the full range of IIT, with some industries heavily export-oriented, others primarily import-competing, and others experiencing high levels of two-way trade (IIT).

These two cases also contain significant variation on the dependent variable, the political organization of industries. In each agreement, we observe industries in which associations are highly active with a strong stance on policy preferences, others in which associations formally register a neutral or ambivalent stance, and still others in which associations do not lobby at all and all political activity is conducted by individual firms. Because industries are affected by both agreements, we can also trace the activity of a single industry across the two trade agreements. Thus, my selection of two trade agreements allows me to observe variation on the dependent variable both across cases, while looking at lobbying over an entire agreement (as opposed to selecting one industry within an agreement) allows for variation on the dependent variable within cases.

7.2 OVERVIEW OF TRADE STRUCTURE IN THE TWO AGREEMENTS

A comparison of US-based lobbying activity over the TPP and TTIP, respectively, is useful to illustrate how lobbying dynamics differ when the structure of international trade differs. In this section, I describe the nature of commercial relationships between the US and its TPP partners, followed by its TTIP partners. In 2014, the 12 members of the TPP represented a combined GDP equal to 36 percent of the world's total (Petri and Plummer, 2016).[4] The TPP would have been the world's largest preferential trade agreement in terms of trade volume among member countries. The aim was, according to the US Trade Representative, to create a "next-generation transformative agreement" that would go far beyond traditional market access issues to address regulatory coherence, rules of origin, government procurement, convergence of standards, and other issues central to the development of regional value chains (USTR, 2011). A wide range of US sectors were expected to be impacted by the TPP, including food and agriculture, manufacturing, natural resources, energy, and services.

With few tariffs remaining between the US and its existing FTA Partners (Canada, Chile, Mexico, Peru, and Singapore), most tariff reductions would affect trade between the US and the remaining five TPP members. The sectors with the largest tariff reductions under TPP would have been footwear, sugar, titanium downstream products, clothing, leather goods, textiles, beef, rice, pork products, and processed foods (USITC, 2016). While the USITC's analysis projected that some of these US industries would expand as a result of the agreement, others were predicted to contract. The agriculture and food sector as a whole was expected to grow, and particularly the beef, dairy, sugar, and processed foods industries, while wheat, rice, and seafood production was expected to shrink. Perhaps more worryingly, USITC estimated that output in manufacturing, natural resource and energy sectors would shrink by \$10 billion by the year 2032, with employment expected to be 0.2 percent lower in this sector. While the government's models predicted gains for the passenger vehicles, clothing, and footwear industries, US-based production of chemicals, textiles, auto parts, electronic equipment, and titanium-based products was predicted to shrink. Other economists criticized the government's modeling approach as severely underestimating the scope of US job losses as a result of the TPP, and one widely cited paper estimated overall employment losses in the US to reach 448,000 over a decade (Capaldo, 2014).

While tariff liberalization was only one of many trade-related issues being negotiated in the agreement, market access issues were nevertheless more salient in TPP than in TTIP because endowments-based trade between the US and its TPP partners was much more significant than between the US and EU. We see evidence for this in the lower levels of intra-industry trade between the

---

4 The parties negotiating the agreement in that year were Australia, Brunei, Canada, Chile, Japan, Malaysia, Mexico, New Zealand, Peru, Singapore, the United States, and Vietnam.

US and TPP countries (excluding Canada and Mexico) compared to TTIP. As seen in Figure 7.1, multilateral IIT between the US and its non-NAFTA TPP partners was 35% in 2013, compared with 55% between the US and its TTIP partners.[5] Several TPP countries are notable among developed economies for the extent to which their trade with the world remains endowments-based, particularly Australia, Japan, and New Zealand, all of whom had IIT levels below 40 percent in 2012 (Madeira, 2014). Furthermore, TPP countries vary much more in their level of development than TTIP countries, all of which are high income. Trade between countries at different levels of development is more likely to be endowments-based, and what IIT does occur among these countries is more likely to be vertical in nature, involving similar products of varying price and quality. We see this reflected in the data as well. Figure 7.2 disaggregates IIT between the US and its TPP and TTIP partners, respectively, and we see that horizontal IIT of similar products constitutes over 40% of total transatlantic trade, while only about 25% of transpacific trade.[6] Figure 7.2 also shows how much more important vertical IIT is as a proportion of total IIT in US–TPP trade compared to US–TTIP trade. Vertical IIT makes up

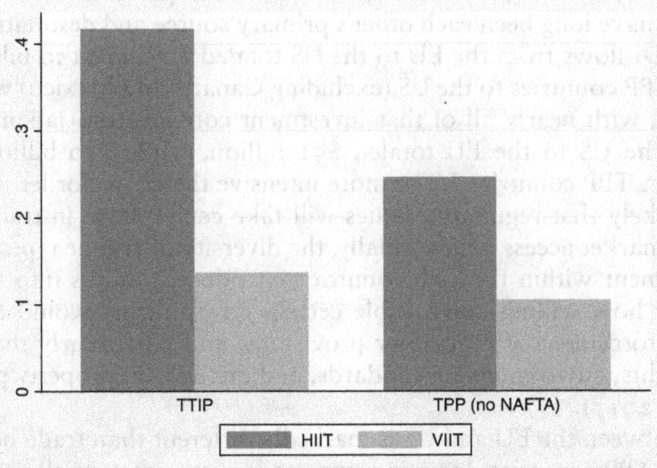

FIGURE 7.2 Horizontal and vertical IIT as a proportion of total trade in TTIP and TPP
Data source: Comtrade.

[5] In this discussion and in the trade statistics provided in this chapter, I exclude the NAFTA countries. This is because the NAFTA partners are already part of a free trade area; what was relevant (and contentious) for TPP negotiations was liberalization between the US and its non-NAFTA partners.

[6] Slight differences in the total share of IIT represented in Figures 7.1 and 7.2 is due to how I weighted industry-level IIT in the two figures. IIT is trade-weighted in Figure 7.1 but not in Figure 7.2, in order to simplify the calculations of HIIT and VIIT.

nearly a third of all IIT between the US and TPP countries, while VIIT represents only about a quarter of transatlantic IIT. The greater relative importance of vertical IIT in transpacific trade is notable because this type of trade takes on characteristics of endowments-based trade between lower- and higher-income economies: It is based on differences in factor prices and generates some of the same distributional effects as inter-industry trade. The presence of varieties gives more firms the opportunity to adjust, yet the presence of lower-cost varieties nevertheless puts considerable pressure on firms and industries and drives some to exit.

The differences in trade structure between the US and its TPP versus TTIP partners is not only a feature of differing levels of development but of the much lower participation of the TPP countries in global value chains (Ravenhill, 2017). In 2009, Canada, New Zealand, and the US had the lowest participation in global value chains of all the OECD countries (along with Turkey) (de Backer and Miroudot, 2014). While the most intensive regional supply chain links exist within NAFTA, NAFTA was also the least integrated of all regions with the rest of the world at this time (Baldwin and Lopez-Gonzalez, 2015; Los et al., 2015). Market access issues will be more problematic where trade within global value chains is lower. Relatedly, FDI between the US and TPP countries, while significant, was also lower compared to US–EU FDI. The EU and US have long been each other's primary source and destination of FDI. In 2012, FDI flows from the EU to the US totaled around $150 billion, while FDI from TPP countries to the US (excluding Canada and Mexico) was around $22 billion, with nearly all of that investment coming from Japan. Outward FDI from the US to the EU totaled $91 billion, while $50 billion went to non-NAFTA TPP countries.[7] The more intensive the cross-border investment, the more likely that regulatory issues will take center stage in trade negotiations over market access issues. Finally, the diversity of regime types and levels of development within the TPP countries introduced doubts into the negotiations over how willing and/or able certain governments would be when it came to enforcement of regulatory provisions, and particularly those related to labor rights, environmental standards, and intellectual property protections (Ravenhill, 2017).

Trade between the EU and US is markedly different than trade between the US and the TPP countries. Intra-industry trade grew substantially as a portion of the trading profiles of the US and the European countries in the postwar period, when European states liberalized their markets regionally through the creation of the European single market as well as multilaterally through the General Agreement on Tariffs and Trade (GATT). Until 2020, the EU and the US enjoyed the world's largest bilateral trade relationship, and this trade occurs primarily in two-way trade of manufactured goods such as medical

---

[7] Sources: Eurostat and OECD.

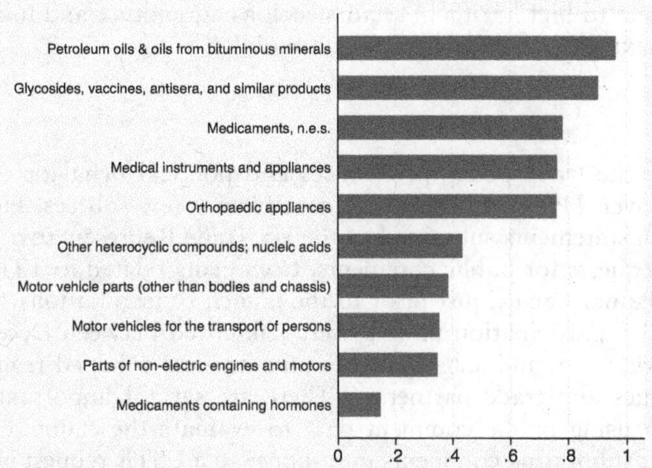

FIGURE 7.3 IIT in ten highest volume product categories, EU–US trade, 2013
Data source: Comtrade.

equipment, automobiles and their parts, chemicals, and pharmaceutical products.[8] In 2013, manufactured goods comprised 88% of the EU's exports to the US, as well as 80% of EU imports from the US. Figure 7.3 shows the extent to which trade between the US and the EU is two-way in the ten highest-volume product categories.

With low tariffs and high levels of transatlantic FDI, TTIP negotiations centered on regulatory harmonization. The one major exception to this was in agriculture and government procurement, where market access issues remained central (Young, 2016). An implication of the intensive transatlantic supply chain linkages is that in 2012, half of EU–US trade in goods was between related parties. This trade between firms and their affiliates abroad was concentrated into a few key sectors – chemicals, machinery, computer and electronic products, and transportation equipment – and was more intensive in capital goods and intermediate goods than EU–US arms-length trade, which is relatively more intensive in final products (Lakatos and Fukui, 2013). A final important feature of transatlantic trade is that related party trade is more sensitive to tariff liberalization: Lakatos and Fukui (2013) estimate that given a 1% reduction in EU–US tariffs, related party imports will increase 4.8% more than arm's length imports. This suggests that transatlantic trade liberalization benefits multinationals more than domestic firms, and in fact could increase competition for domestic firms as multinationals reap greater efficiency gains post-liberalization. While transatlantic tariffs are on average low, EU–US trade

---

[8] In 2020, China overtook the US as the EU's leading partner for goods, though the EU and US remain each other's largest trading partners by far when services and investment are included.

is still subject to high tariffs in sectors such as agriculture and food products, footwear, textiles and clothing, and automobiles.

7.3 DATA

To analyze the trade policy preferences and political behavior of firms and industries over TPP and TTIP, I use data from a few sources. First, I examine position statements submitted to the US Trade Representative in response to USTR requests for public comments. Comments related to TTIP were submitted in January 2013, just prior to the launch of negotiations.[9] Comments related to US participation in TPP were submitted between December 2009 and January 2010, and subsequent comments were solicited regarding more specific issues and trade partners.[10] There are several important considerations when using public comment data to evaluate the claims made in this book. First, submitting comments in response to a USTR request is a relatively low-cost form of lobbying. Small firms are more able to submit comments than they are to donate to political campaigns or host expensive lobbying events in Washington. So although I have argued that IIT can create the appearance of less contention within industries because small firms are much less likely to engage in political activity than large firms, I would expect to observe more intra-industry division within the data on public comments than in alternative data sources, such as lobbying expenditures.

Second, my theory predicts that industry associations will have a more difficult time generating consensus among their members in high-IIT industries, causing them to reduce their political activity. This dynamic is more likely to be observed in lobbying expenditure data. Public comments are a tougher case because it is easier for an industry association to file a boilerplate submission without angering dissenting member firms than it is for the industry association to engage in costlier, higher-profile lobbying efforts. Thus, we may not observe quantitative differences in activity in the public comments data: Industry associations in high-IIT industries may be just as likely to file submissions as industries in low-IIT industries where there is more consensus among members about trade policy. Yet we would expect to observe *qualitative* differences in activity. We would expect industry associations to take a stronger stance in industries with lower levels of IIT, and comments in industries with high-IIT would either be missing altogether, or contain weak or ambivalent language or a declaration of staying formally neutral.

I supplement the public comments data with transcripts from public hearings about the trade agreements hosted by USITC, articles from *Inside U.S. Trade*, a leading US publication specializing in trade-related news, and position

---

[9] See docket USTR-2013-0019 available at www.regulations.gov/docket/USTR-2013-0019.
[10] See docket USTR-2009-0041 available at www.regulations.gov/docket/USTR-2009-0041.

statements and industry analyses published to company and industry association websites. Finally, I use lobbying activity and expenditures data reported to the Senate Office of Public Records and provided by the Center for Responsive Politics.[11] Using these sources together allows me to cross-validate my claims about firm and industry positions, as a lobbying actor's activity typically shows up in more than one of the above sources.

7.4 LOBBYING OVER THE TRANS-PACIFIC PARTNERSHIP

In promoting the TPP, a cornerstone of his foreign policy, President Obama had praised it as a "new type of trade deal that puts American workers first" as it "sets new, high standards for trade and investment in one of the world's fastest growing and most important regions" (White House, 2016). A major focus of the agreement was on trade-related, "behind the border" issues of regulatory convergence aimed at increasing the development and efficiency of global value chains. The Obama administration and other supporters justified the TPP based on the way it would facilitate trade and investment through reforming rules of origin, technical barriers to trade, intellectual property rights, competition policy, government procurement rules, strengthened dispute resolution procedures, and enforceable labor and environmental standards (Schott, 2016).

There were several reasons why the Obama administration (and observers) expected the TPP would be successfully concluded and ratified without much controversy. First, market access issues were less central to the agreement (though still extensive – TPP members agreed to eventually eliminate 99 percent of their tariff lines). Second, the administration sought to minimize opposition by including enforceable environmental and labor safeguards in the agreement. Third, the TPP continued the trajectory of US trade policy since the 1990s, adopting many of the same "WTO-plus" provisions that characterized the US's most recent FTAs with Colombia, Korea, and Panama. Given all of this, the Obama administration did not expect the fierce opposition to the agreement that peaked during the presidential campaign of 2016. By 2015, this opposition had "coalesced into a movement" of over 2,000 organizations campaigning first to block fast-track negotiating authority for the Obama administration, and then to block Congressional ratification of the agreement (Chodor, 2019).[12] The opposing groups were diverse, including labor unions, NGOs working on an array of environmental and human rights-focused causes, academics, consumer advocates, small businesses, and agricultural interest groups, among many others. The anti-TPP movement staged protests, wrote petitions, and disseminated leaked draft text of the agreement. Ravenhill (2017) observes that the position of peak labor organizations shifted from

[11] This data is available at OpenSecrets.org.
[12] See letters to Congress posted publicly by the Citizens' Trade Coalition at www.citizenstrade.org.

"initial scepticism to outright hostility." Though negotiations concluded successfully and the Obama administration signed the agreement in 2015, by 2016 all three leading presidential candidates repeatedly declared their opposition to TPP. President Trump formally withdrew the US from the agreement during the first week of his presidency.[13]

Peak Associations and Cross-Sectoral Coalitions

Though public opinion and civil society actors were highly critical of the TPP, peak business organizations were united in their support for the agreement. The US Chamber of Commerce was the most active lobbying actor in support of TPP, mentioning the agreement 158 times in reports filed between 2007 and 2020. The Business Roundtable, Emergency Committee for American Trade, National Association of Manufacturers and National Foreign Trade Council were other peak business organizations that spent heavily in support of TPP and filed supportive comments to USTR.[14]

All of the organizations above are longstanding, permanent business coalitions, but an interesting feature of trade politics since the 1990s and the NAFTA debate is the formation of ad hoc coalitions specifically for the purpose of lobbying for or against specific trade agreements (Osgood, 2021). Notably, these ad hoc groups are cross-sectoral and often temporary, bringing a range of actors together on the basis of shared preferences. Two highly organized ad hoc coalitions formed in support of TPP, with memberships consisting of leading firms and industry associations: the US Coalition for TPP and the TPP Apparel Coalition. Several permanent cross-sectoral coalitions opposed TPP, including the Alliance for American Manufacturing, American Manufacturing Trade Action Coalition (AMTAC), Coalition for a Prosperous America, US Business and Industry Council, National Family Farm Coalition, and the National Farmers Union.

The importance of these cross-sectoral business organizations is a relatively recent phenomenon in US trade politics. Liss (2021) documents a major shift in the structural landscape of US trade politics that took place in the late 2000s. At this time, domestic-oriented manufacturers began to break away from industry associations and peak organizations that they viewed as dominated by MNCs. The issue sparking this schism was Chinese currency manipulation, which created heavy import competition for US manufacturers. In 2007, a diverse group of manufacturers, farmers, labor unions, and ranchers formed the Coalition for a Prosperous America to represent "exclusively domestic producers across many sectors."[15] In the same year, a coalition of US

---

[13] The other eleven TPP signatories went on to renegotiate a successor agreement without the US, called the Comprehensive and Progressive Agreement for Trans-Pacific Partnership, which entered into force in December 2018.

[14] Center for Responsive Politics data.

[15] www.prosperousamerica.org.

steel producers and the United Steelworkers formed the Alliance for American Manufacturing. Both of these groups (and others, such as AMTAC) lobby on behalf of US manufacturers and advocate for higher US tariffs and enforceable rules to prevent currency manipulation in order to address what they view as unfair import competition primarily from China but also from TPP members. When TPP negotiations ramped up under the Obama administration, these groups actively opposed the agreement (AMTAC, 2010; Alliance for American Manufacturing, 2015; Coalition for a Prosperous America, 2016). Cross-sectoral coalitions tended to pit alliances of pro-TPP MNCs against anti-TPP domestic-oriented firms, which found strong partners in labor and environmental groups.

Low-IIT Industries

At the same time, many industries were united and actively lobbied either in support of or against the agreement. Industries supporting TPP gave nine times more money in campaign contributions than industries opposing the legislation.[16] Industries whose associations lobbied in support of TPP (or publicly expressed support of the agreement) tended to be strong exporting industries, as we would expect, but they also tended to trade on an inter-industry basis with TPP partners, largely based on endowments. Examples are agricultural associations such as the American Corn Refiners Association, American Feed Industry Association, American Potato Trade Alliance, American Soybean Association, National Chicken Council, National Oilseed Processors, National Pork Producers Council, US Grains Council, and US Wheat Associates.[17] In Table 7.1, I list each of these industries and the proportion of their trade with TPP partners in the year 2013 that was intra-industry. Each of these associations is net-exporting, but what is notable is how low IIT is. It is also important to note that US agricultural tariffs on TPP imports were much lower than the tariffs facing US exports in the three most significant agricultural markets with whom the US did not already have a free trade agreement: Japan, Vietnam and Malaysia (McMinimy, 2016). Despite facing very high tariffs in some markets as well as significant trade-impeding sanitary and phytosanitary measures, US agricultural exports to the TPP zone represented 42 percent of the sector's total exports. For many industries, with so little import competition, there was little to no opposition among producers to additional trade liberalization within the agreement. Thus, these industries could engage in collective action and their associations were able to take strong supportive positions.

---

[16] https://maplightarchive.org/story/industries-supporting-trade-bill-contribute-nearly-nine-times-more-than-opposing-industries/.

[17] All of these associations either submitted statements in support of TPP via the USTR's request for comments, or these industries were listed as supporters on USTR's website, available here: https://ustr.gov/about-us/policy-offices/press-office/blog/2015/october/what-they're-saying-completion-trans-pacific.

TABLE 7.1 *US agricultural industries supportive of TPP*

Industry Association	SITC four-digit industries	IIT
American Corn Refiners Association	4216	0.04
American Feed Industry Association	0819	0.156
American Potato Trade Alliance	0541	0.0004
American Soybean Association	2222, 4211	0.019
Distilled Spirits Council of the US	1124	0.124
National Cattlemen's Beef Association	0111, 0112	0.51
National Chicken Council	0123	0.49
National Oilseed Processors	0813, 4211-4229	0.18
National Pork Producers Council	0122, 0161	0.004
US Grains Council	0430, 0441, 0449	0.034
US Wheat Associates	0411, 0412	0.002

Data source: USTR Press Office, WITS trade data.

Conversely, other agricultural industries were united in opposition to TPP, and these industries had active associations as well. Several of these industries emphasized their lack of global competitiveness and their reliance on the US market. In other words, these were comparative disadvantage industries facing existential threats from import competition. In an impassioned submission to USTR, the California Olive Association stated that their industry is "vigorously opposed to the expansion of duty-free status on any processed canned black ripe olives from any country," giving a history of the industry's "unfortunate experiences" with competition from low-priced imports that have contributed to the "near extinction" of the industry (California Olive Association, 2010). A domestic-oriented industry, the association's statement detailed the growth of import competition in the US market and said nothing about export opportunities that might be created by TPP. Similarly, the California Cling Peach Board filed comments with USTR, emphasizing that the industry depends on the US market for 95 percent of canned peach sales and that its export market is unsustainable in the presence of low-priced canned peaches abroad. The association expressed particular concern about competition from Chile and Australia as "competitive producers and exporters of canned peaches, fruit mixtures and frozen peaches," arguing for continued import-sensitive treatment and the longest possible tariff phase-out periods and strict rules of origin (California Cling Peach Board, 2010). The American Sugar Alliance (IIT=0.002 in 2013) lobbied strongly against market liberalization within TPP, and the association ultimately supported the agreement once it was assured that its objectives had been met (American Sugar Alliance, 2010; McMinimy, 2016). The American Shrimp Processors Association told USTR in 2010 that "US shrimp producers and processors have struggled to maintain their livelihoods amid a rising tide of low-priced shrimp imports, particularly from the Asia-Pacific region," though the group remained optimistic that TPP may be an opportunity "to address many of the underlying distortions that result in unfair and imbalanced trade in this sector" (American Shrimp Processors Association, 2010). Seven years later, the executive director of the association communicated that the industry opinion had changed. "We think it [TPP withdrawal] is positive. I speak from the perspective of the domestic shrimp industry. If I exported a lot of product, I wouldn't think that."[18]

Similar patterns play out in manufacturing industries. The steel sector, a comparative disadvantage industry engaging in little two-way trade with TPP countries, was able to engage in powerful collective action, delegating lobbying to its associations. Steel producers were united in their comments to USTR in 2010, which were submitted jointly by four US steel associations, who described themselves as representing the "vast majority" of steel production in the US. These comments put a heavy emphasis on the steel sector's "great concern" about what it viewed as unfair competition from Vietnam, due to currency intervention and other forms of government intervention in the steel industry (American Iron and Steel Institute, 2010). In 2015, at the close of the negotiations, the Industry Trade Advisory Committee (ITAC) on Steel concluded in a letter to USTR that its objectives were not prioritized in the negotiations and went largely unmet. Steel associations emphasized the huge trade deficit between the US and the TPP countries. In its report, the ITAC noted that "steel trade with TPP countries excluding NAFTA is extremely unbalanced, with imports at 3,000,000 tons and exports at only 128,000 tons in 2014."[19] The ITAC stated in its report that it is "unable to render an opinion either in support of or in opposition to the TPP," stressing that this was because "it is not possible" to thoroughly review the 5,600+ page text within the 30-day statutory deadline. The Committee goes on to conclude that the TPP does not seem to have addressed its key concerns surrounding currency manipulation and rules of origin. The only steel company that lobbied individually through the USTR comment process was US Steel, and its positions echoed those of the associations. Winemakers, facing strong import competition from Australia and New Zealand (and low IIT at 0.21), lobbied jointly via their associations (the Wine Institute, the California Association of Wine Grape Growers, and Wine America) to request the longest possible tariff phaseout schedule. The ceramic tile industry, also heavily import-competing (IIT=0.17 in 2013), was represented by its industry association, the Tile Council of North America, whose testimony at a USITC hearing in 2016 emphasized the industry's concern with further "import penetration" and asked for continued protection (Tile Council of North America, 2015).

The case of the auto industry is an interesting one. Before Japan's entry into the TPP talks, automakers were united in support of the agreement, and their

---

[18] C. David Veal, quoted in "Seafood Leaders React After Trump Kills TPP." January 24, 2017. Available at https://americanshrimp.com/aspa-news/seafood-leaders-react-trump-kills-tpp/.
[19] Report available at https://ustr.gov/sites/default/files/ITAC-12-Steel.pdf.

industry association, the American Automotive Policy Council (AAPC) actively lobbied in favor. Without Japan in the agreement, US automakers enjoyed a strong trade surplus with the TPP countries and IIT was very low (IIT=0.13 in 2013, net-exporting) (American Automotive Policy Council, 2010). Upon Japan's entry into the trade agreement, which AAPC strongly opposed, the situation facing US automakers largely reversed itself, giving them a massive trade deficit (IIT=0.14 among TPP partners including Japan in 2013, net-importing). At this time, the industry position flipped, and AAPC informed USTR that "it would be impossible for AAPC to support the TPP agreement" without enforceable provisions to address currency manipulation (American Automotive Policy Council, 2013). In both scenarios, there was low two-way trade, and the industry could engage in strong collective action via their association, with Ford supplementing AAPC's activity with its own strong lobbying effort against Japan's entry.

In contrast to net-importing manufacturing industries, strong exporting industries (net-exporting, low IIT) took strong pro-trade positions and similarly delegated lobbying through the USTR comment process to associations. The pesticides industry, a strong exporting sector with moderate IIT (IIT=0.41), expressed its strong support of TPP collectively via a submission from the industry association CropLife America. Another strong exporting industry, toiletries, and personal care products (IIT = 0.25), represented itself collectively through the Personal Care Products Council with no submissions from individual firms. The distilled spirits industry (IIT=0.124) lobbied collectively through its association, the Distilled Spirits Council. It is notable how few industry associations that submitted comments to USTR represent strong exporting industries with low IIT. The three industries discussed above are the only industries represented in this data that fall into this category. Though there are other US industries that are net-exporting vis-à-vis TPP partner countries, their relative lack of political engagement could be a result of a few factors. First, cross-sectoral business organizations such as the National Association of Manufacturers, the US Chamber of Commerce and the Emergency Committee for American Trade (which represented many leading US firms) were very active in the negotiations over TPP, in the 2010 USTR rulemaking process and in all lobbying forums. Exporting firms and industries relied on these politically powerful lobbying groups to effectively represent them, which aligns with the theory developed in this book. Comparative advantage industries, without significant import competition and thus without significant opposition to liberalization from small producers within their industries, have an easy time delegating political activity to associations and peak-level organizations, the latter of which are well-represented in the lobbying data. By 2015 over thirty manufacturing industry associations had joined the ad hoc, cross-sectoral US Coalition for TPP (alongside many leading firms), which lobbied strongly in favor of the agreement. Second, in its submission to USTR, the National Association of Manufacturers pointed out that the vast majority of manufacturing trade between the countries that were part of TPP negotiations in 2010 was already covered by existing FTAs, and tariffs within these FTAs had already been brought to zero or were on schedule to reach zero in the future (National Association of Manufacturers, 2010).[20] Given relatively modest additional gains from trade liberalization with the remaining TPP partners, industry associations may have further calculated that delegating action to powerful peak organizations and ad hoc coalitions was the best use of their resources.

Trade between the US and its non-NAFTA TPP partners at the time of TPP negotiations primarily took the form of inter-industry, comparative advantage-based trade, as indicated by the overall low level of IIT between the US and these countries as shown above in Figure 7.1. The lobbying dynamics described above conform to my expectations about how industries engage politically when trade is heavily import-competing or heavily export-driven. As was clear in the heated public debate over TPP, many industries took a strong position on the trade agreement, either supportive or in strong opposition. These industries were able to engage in sustained collective action via their associations, which submitted comments to USTR, joined cross-sectoral coalitions, wrote joint letters to members of Congress, took strong public positions in the media and on their own websites, among other forms of lobbying. Part of what made the public debate over TPP so contentious is that when industries are unified, they can be highly politically active, as most of the industries discussed above were. Many partnered with labor unions that took similar positions. Leading peak labor organizations and labor unions strongly opposed the TPP, such as the AFL-CIO, Communications Workers of America, the International Association of Machinists and Aerospace Workers, United Autoworkers, United Steelworkers, Aerospace and Agricultural Implement Workers of America, and the Teamsters. These organizations were very engaged, submitting comments to USTR, testifying in USITC's public hearing in January 2016, giving many media interviews, taking strong public positions and reporting significant lobbying expenditures specifically on TPP.

High-IIT Industries

Despite low levels of IIT between the US and TPP partners overall, there were nevertheless a few high-profile industries with higher levels of two-way trade. Debate over the TPP highlighted the deep divisions within these industries over the agreement's potential costs or benefits, and lobbying dynamics correspond to those I have predicted in this book. The auto parts industry faced moderate levels of two-way trade (IIT=0.5 in 2013). US-based manufacturers of automotive parts and equipment were divided over TPP, and debate centered around enforcement processes and rules of origin, which were overall weaker than those in NAFTA. Small, US-based producers of less complex parts expected

---

[20] Existing FTAs were already in effect between the US and Australia, Chile, Peru, and Singapore.

significant new competition from low-cost suppliers of similar parts based in non-TPP countries such as China, while US makers of more sophisticated components expected little import competition as well as new export opportunities within the bloc. These intra-industry divisions manifested themselves in the industry's lobbying in the following ways.

First, the auto part industry's association, the Motor & Equipment Manufacturers' Association (MEMA) engaged in limited lobbying, did not take an official position until late in the negotiating process, and then its support was measured, reflecting the division among its membership. MEMA did not participate in USTR's 2009 rulemaking process. Despite lobbying on other issues, MEMA did not report any TPP-related lobbying until 2012, when negotiations were well underway. By 2015, MEMA officials told media that their association was "not taking as specific a position" as its counterparts in Canada and Mexico, who strongly opposed the proposed TPP rules of origin.[21] IIT is low between Canada and Mexico and non-NAFTA TPP countries, as the vast majority of both countries' auto parts exports go to the US. Thus, Canadian and Mexican auto parts makers were united in opposition to weak rules of origin in TPP, which would have increased low-cost imports into both countries, and industry associations in these countries took a stronger position than MEMA. In a joint letter that the associations of all three NAFTA countries sent to USTR in September 2015, demands "appeared to straddle the line between the firm demand by Canadian and Mexican auto parts industries for a regional value content of 50 percent and the more flexible position being taken by MEMA."[22] In January 2016, USITC held a three-day public hearing soliciting comments from stakeholders. Over 100 firms, associations, labor unions, and other organizations submitted written or oral testimony, but MEMA did not. That month MEMA did release a statement announcing its support for the TPP, but the statement explicitly acknowledged that some US manufacturers would be hurt by the deal, saying "MEMA is concerned the TPP may not provide adequate long-term protections for small, regional US suppliers that provide employment in all 50 states" (Motor & Equipment Manufacturers' Association, 2016).

Given equivocal, delayed, and muted messaging from their industry association, individual firms within the industry were very active representing themselves. At the 2016 USITC public hearing, at which MEMA was absent, four individual firms submitted written testimony, all voicing strong support for TPP and the export opportunities it would bring. The only domestic firm that testified in opposition to TPP at the hearing was Penn United, a small machine tools manufacturer that supplies parts to the automotive industry (among other industries). In a submission to USTR as part of the 2009 request for comments, Penn United stated its strong opposition to TPP:

"The proposed trade agreement will simply let the multinationals expand production facilities in East Asia to gain more unfair mercantilist trade advantages there. Then they will dump more under-priced foreign goods here to compete with domestic producers like us. And we have neither the money nor the political power to get our government to enforce the law and stop this unfair trade from destroying our business and industry" (Penn United, 2009).

In the face of division within their industry and limited collective action, individual firms were active in the auto parts industry representing their own interests, and as we would expect, larger, internationally oriented firms were more active than small, domestic-oriented firms.

Finally, it is instructive to compare MEMA's lobbying activity over TPP to its lobbying activity in the period immediately after President Trump withdrew from TPP and announced plans to renegotiate NAFTA. MEMA's average lobbying expenditures on NAFTA/USMCA issues in 2017–2020 were more than triple the association's average annual expenditures on lobbying for TPP-related issues over the period of 2012–2016.[23] MEMA's much more decisive political activity during this period was likely a reflection of the greater unity within the industry around the proposed rule changes within NAFTA, a market that was already fully liberalized.

Other industries with high IIT were subject to similar dynamics, incentivizing lobbying by individual firms. The pharmaceutical industry (IIT=.54 in 2013) behaved in the ways we would expect of an industry whose producers are divided over the differential effects of two-way trade, though the particularities of this industry meant that there were existing associations to represent those two sets of firms. Generics producers and brand-name manufacturers had opposing interests over intellectual property (IP) rules within the agreement, and this was reflected in the industry's lobbying. PhRMA, representing brand-name firms, and the Generic Pharmaceutical Association, representing generics producers, each lobbied heavily in pursuit of different approaches to IP protections and were among the most active business organizations out of any industry during TPP negotiations. Given this lack of consensus, individual firms also lobbied heavily in support of their industry's position, such as Pfizer, Merck, and Eli Lilly on the brand-name side, and Teva Pharmaceuticals on the generics side.[24] The division between generics and brand-name producers is not identical but is similar to the divisions that arise among producers of differentiated products: Low-priced producers (generics) may anticipate greater

[23] Annual lobbying expenditure data on specific trade issues is available from the Center for Responsive Politics. It is worth noting that MEMA's reporting expenditures on TPP often included mentions of TTIP as well, while reports of expenditures on NAFTA renegotiation also may have also included lobbying over President Trump's proposed Section 301 tariffs on steel and aluminum.

[24] According to OpenSecrets.org, in 2013, PhRMA, Pfizer and Merck were all among the top ten most active lobbyists from any industry on issues related to international trade.

market opportunities from trade liberalization while producers of higher-price goods are more concerned with competition from lower-priced substitutes.

7.5 LOBBYING OVER THE TRANSATLANTIC TRADE AND INVESTMENT PARTNERSHIP

Simultaneously with negotiations over TPP, the Obama administration was engaged in much less publicly salient negotiations over the Transatlantic Trade and Investment Partnership between the EU and US. As discussed earlier, part of what was notable about the TTIP was the fact that no one (in the US, at least) seemed to have heard of it. While TPP was one of the most hot-button issues during the 2016 US presidential campaign, there was almost no public debate in the US about TTIP (Birchfield, 2015; Madeira, 2018; Young, 2017).

TTIP was considered by experts and policymakers involved in the process to be both a no-brainer and a game-changer (Ville and Siles-Brügge, 2015). It was a no-brainer because the EU and US shared not only the world's largest bilateral trading relationship but also the world's largest investment relationship. It was a game-changer because with most transatlantic tariffs already near zero, TTIP's primary focus was on the harmonization of standards, investment protections, regulatory cooperation, intellectual property rights, procurement rules, and other nontariff barriers, which would allow firms operating in both economies to reap substantial efficiency gains. Because firms from both sides of the Atlantic were invested so heavily in the other, there were many issues on which EU and US firms advocated common positions. Ville and Siles-Brügge (2015) also observe that policymakers in both economies were especially motivated to conclude the long-discussed agreement because of the failures of the multilateral trading system to achieve "deep liberalization" within the Doha Round. Both the EU and US had turned their efforts to bilateral agreements with willing partners, and the successful conclusion of a transatlantic agreement would allow the EU and US to jointly set standards for continued liberalization of the global economy.

The Obama administration formally announced the start of TTIP negotiations during the 2013 State of the Union address, after a high-level working group commissioned by the European Commission and USTR had submitted a report which found that greater transatlantic trade and investment would lead to job creation and increased competitiveness in both economies. The negotiation teams focused on three pillars. The market access pillar focused on tariff liberalization for goods and services as well as investment and procurement liberalization and the development of investment protections, including the development of an investor-to-state dispute settlement (ISDS) system. The second pillar concerned regulatory cooperation, technical barriers to trade, sanitary and phytosanitary (SPS) measures, and the harmonization of regulatory processes. The third pillar sought to develop rules to govern trade-related issues of importance within the TTIP but also in future PTAs with other countries, such as intellectual property rights. Despite high tariffs remaining in certain sectors and procurement rules (particularly in the US) that impeded market access for some producers, business interests that operated transnationally were overwhelmingly concerned with regulatory issues. Thus, market access issues were far less central in TTIP negotiations than in TPP negotiations. Though transatlantic business groups agreed on many negotiating priorities and in several industries advocated common positions, as I will discuss in more depth later, there were nevertheless serious difficulties in some areas, such as government procurement rules, which was a high priority for EU negotiators (Hansen-Kuhn, 2016). Leaked negotiating documents in 2016 described the talks as being at an impasse due to "irreconcilable" differences among the parties (Neslen, 2016).

Over the course of fifteen negotiation rounds held between 2013 and 2016, the EU and US held stakeholder events during each round, in Brussels and Washington. These events included a mix of meetings, hearings, and calls for written comments, including joint EU–US requests for societal submissions. Business interest groups on both sides of the Atlantic were heavily involved in shaping the TTIP negotiations, but what was unusual about TTIP was the intense, organized, and effective public opposition to the agreement from civil society organizations in Europe, while there was very little organized opposition in the US (Buonanno and Dudek, 2015). Corporate lobbying in favor of the agreement was intense, and European and US civil society groups both framed TTIP as a gift to multinational corporations, whose lobbyists ostensibly helped draft the text in secret and enshrined mechanisms designed to maximize corporate profits at the expense of the public interest. Opposition in Europe coalesced around Europeans' fears that TTIP would erode European food safety regulations, which were widely perceived to be stricter than US food safety laws, as well as public anger over the ISDS mechanism, which was perceived to erode public sovereignty for the benefit of corporate profits. This latter concern drove public interest group opposition in the US as well, particularly among consumer safety and environmental groups (Ville and Siles-Brügge, 2015).[25]

Amid widespread public anger and an organized anti-TTIP campaign in Europe, support for TTIP began to crack among center-left parties in Europe, notably in Germany. With the ascendancy of Donald Trump in the US, the rise of anti-trade attitudes among Americans, vehement public opposition to TTIP in Europe, as well as genuine difficulties concluding negotiations, the transatlantic agreement stalled. The US withdrawal from TPP in January 2017

---

[25] Both governments engaged in intense public relations efforts to reassure Europeans that their grocery stores would not be flooded with GMOs and chlorine-washed chickens and that ISDS mechanisms were in the public interest. See, for example, the interview between then US Ambassador to the EU Anthony L. Gardner and *European Views*, an EU-focused news website. Available at www.european-views.com/foreign-affairs/us-ambassador-anthony-l-gardner-to-debunk-the-ttip-myths/.

seemed to put the nail in the coffin, and at the time of this writing, there has been no talk of reviving TTIP.[26]

Intra-industry trade, and particularly horizontal IIT in similar products, is much higher between the EU and US than between the US and the TPP bloc (as shown in Figure 7.1), so I expect that lobbying dynamics over TTIP differed from those of TPP. Additionally, the proportion of IIT that is comprised of horizontal IIT (differentiated products of similar price and quality) is higher in TTIP, whereas IIT between the US and TPP members is more likely to be vertical in nature (products differentiated by price and quality), as shown in Figure 7.2. Finally, as discussed, supply chain linkages are much deeper in the transatlantic region than in the TPP region, and there is far more FDI between the EU and the US than between the US and TPP partners. I expect that these key structural differences in the nature of trade and investment relationship within the TPP and TTIP will result in different dynamics in terms of how industries mobilized politically to shape the two agreements.

Peak Associations, Small Business Coalitions, and Cross-Sectoral Coalitions

First, I expect to observe evidence of intra-industry division over the benefits of TTIP, with large, multinational firms supportive of the agreement and SMEs and/or domestic-oriented firms less supportive. The organizer of an SME-led anti-TTIP campaign in Europe put the concerns of some small business owners clearly: "fewer than 1% of European SMEs export to Canada and the US. For the other 99% CETA [Canada-US Trade Agreement] and its twin TTIP increase the competition in their main market, which is the European."[27] Reports of a meeting at the European Commission between leading business organizations and Directorate-General Trade officials indicate that MEDEF, the largest employer federation in France, was well aware of these divisions among its membership. MEDEF asked trade officials how it could "reassure the 19 million European SMEs which do not export and which will face increased competition" about the value of TTIP.[28] The inclusion of a chapter devoted solely to the needs of SMEs (the shortest chapter in the agreement, focused on assisting SMEs to overcome barriers to exporting and importing) appears to have been the attempted solution. Peak business organizations and

---

[26] The Biden administration and the EU focused instead on achieving progress on regulatory cooperation through the Transatlantic Trade and Technology Council, which has a more limited scope.

[27] See "Small and medium-sized enterprise from across Europe call on European governments to reject the CETA agreement." Joint press release from KMU Gegen TTIP (Germany), KMU Gegen TTIP (Austria), and Ondernemers van NU (Netherlands), September 23, 2016. Available at www.noalttip.org/wp-content/uploads/2016/11/2016-09-23-SME-against-CETA_TTIP-press-release.pdf, accessed March 5, 2023.

[28] See https://corporateeurope.org/en/international-trade/2015/08/dont-believe-hype-ttip-not-small-companies.

industry associations in the EU as well as the US could advocate for the inclusion of such a chapter as a way to demonstrate to SME members that their needs were being represented. Speaking not about SMEs but about divisions within the US textile industry over rules of origin, the president of the National Council of Textile Organizations said: "It just shows you that that policy is driven by the international brands, who have the same overall objective that they do on almost any trade agreement, which is: 'we don't care where it's made, we just want the duties to come down.'"[29]

Another indicator of intra-industry division is the activation of cross-sectoral, often ad hoc coalitions that unite like-minded firms across industries. This strategy aims to demonstrate the breadth of support behind a particular position, and it is even more important if industries are internally divided. Cross-sectoral coalitions were very active during TTIP negotiations. Groups like the Trade Benefits America Coalition, the US Council for International Business, the US Chamber of Commerce and the Emergency Committee for American Trade lobbied strongly in favor of the agreement. Two cross-sectoral organizations representing domestic manufacturers expressed concerns about TTIP. The Alliance of American Manufacturing submitted a letter to USTR in 2013 that remained open-minded about the agreement, yet emphasized its primary objective was to prevent any liberalization of US government procurement rules, a substantial form of protection for firms in a range of industries (Alliance for American Manufacturing, 2013). The Coalition for a Prosperous America was far more critical, objecting to TTIP but on the grounds that it ceded power to "transnationals" to set global trade and investment rules.[30] In Europe, SMEs united across industries to mount highly visible campaigns against TTIP, which were likely consequential in increasing public opposition to the agreement in Europe and eroding support among national policymakers. SMEs were far more politically active against TTIP in the EU than in the US. This is in part because many European SMEs expected not only to be disadvantaged relative to European multinationals but also relative to small US companies, as regulatory standards are uniform across Europe but may diverge internally across US states, leading many (though not all) European SMEs to believe they would be the "losers" of TTIP in terms of the costs associated with accessing export markets (Götz, 2019). In the US, the leading association representing small businesses, the National Federation of Independent Business, did not lobby over TTIP or TPP, citing a lack of consensus among its members over trade policy.[31]

---

[29] See "Official Urges More Joint Industry Work on TTIP Textiles; Fault Lines Emerge." *Inside U.S. Trade*, April 18, 2014.

[30] See https://prosperousamerica.org/ttip-is-dead-or-maybe-theyre-making-progress/.

[31] Interview with representative of the National Federation of Independent Business, April 21, 2021.

One distinctive and unusual feature of lobbying over TTIP, which Young (2016) documents and analyzes in depth is the formation of transnational business alliances between US and European firms and industry associations, a dynamic which was nearly entirely absent from TPP lobbying. This aspect of TTIP lobbying is also a departure from conventional understandings of trade politics, which expect industries from two trading states to have competing preferences. According to Young, the frequency with which US and EU industries formed transnational alliances – adopting common positions and engaging in joint lobbying – was a result of the high levels of transatlantic FDI. For firms with cross-border investments, the transatlantic relationship is more about investment than about trade. Firms operating in either market benefited from regulatory harmonization, investment protections, and increased regulatory cooperation. Young counts twenty-eight US- or EU-level sectoral and industry associations that allied themselves into thirteen transnational alliances submitting joint comments to EU and US solicitations on behalf of their respective industries. Two peak business alliances (comprised of five EU or US peak associations, such as BusinessEurope and the US Chamber of Commerce) submitted joint comments, while only one agricultural alliance formed, representing the starch industry.[32] The absence of common transnational positions among agricultural producers is consistent with the market access logic of agricultural trade, but how were industry associations with high levels of two-way trade not only able to put forth strong industry positions but also to adopt common positions transnationally?

While my arguments about the effects of intra-industry division over trade politics expect that like-minded firms from different sectors will form ad hoc coalitions, something we observe in lobbying over TPP as well as TTIP, what differs about these coalitions is that they are (1) transnational and (2) occur among associations, rather than individual firms. Industries that formed transatlantic alliances have high levels of IIT for the most part: chemicals, pharmaceutical goods, personal care products, and auto parts, for example. Yet some industries did not have extensive two-way trade, and they also managed to form common positions on trade preferences. For example, two-way trade is relatively low in finished automobiles, textiles, apparel, and footwear, with the EU capturing a sizeable trade surplus in all these industries and substantial tariff barriers remaining. Yet EU and US industry associations, such as the American Apparel & Footwear Association (AAFA) and the European Apparel and Textile Confederation (Euratex) still were able to lobby jointly. These unusual dynamics only make sense when considered in light of the politics of FDI and the focus of these alliances on regulatory and investment issues, rather than market access issues. Transnational alliances also make sense

---

[32] There was also an alliance between biotechnology associations working in agriculture: BIO and EuropaBio.

in the context of transatlantic supply chains, which are much more prominent than transpacific supply chains: For example, AAFA represents American apparel importers (who are leading importers of European-produced fabrics) and Euratex represents European textile manufacturers. These supply-chain linkages create joint interests and facilitate transnational collective action, at least among large firms that dominate these associations. The policy positions submitted by transnational business alliances overwhelmingly focus on regulatory harmonization and other efficiency concerns within transatlantic supply chains, though they also ask for tariff elimination. The choice to emphasize efficiency is strategic because efficiency through regulatory harmonization creates the potential for gains for all firms, large or small, on either side of the Atlantic, facilitating collective action.

Low-IIT Industries

Yet in industries/sectors where FDI is low, transatlantic collective action breaks down and market access issues predominate. When IIT is also low, collective action through industry associations is the most common form of political organization, as I expect. For example, agriculture industries acted primarily through national associations, as in TPP, as these are low-IIT industries based on comparative advantage. Only a very few business associations opposed tariff liberalization (Tile Council of North America, American Sugar Alliance, California Cling Peach Board, California Olive Association) and these were in low-IIT, net-importing industries facing heavy competition from European producers. In textiles, IIT is fairly low between the EU and US (averaging 0.4 in textile products in 2013) and the US industry is net-importing. The National Council of Textile Organizations (NCTO) focused exclusively on trade and market access issues, advocating for an eventual agreement with strict rules of origin, import-sensitive treatment for certain products, long tariff phase-out periods, and no weakening of government procurement rules.[33] Other textile associations (US Industrial Fabrics Institute, Agathon Associates) also expressed their strong objection to any weakening of procurement rules, which EU negotiators had indicated was one of their key objectives. Many domestic-oriented US firms rely on Buy American provisions for their continued survival, particularly textile, footwear, and apparel firms granted preferential access to US military contracts under the Berry Amendment. In these import-competing industries, even associations such as the American Apparel and Footwear Association which represent many importing brands mobilized strongly behind the Berry Amendment through an ad hoc coalition called the Berry Amendment Textile Coalition. Finally, the Rubber and Plastic Footwear Manufacturers Association, representing made-in-USA shoe manufacturers subject to very

---

[33] NCTO's vision for TTIP is consistent with what Anne O. Krueger called "trade agreements as protectionist devices" (Krueger, 1997).

heavy import competition, was highly critical in public comments of any reduction in tariffs or too flexible rules of origin.[34]

High-IIT Industries

We observe more internal division and political challenges in high-IIT industries, as well as more lobbying by individual firms. A few small US firms in high-IIT industries lobbied for themselves to express concerns about import competition. The surge protective device industry, for example, was characterized by very high two-way trade in 2013 (IIT = 0.78). Its industry association, the National Electrical Manufacturers Association, lobbied took a strong pro-TTIP position: "NEMA supports complete and immediate U.S. and EU tariff elimination for products within its scope" (National Electrical Manufacturers Association, 2013). This prompted three small businesses within this industry (two manufacturers and one contractor who said her clients are "all small business entities") to submit separate but nearly identical statements registering strong objections to tariff liberalization within TTIP. The two manufacturers wrote: "The passage of a TTIP will indeed have a direct impact on our business as well as many other small business entities throughout the USA" (ECS International, 2013; Surge Suppression Incorporated, 2013). All three actors emphasized the importance of "Buy American" laws, opposed liberalization of procurement, and also mentioned the burdens of compliance with European standards.

Another high-IIT industry (0.64 in 2013) was ball bearings. An owner of one of the global leaders in this industry, Schaeffler (a German multinational with a US affiliate), dined with President Obama when he visited Germany in 2016 to meet with Angela Merkel and attend public events promoting TTIP.[35] Countering this presumably pro-TTIP informal lobbying, a domestic-oriented US manufacturer, the Timken Company, submitted comments to USTR asking for continued protection of its "import-sensitive" industry. Timken is a large, exporting firm, but it emphasized that its "primary production and sales market is the United States." Timken noted the high import penetration of European bearings and requested "the longest tariff phase-out period considered." It noted USITC's own recent conclusion that "producers in France, Germany, Italy and the United Kingdom are highly export oriented, ranking among the largest [ball bearing] exporters in the world." Notably, the American Bearings Manufacturing Association (ABMA), the industry group representing both Schaeffler USA and Timken, did not lobby, though Europe is a major market and ABMA has reported lobbying expenditures on other trade issues in recent years.

---

[34] See *Inside U.S. Trade*, "U.S. shoemakers, importers could clash over TTIP footwear provisions." July 15, 2016.

[35] *Politico*, April 25, 2016. See www.politico.eu/article/politico-pros-morning-trade-merkel-we-should-hurry-up-with-ttip-obama-defends-isds/.

Several high-IIT manufacturing industries revealed internal division over government procurement rules. Domestic iron, steel, and manufactured goods producers benefit from preferred access to federal projects under the Buy American Act, and the Steel Manufacturers Association and American Iron and Steel Institute expressed strong opposition to liberalizing government procurement rules. Yet large, US-based multinational firms in the same industry do not qualify for Buy American provisions if they source inputs from global supply chains. The US Chamber of Commerce and US Council for International Business explicitly asked for procurement rules to be relaxed, reflecting the preferences of multinational firms (US Chamber of Commerce, 2013; US Council for International Business, 2013), while another peak organization, the National Association of Manufacturers said nothing about procurement in its otherwise detailed and lengthy comments (National Association of Manufacturers, 2013). As we would expect given lack of consensus among peak organizations, one US-based multinational submitted individual comments regarding this issue, asking for liberalization of procurement rules to deter foreign governments from retaliating against US exports (Ingersoll Rand, 2013). Given the steel associations' heavy emphasis on import competition in their comments (in addition to procurement, both associations prioritized trade remedies, rules of origin, and customs fraud), a small individual producer of steel tubing, Omega Flex, lobbied alone to ask USTR to remove nontrade barriers to EU market access for its products (Omega Flex Inc., 2013). A leading steel producer, Nucor, also lobbied alone, mentioning TTIP eighteen times in lobbying reports submitted since 2006.[36] Given inconsistent positions from peak organizations regarding procurement, as well as ambivalent submissions from leading steel associations that put a heavy emphasis on protection from import competition while also expressing support of liberalization, firms mobilized individually to represent themselves and their specific needs.

Though there were clearly objections to TTIP as a whole or to key liberalizing components of TTIP from subsets of firms within industries, small firms are far less able to lobby than large firms, and this is even more apparent in the lobbying expenditures data reported to the Senate Office of Public Records, where virtually all of the 116 firms that reported TTIP-related lobbying expenditures were multinationals.[37] Large firms strongly supported the agreement and lobbied on many firm-specific issues, such as regulatory harmonization or mutual recognition of standards relevant to their particular product varieties. Since so much of TTIP concerned investment and regulatory issues rather than market access, associations could address the concerns of both multinational and domestic-oriented producers in their comments. National associations could also forge consensus with their counterparts across the Atlantic on regulatory

---

[36] It is not possible to see the content of those lobbying reports. Lobbying report data available from OpenSecrets.org.

[37] OpenSecrets.org.

and investment concerns that were important to multinationals without alienating domestic-oriented producers, who could benefit from easier access to export markets. Nearly all associations strongly supported the removal of non-tariff barriers to trade, while many also advocated continued protection for domestic-oriented producers through restrictive procurement rules and strict rules of origin, as well as long tariff phaseout periods in some cases. The disconnect between these positions was an attempt to satisfy diverse producers in the context of high IIT: For some producers, TTIP's effects would primarily be greater import competition or more competition from multinationals, while for others it would allow greater gains from trade and foreign investment. For all firms, however, horizontal IIT creates lower adjustment costs than vertical IIT and trade based in comparative advantage. Given all of these dynamics, multinationals and transnational business alliances dominated the politics of TTIP, and we might have expected they'd get what they were after.

7.6 CONCLUSION

Both TPP and TTIP ultimately failed. The failure of TPP seems more straightforward. In the context of trade among countries at very different stages of development, with different endowments and different factor prices, trade was more heavily based on comparative advantage. What intra-industry trade did occur was far more likely to be vertically differentiated on price, with potentially high losses for US firms with higher costs. As political economists have long understood, comparative advantage-based trade unites industries, facilitating powerful collective action, and crucially, it also unites labor unions. Comparative disadvantage industries in the US, facing highly imbalanced trade with TPP countries, were well-positioned to mount coherent, strong lobbying campaigns via national associations.

Their positions were supported by the peak labor unions, which fiercely opposed the agreement, anticipating heavy job losses to countries with far lower labor costs and fewer worker protections. The AFL-CIO, International Association of Machinists, the Teamsters, and the United Auto Workers found the agreement's provisions on the environment and labor to be weak, unlikely to be enforced, and they were scathing in their criticisms.[38] Though many leading firms and industries strongly supported the agreement, and these industries far outspent industries that opposed TPP, the concerns voiced by labor unions as well as anti-TPP business groups mobilized civil society actors. Public interest groups objected to the weakness of the environmental and labor chapters, as well as intellectual property provisions that they feared could jeopardize access to affordable medicines, and to the proposed ISDS mechanism, which was widely scorned as eroding the public's ability to pursue health and safety objectives (Ravenhill, 2017). Liss (2019) argues that this alliance

---

[38] See Hoffa (2017); Martinez (2016); Trumka (2016); United Auto Workers (2016).

between labor, public interest groups, and the new domestic-oriented manufacturing groups such as the Alliance for American Manufacturing and Coalition for a Prosperous America doomed TPP by gaining influence in Congress, and particularly with newly elected House Republicans. Given the breadth of societal opposition to TPP as well as the looming 2016 Presidential election, Congress was unwilling to put the agreement to a ratification vote. Even a lame-duck session of Congress wouldn't ratify the agreement once the three leading Presidential candidates all declared their opposition.

High levels of inter-industry, endowments-based trade among the TPP countries unified industries that expected losses and facilitated collective action by business, labor, and civil society groups to thwart the agreement, but how can we make sense of the failure of TTIP? Trade among developed countries is far less controversial, far less damaging for industries, and tariffs were already very low. Business lobbying in the US over TPP was far higher than lobbying over TTIP. There were 4,506 mentions of TPP in US lobbying reports filed from 2006 onward, while TTIP was only mentioned 1,874 times during the same time period.[39] Intra-industry trade has long been thought to be easier to liberalize than endowments-based trade because it benefits firms and industries in both trading partners, and distributional effects are felt at the firm level, rather than the industry level. Small firms may be hurt by increased import competition, but they may also find export markets for their products, and in any case, their concerns are overwhelmed politically by the intense lobbying from leading, internationalized firms that stand to gain from liberalization. These dynamics should have made TTIP negotiations far easier to conclude than those over TPP, yet TTIP became a lightning rod of controversy in Europe, a key factor in its demise.

There are three compelling explanations for the death of TTIP, all of which relate to claims I have made in this book about the different political effects of inter- versus intra-industry trade. The first is that the controversy over TPP created a populist backlash to trade that would have doomed any other trade agreement that found itself in the unfortunate position of being negotiated at exactly the same time. The partnership between anti-TPP business groups and labor unions facilitated intense lobbying efforts by these actors, which increased public salience. While only ten public interest groups submitted comments as part of USTR's consultation in 2009, as details of the draft text emerged and labor unions publicly declared their opposition, civil society opposition grew into a full-blown movement (Chodor, 2019). As salience increased, civil society groups mobilized, generating a populist backlash which

---

39 These calculations are based on lobbying report data available from OpenSecrets.org. It is not possible to tabulate expenditure differences with the available lobbying report data, as lobbyists report expenditures on the trade issue area more broadly and often list several trade agreements on a single lobbying expenditure report. The significant difference in how many more times TPP was mentioned on lobbying reports compared with TTIP mentions, however, does suggest much higher lobbying expenditures on TPP.

would have been unlikely in the US over TTIP alone, given the intra-industry structure of trade between the EU and US and the relative ease with which past agreements with other developed countries have been concluded.

To be sure, there was such a populist backlash in Europe, leading to the second explanation for TTIP's demise. The heated opposition to TTIP among the European public and civil society groups, which centered around fears about European food health and safety standards being undermined by perceived lower US standards (such as the infamous chlorine-washed chickens), mobilized opposition among SMEs that may otherwise have not been politically active. Out-lobbied and outspent by the powerful Eurofederations and transnational business alliances, European SMEs, like US SMEs, may have pursued a strategy of adjustment to a more open trade and investment environment. The intensity of public opposition to TTIP in Europe, however, likely changed the lobbying calculus for the subset of SMEs that either anticipated losses or few new market opportunities in the US post-TTIP. With civil society groups from the "STOP TTIP" movement as powerful allies, some SMEs may have expected their lobbying efforts could now be more effective, leading to more political engagement from SMEs than we would typically expect (and certainly more than we saw in the US). This interpretation is supported by the fact that SMEs in Europe did not initially oppose TTIP; anti-TTIP campaigns by small businesses did not take shape until 2016 (Chan and Crawford, 2017).

Finally, this book documents a new model of interest representation in a world of intra-industry trade: Individual firms, and specifically, large and internationalized firms, lobbying alone for firm-specific, free-trading preferences. Given the power and influence of corporate actors, the often more ambivalent positions taken by industry associations representing diverse producers, and the limited involvement by small firms, the public perception of trade and investment agreements during the debate over TPP and TTIP is that they promote a form of "hyperglobalization" that advances corporate interests at the expense of broader public interests, worker interests, and small business interests. While TPP was criticized over fears of severe job losses in US manufacturing, what criticism did exist of TTIP in the US focused on its lack of transparency, its "corporate-ness," its perceived giveaways to multinational corporations and its prioritization of "investor rights." Corporate actors certainly won the day with USTR, whose draft text aligned closely with corporate demands, particularly in the investment protections chapter and in the inclusion of ISDS (Liss, 2019). Yet for all the intense corporate lobbying over TTIP and the near absence of true business opposition, the agreement failed to convince the US Congress, the public, and the president elected in 2016.

Though TTIP would have likely created jobs in the US as a result of increased investment by EU firms, and it would have reduced the costs of imports from Europe, making consumers and importing firms better off, mega-agreements like TTIP that seek deep integration far beyond tariff liberalization likely require a measure of broad societal support in order to appear legitimate. That support was not apparent in the lobbying over TTIP, and I argue that this is in no small part a result of the ways that IIT incentivizes corporate lobbying and disincentivizes counter-lobbying by industry associations and by labor unions, for either substantive or strategic reasons. Labor unions were not overtly hostile to TTIP and expressed cautious optimism that an agreement "could" create jobs for US workers as well as lead to stronger labor standards in the US (AFL-CIO, 2013). Without stronger support from labor, and with little opposition from industry groups, the public perceived the process as being subject to undue influence from multinational corporations, and this contributed to the agreement's failure. This is also perhaps a particular hazard of intra-industry trade in the era of popular fears about hyperglobalization: As firms increase their lobbying for firm-specific interests, and as labor and industry associations mount few objections (whether because they are unable or unwilling), public trust erodes.

8

Conclusion

This book offers a theory of the relationship between the structure of international trade and the dynamics of trade politics that can explain one of the most important changes in contemporary trade politics: The rise of the firm as an individual political actor. My primary contribution has been to build on the canonical models in the field, which explain longstanding cleavages and coalitions that form for or against trade openness, but which do not predict the rise of individual firm lobbying over trade and the relative decline of industry associations, long among the most influential societal actors in trade policy debates. My model here is based on the newest, firm-centric economic theories of international trade. I have shown that the structure of trade has changed significantly in the post-World War II era, as developed economies trade increasingly with other developed economies for different varieties of goods that they also produce themselves. This is a fundamental shift in trading patterns that demands new models of winners and losers and new theories about societal trade preferences, societal mobilization over trade policies, the structure of trade policy coalitions, and trade policy outcomes themselves. The canonical political economy models of international trade are based upon economic models that do not and cannot explain intra-industry trade. The explanatory power of these analyses still stands, but their theories of trade politics only apply when trade is of the classic, inter-industry structure on which the older economic models were built. In this way, my analysis is complementary to these leading contributions in the trade politics literature, and I enlarge our understanding of trade politics by providing a theoretical rationale for the rise of the firm and the increasing difficulties industries face engaging in collective action.

I have argued that the economics of intra-industry trade – its sources and its distributional effects – change the structure of societal demands over trade policy in ways that undermine existing coalitions and incentivize firm-level lobbying in support of freer trade. To do so, I drew on two field-changing literatures from economics that changed the way economists understood the sources and economic effects of international trade, but which have been underutilized by political economists until recently. First, I referred to the contributions of the "new trade theory" literature, which demonstrated that unlike comparative advantage-based trade, intra-industry trade is driven by economies of scale, increasing returns, and consumer love of variety. I also rely on a newer generation of economic models, currently known as the "new new trade theory," which demonstrate how the costs and benefits of trade fall on individual firms rather than on entire factor-owning classes or entire sectors. In industries subject to two-way trade, internationalized firms gain from liberalization while domestically oriented firms suffer losses.

Building on these insights, I developed a model of the political implications of intra-industry trade. In Chapter 3, I argued that intra-industry trade undermines industry consensus over trade policy, pitting exporters against import-competing firms within the same industry. The breakdown in industry preferences makes it difficult for industry associations to take a strong political position when trade policies are negotiated, and firms instead take up the lobbying burden alone. Exporters have an incentive to lobby for liberalization in the context of reciprocity-based trade negotiations, while import-competing firms within their same industry seek continued protection. Crucially, exporting (and importing) firms are more likely to engage politically, as these are industry-leading firms with the resources to lobby effectively, while firms benefiting from protection are more likely to be small firms without the capacity for political action. The result of this is a lobbying landscape that skews strongly in favor of free trade interests, even as there continue to be many firms that are worse off in a more liberal trading environment.

The rise of intra-industry trade has important implications for trade policy outcomes. One implication is economic: Firms may find it easier to adjust to two-way trade in similar varieties, as they can often find a market for their particular variety. This is likely to reduce demands for protection, compared to comparative advantage-based trade between countries at different levels of development. The second implication is political: Protectionist and free-trading firms are nowhere near matched in their ability to engage politically. Free-trading firms politically overwhelm domestic-oriented firms that may prefer protection. Thus, policymakers receive far more demands for liberalization than for protection, facilitating tariff reductions. The availability of nontariff measures of protection also allows policymakers to supply regulatory forms of protection even as they reduce tariffs.

My empirical analyses in Chapters 4–7 yielded support for my theoretical claims. In Chapter 4, I tested my hypothesis that as intra-industry trade increases, coalition-based lobbying should decrease relative to lobbying by individual firms. I found empirical support for this claim using lobbying data from US manufacturing industries. Even controlling for leading alternative explanations for firm-based lobbying, I still found that intra-industry trade has an independent effect on political activity. Among US manufacturing industries, individual firms are more politically active relative to coalitions when intra-industry trade is higher. I also found that overall industry lobbying expenditures decline as IIT increases, and this drop is driven by the drop in spending by industry associations, providing further support for my arguments. In Chapter 5, I supported these arguments with an original dataset of lobbying over trade policy in the European Union. This is an important contribution that shows that my theory is generalizable across very different policymaking contexts. While much of the lobbying literature focuses on the US context, here I contribute to our broader understandings of the way that shifts in trade structure change domestic politics in democracies more generally.

In Chapter 6, I found that IIT is consistently associated with lower tariffs but higher nontariff measures in developed economies. This relationship holds even when controlling for other factors that should influence protection, such as export dependence, import penetration, and institutional responsiveness to special interest groups. While my results in Chapter 6 do not tell us about the causal process linking intra-industry trade with levels of protection, I contend that when we consider them in conjunction with my analyses of lobbying in Chapters 4 and 5, the evidence is supportive of my theory. Taken together, the results support my argument that intra-industry trade undermines industry consensus and incentivizes relatively more lobbying by individual firms, and especially exporters. As exporters realize the gains to be made from specialization, returns to scale, and production for foreign markets, they become increasingly politically active to lobby for tariff reductions and regulations that benefit them at the expense of smaller producers. Policymakers provide both of these things, and in this way the structure of trade policy shifts to doubly advantage exporting firms at the expense of domestic-oriented firms.

In Chapter 7, I explored the dynamics of firm and industry lobbying over the TTIP and TPP in the US. Examining position statements and the content of written submissions to trade policymaking debates, I showed how it is more difficult for industry associations to form strong positions over particular pieces of trade policy legislation when IIT is high. There was far more organized opposition to TPP than TTIP because trade between the US and its prospective TPP partners is more inter-industry in nature, and comparative disadvantage industries in the US – alongside labor unions – were able to mount united campaigns in opposition to the agreement. I also showed that industries with high two-way trade with TPP partners, such as auto parts, were divided in their preferences regarding the agreement, which made collective action difficult. TTIP, by contrast, aimed to further liberalize the already very open trading environment among countries at similar levels of development. Large, internationalized firms lobbied hard for firm-specific priorities, and small firms in the US largely sat out the political process, so business lobbying over TTIP was overwhelmingly supportive on the US side. Industry associations, though overall supportive of the agreement, nevertheless expressed ambivalence in their comments over key provisions, such as government procurement and rules of origin, reflecting divisions among their member firms. This ambivalence is likely a reason that so many firms lobbied individually to express their particular preferences over these and other issues.

8.1 IMPLICATIONS FOR THE FUTURE OF INTERNATIONAL TRADE AND FOR THOSE WHO STUDY IT

In this book, I have aimed to show that the rise of intra-industry trade provides a powerful explanation for the rise of firm-level lobbying, one of the most dramatic changes in the politics of trade in recent decades. But the political implications of a new model of interest representation dominated by individual firms go far beyond academic debates about cleavage, coalition, and collective action. Both the economics and politics of intra-industry trade have major consequences for the future of firms, workers, and the broader public in globally integrated economies. This suggests several important avenues for future research.

First, the combination of rising intra-industry trade and firm-level lobbying has troubling implications for income inequality within societies and the future prospects of small firms in globalized industries. IIT reallocates economic resources within industries, as large firms expand global market share and smaller firms face greater import competition. Economic research has demonstrated that wage inequality rises with IIT, both across and within sectors, as the most competitive firms demand more high-skilled workers, who gain at the expense of less-skilled workers (Beaulieu et al., 2011; Sampson, 2014). If IIT also advantages large firms in the political process and makes it more difficult for industry associations to represent the interests of small firms, the income disparities between large and small firms – and their workers – will only grow. Relatedly, I found that IIT is associated with lower tariffs but higher NTMs. This also benefits the most competitive, globally integrated firms at the expense of small firms. Large international firms often support restrictive regulatory measures that increase their trade volumes while severely damaging small firms' ability to compete (Fontagné et al., 2015; Gulotty, 2020). This was an argument that owners of small and medium-sized firms in Europe made explicitly as part of the "Stop TTIP" movement, and domestic-oriented US firms also articulated this concern when critiquing TTIP as written by "transnational corporate lobbyists."[1] In sum, IIT tends to consolidate industries, giving ever greater market share to the tiny minority of firms that are globally integrated. Firm-level lobbying and regulatory protection should speed up this process, concentrating wealth and political power ever further into the hands of the global business elite.

---

[1] See https://prosperousamerica.org/ttip-is-dead-or-maybe-theyre-making-progress/.

Second, there are troubling economic implications for the broader economy of a policy space dominated by the narrowest of particularistic interests, the individual firm. Recent work has demonstrated inefficiencies associated with firm-level lobbying, which may generate private benefits for politically active firms while reducing the economy's aggregate productivity. This includes higher tax breaks for lobbying firms and the misallocation of public expenditures, benefiting lobbying firms at the expense of the broader economy (Huneeus and Kim, 2018; Radhakrishnan, 2022; Richter et al., 2009). Other researchers have found that when the business community is fragmented within and/or across industries, there is reduced business support for social programs and active labor market policies (Martin and Swank, 2004; Mizruchi, 2013). The influence of very narrow special interests is a source of inefficient policy outcomes and ultimately, as Olson (1982) warned decades ago, may be a cause of economic decline.

Yet policymaking and electoral institutions vary considerably across countries, and some are far more responsive to particularistic interests than others. This affects the decision to lobby in the first place, suggesting that IIT will not have uniform effects on policy outcomes across countries. Where elected officials are less responsive to individual firms, these firms may seek regulatory forms of protection through bureaucratic channels. This has important implications for the structure of trade protection, for the distortionary effects of trade policies and for public opinion about whose interests are represented in trade agreements. In what institutional contexts are corporate demands most often adopted in PTAs, and how does this affect public opinion and the likelihood of successful conclusion of trade agreements? What types of institutions most effectively moderate the trade policy demands of narrow interest groups, and do countries with these institutions have more success maintaining open economies while also ensuring that the benefits of globalization are distributed throughout the economy?

Third, and relatedly, the rise of firm lobbying for firm-specific interests is likely partly responsible for the populist backlash to "hyperglobalization" that poses a real threat to the liberal world order. When the public sees corporations heavily involved in the policymaking process, acting individually without broad coalitions or partnerships with labor unions, this undermines the public's trust in representative democracy as well as the public's belief that trade agreements will advance broad societal interests or the economy in the aggregate. This is well-represented in the nature of the critiques levied by civil society actors, which typically characterize trade and investment agreements as corporate power grabs that undermine national sovereignty to pursue the public interest, harming workers, consumers, and the environment in the process. Citizens perceive little voice in the trade policymaking process, as the institutional location for trade policymaking has increasingly moved away from Congress toward bureaucratic and judicial arenas, a process that Chorev (2007) shows was driven in part by the efforts of multinationals and other internationalized firms and investors. There is also little hope that international institutions are more insulated from corporate lobbying, as an emerging literature documents how firms are increasingly dominating political processes at the international level as well, a dynamic that will only deepen the democratic deficit within global governance institutions (Brutger, 2024; De Bièvre et al., 2016; Kim and Spilker, 2019; Ryu and Stone, 2018). The globalization backlash is perhaps most evident in voting behavior, as voters across the West have increasingly embraced radical-right parties with antiglobalization platforms, and, still more concerning, platforms that are skeptical of liberalism more broadly (Walter, 2021). Although IIT is associated with lower tariffs, easier trade liberalization more generally, and less contentious trade politics, as it empowers firm-based lobbying and undermines broader consensus, will we observe a greater backlash to globalization emerge in countries with higher IIT, more active firms, and perhaps bolder corporate demands?

Finally, what do the politics of intra-industry trade suggest about the future of North–South trade or about South–South trade? Intra-industry trade is associated with lower adjustment costs than trade based in comparative advantage, and it also is associated with economic development. As the rich countries developed, so did their trade with each other for varieties of consumer and industrial goods. As once poor countries have successfully developed and joined the ranks of upper-middle income or high-income countries in the last several decades, most did so by upgrading their manufacturing capabilities to produce these same consumer goods and engage in more two-way trade with advanced economies. Indeed, many developing countries are now producing different varieties of goods that rich countries also produce, but the crucial difference between North–North two-way trade and North–South two-way trade is that the former is differentiated on variety, while the latter is differentiated on price.

Thus, North–South vertical IIT will be more difficult for firms in developed countries to adjust to, and it is therefore more controversial than horizontal IIT between rich countries. This was clear in the debates over TPP, as manufacturing firms based in the US feared existential threats from varieties produced at much lower cost in TPP countries. Importantly, this did not make unified industry lobbying any easier: It seemed to completely undermine associations like MEMA who faced the seemingly impossible challenge of satisfying small auto-parts producers that feared certain exit and the large, globally competitive member firms that pay the bulk of the association's dues. Largely due to heavy opposition from organized labor in the US, TPP failed, an indication of the difficulties emerging markets face in accessing rich country markets for industrial goods. Thus, the relative ease with which rich countries liberalized trade among themselves is unlikely to extend to developing countries even as they produce increasingly similar goods as rich countries – at least not until factor prices converge. Future research should explore the different dynamics surrounding North–South PTAs that seek to liberalize primarily endowments-based trade and North–South PTAs that would primarily liberalize intra-industry trade. How does trade composition affect the ability of emerging market exports to access developed country markets, a crucial driver of development?

8.2 POLICY RECOMMENDATIONS

There are two sets of recommendations that follow from the discussion above: recommendations for societal stakeholders and recommendations for policymakers. First, firms would do well to redouble their efforts to form broader coalitions domestically, rather than with their counterparts transnationally, as was their strategy in the negotiations over TTIP. Broad-based collective action focused around points of common interest rather than particularistic firm-based demands will inspire more confidence in the public and in their elected representatives in government. Pro-trade firms have certainly attempted to do this in debates over recent FTAs; Osgood (2021) counts more than fifty ad hoc or permanent cross-sectoral pro-trade coalitions that US firms have formed since the 1990s, such as the US Coalition for TPP and the US–Korea Business Council. These coalitions are attempts to demonstrate the breadth of business support for FTAs, yet they typically are composed nearly exclusively of multinational and other very large firms as well as industry associations; there is very little heterogeneity of firm size and typically no partnerships with labor or civil society groups. Owners of SMEs in Europe often took positions that directly opposed those of large firms, and many argued that ISDS and regulatory cooperation mechanisms would disproportionately benefit large firms. Pro-trade firms need to focus on building more diverse coalitions that bring in stakeholders from labor, public interest groups, and small firms. This will require, to paraphrase Rodrik, a refocus on the essentials of global economic openness, even if this falls short of the "hyperglobalist ideal" (Rodrik, 2019). This is likely to be difficult for the US business elite at least, whose unity and ability to act collectively has fractured in recent decades over a range of issue areas, as CEOs are increasingly preoccupied with short-term gains for shareholders rather than long-term problems facing the country as a whole (Mizruchi, 2013).

Second, the economic and political implications of IIT suggest that labor and civil society groups need to rethink their own political strategies. The intra-industry reallocation of resources away from small firms and toward internationalized firms suggests that workers are likely divided in their trade preferences in a similar way that firms are, yet in the US, workers at large firms are far more likely to be unionized than workers at small and medium-sized firms (Dinlersoz et al., 2014). IIT benefits workers at large firms as these firms expand market access abroad, invest in scale production with advanced technologies, and hire more skilled workers. Furthermore, trade liberalization between high-wage countries with strong labor rights protections is unlikely to cause a race to the bottom in labor standards or offshoring. All of this suggests that unionized workers may benefit from trade liberalization in IIT industries, even as workers at small, likely nonunion firms are made relatively worse off.

This creates a serious dilemma for labor unions. If unions support agreements between developed economies that are job-creating at leading, unionized firms, this could undermine support for organized labor among nonunion workers at smaller firms (the vast majority of US workers) that are harmed by increasing IIT. This could explain why US peak labor unions vehemently opposed TPP, which they anticipated would make American workers worse off across the board, while they gave only cautious support to TTIP.[2] Labor leaders may have believed that if they took fairly ambivalent positions, expressing cautious optimism while also voicing concerns and objections to certain provisions, the agreement would be concluded without them having to take a stronger position that would be controversial among workers. Yet it appears that the opposite may be true: Without labor as a partner, the public may view pro-trade corporate lobbying with enough suspicion to erode Congressional support and doom any agreement. The new politics of heavy firm lobbying for firm-specific, hyperglobalist interests suggest that if labor unions do support an agreement, they need to loudly support it. More research is needed on the effects of IIT on organized labor, and especially on the conditions under which labor is more successful in shaping the design of PTAs.

Finally, my research suggests several important implications for policymakers in advanced economies with substantial two-way trade and heavy firm lobbying for firm-specific interests. First, recent research shows that including social standards in trade agreements – such as labor, environmental, and consumer protection provisions – increases public support for free trade agreements in developed countries. Bastiaens and Postnikov (2020) argue that social standards can function as *ex ante* mechanisms to reduce the likelihood of societal dislocation from trade liberalization, reducing opposition to trade among those who otherwise would anticipate losses. Social standards not only reassure workers, but they are also demanded by fair-trade activists whose opposition to trade has been a central part of the globalization backlash in recent years (Ehrlich, 2018; Winslett, 2021; Young, 2016). Enforceable standards are also at the heart of labor union demands, and the recent battles over TPP and TTIP should make clear to policymakers that their inclusion is key to securing the support of organized labor, which may be critical to passage of an agreement.

Social standards play a similar role to compensation policies, which governments should also provide to reduce the disruptive impacts of trade openness. For example, the US government should invest in its TradeAdjustment

---

[2] Richard Trumka, former president of AFL-CIO, used language like "I'm somewhat optimistic" about TTIP. See https://aflcio.org/speeches/trumka-executive-council-diplomacy-public-wants-justice-not-more-same.

Assistance program. Kim and Pelc (2021) show that approximately forty times more firms filed for TAA assistance than filed an anti-dumping petition, demonstrating that the lack of demands for protection is not a result of lack of injury, but of collective action problems. Producers must overcome considerable challenges in order to file anti-dumping petitions, marshaling support from a representative portion of the industry. By contrast, they can file for TAA individually, so many more of them do. This supports claims I have made throughout this book that the overwhelmingly pro-trade bias of lobbying over trade policy, and particularly when trade is intra-industry in nature, is not because there are no firms that suffer losses from deeper liberalization. Rather, the losers of trade face steep barriers to lobbying. More robust TAA support for firms is likely to reduce opposition to liberalization that manifests more in public opinion and public interest opposition than it does in business lobbying.

Finally, because of these collective action problems, governments need to more actively solicit input from labor, public interest groups, small firms, and even industry associations. Due to intra-industry conflicts, associations representing domestic producers are sometimes excluded from industry attempts to promote a united, industry-level position. For example, footwear industry associations representing made-in-USA producers were excluded by associations representing global brands (importers) and retailers when the importers and retailers formulated a joint industry position with their European counterparts over footwear provisions in TTIP.[3] US trade negotiators should prioritize representative positions from US industry, rather than encouraging the formation of transnational positions, which advance the interests of the "happy few" global firms (to borrow the language of Ottaviano [2008]) while excluding or neglecting the interests of domestic-oriented firms. Even when trade liberalization has positive economic consequences overall, more inclusion of the voices of those who are made worse off will push policymakers to provide the kinds of compensation policies that are critical to maintaining support for a liberal global economic order.

The theory and findings presented in this book imply that the rise of firm-based lobbying and firm-specific trade policy demands means that trade agreements among rich countries will not be as easily negotiated as they once were, with worrisome normative implications. Intra-industry trade creates winners and losers at the firm level and undermines the ability of industries to act collectively. The winning firms are the best prepared to engage politically in order to influence trade rules to advance firm-specific interests, and their lobbying contributions overwhelm those of small firms that are harmed by increased import competition. It is these political effects of intra-industry trade, not intra-industry trade itself, that create the most troubling societal consequences. When pro-trade firms are successful in their political efforts to secure

---

[3] See "U.S. Shoemakers, Importers Could Clash Over TTIP Footwear Provisions," *Inside U.S. Trade*, July 15, 2016.

their preferred trade, investment, and regulatory preferences, the result may be trade agreements that reduce the overall productivity of the economy and increase inequality. Worse, heavy corporate lobbying may distort the workings of representative democracy itself, by pressing for changes to the trade policymaking *process* that further erode the ability of voters, labor unions and civil society groups to meaningfully participate. Democratic governments – and international organizations – would do well to cultivate a political economy of broad participation in the design of the global economic order, rather than cede to the demands of every firm for itself.

Appendix A

Appendix to Chapter 2

Low income and lower-middle income:
Bolivia, Brazil, Colombia, Ecuador, Egypt, Guatemala, Honduras, Indonesia, India, Jordan, Morocco, Nicaragua, Pakistan, Peru, Philippines, Paraguay, El Salvador, Thailand, and Tunisia

Upper-middle income:
Argentina, Barbados, Chile, Costa Rica, Hungary, Mexico, Malaysia, Panama, Turkey, and Venezuela

High income:
Australia, Austria, Belgium, Canada, Switzerland, Germany, Denmark, Spain, Finland, France, United Kingdom, Greece, Hong Kong, Ireland, Iceland, Israel, Italy, Japan, Korea, Malta, Netherlands, Norway, New Zealand, Portugal, Singapore, Sweden, and the United States

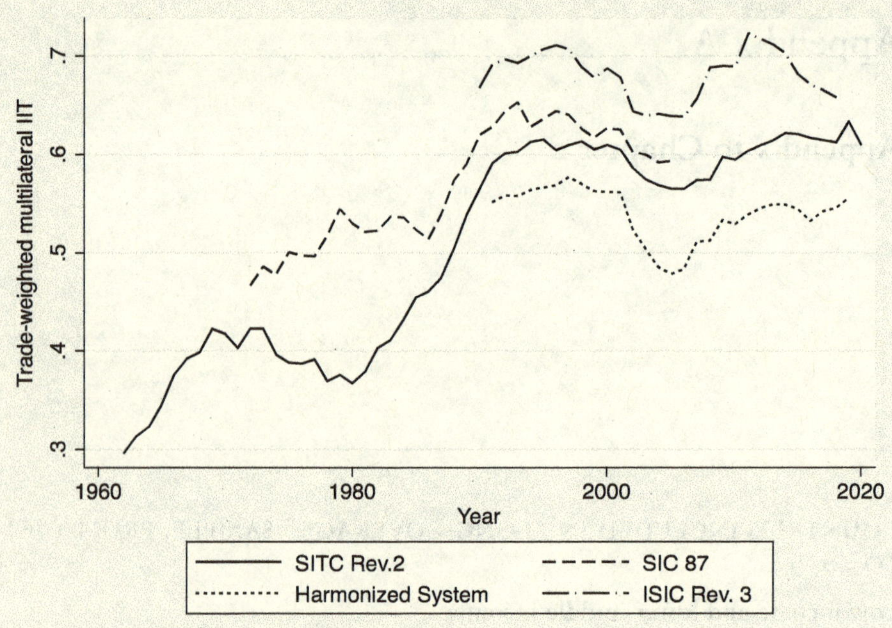

FIGURE A.1 Comparison of different industry classification systems: United States multilateral IIT over time
Data source: Author's calculations based on trade data from Atlas of Economic Complexity, WITS, UNIDO, and US Census Bureau, as described in this book. All measures disaggregated to four-digit level.

Appendix B

Appendix to Chapter 4

TABLE B.1 *Summary statistics for all 459 four-digit manufacturing industries, minus missing data. Average firm size, industry size, political contributions, and the three domestic lobbying expenditure variables are in millions of USD*

	Mean	SD	Min	Max	N
Proportion of industry lobbying by individual firms	0.66	0.40	0	1	338
Intra-industry trade	0.59	0.27	0	1	388
Industry concentration	39.27	19.26	0	100	453
Average firm size	32.45	120.95	0.71	2,250.21	458
Elasticity of substitutability	4.78	6.06	1.15	63.70	386
Average MFN tariff	5.14	25.34	0	350	382
Industry size	8,644.73	17,080.14	57.04	220,608.59	458
Imported intermediates	0.09	0.18	0	1	386
Related-party trade	0.32	0.17	0.01	0.92	339
Export–import ratio (RCA proxy)	1.55	3.35	0	30.27	395
Political concentration	0.03	0.04	0	0.35	452
Geographic concentration	0.44	0.11	0.18	0.79	452
Total domestic lobbying expenditures	0.45	0.82	0	6.53	458
Domestic firm lobbying expenditures	0.30	0.57	0	3.63	458
Domestic industry association lobbying expenditures	0.15	0.57	0	4.66	458

TABLE B.2 *Regression table: Main models*

	(1)	(2)	(3)	(4)
Intra-industry trade	0.342**	0.450***	0.351**	0.354**
	(0.150)	(0.145)	(0.168)	(0.164)
Industry concentration			0.007***	0.007***
			(0.003)	(0.002)
Average firm size			0.001	0.001
			(0.001)	(0.001)
Industry size			−0.000	−0.000
			(0.000)	(0.000)
Elasticity of substitutability			−0.008	−0.008
			(0.005)	(0.005)
Average tariff (MFN)			−0.046	−0.092
			(0.052)	(0.056)
Imported intermediates			−0.477**	−0.323
			(0.206)	(0.213)
Related-party trade			−0.458	−0.341
			(0.287)	(0.295)
Sector fixed effects		−0.262***		−0.246**
		(0.076)		(0.101)
Constant	0.664***	0.737***	0.668***	0.862***
	(0.100)	(0.102)	(0.206)	(0.227)
Observations	294	293	254	254

TABLE B.3 *Robustness check: High-leverage observations removed*

Intra-industry trade	0.334**
	(0.166)
Average firm size	0.000
	(0.001)
Industry concentration	0.007***
	(0.003)
Industry size	−0.000
	(0.000)
Elasticity of substitutability	−0.008
	(0.005)
Average tariff (MFN)	−0.086
	(0.057)
Imported intermediates	−0.329
	(0.213)
Related-party trade	−0.309
	(0.298)
Sector fixed effects	−0.233**
	(0.102)
Constant	0.839***
	(0.232)
Observations	251

Robust standard errors in parentheses. * p<0.10, ** p<0.05, *** p< 0.01.

TABLE B.4 *Alternative specifications of main model: Probit (model 1) and logit (model 2) estimators*

	(1)	(2)
Intra-industry trade	1.396***	2.421***
	(0.491)	(0.909)
Average firm size	0.008	0.013
	(0.005)	(0.009)
Industry concentration	0.012*	0.020*
	(0.007)	(0.012)
Industry size	0.000	0.000
	(0.000)	(0.000)
Elasticity of substitutability	−0.003	−0.007
	(0.018)	(0.028)
Average tariff (MFN)	−0.021	−0.053
	(0.157)	(0.284)
Imported intermediates	−0.409	−0.784
	(0.556)	(0.968)
Related-party trade	−1.505*	−2.678*
	(0.821)	(1.561)
Sector fixed effects	−0.410	−0.625
	(0.265)	(0.475)
Constant	−0.020	−0.018
	(0.592)	(1.041)
Observations	191	191

Robust standard errors in parentheses. * p<0.10, ** p<0.05, *** p< 0.01.

TABLE B.5 *Controlling for political and geographic concentration*

Intra-industry trade	0.371**
	(0.164)
Average firm size	0.001
	(0.001)
Industry concentration	0.008***
	(0.003)
Political concentration	−2.889*
	(1.539)
Geographic concentration	−0.020
	(0.352)
Industry size	−0.000
	(0.000)
Elasticity of substitutability	−0.008
	(0.005)
Average tariff (MFN)	−0.092
	(0.059)
Imported intermediates	−0.304
	(0.219)
Related-party trade	−0.415
	(0.299)
Sector fixed effects	−0.280***
	(0.102)
Constant	0.916***
	(0.250)
Observations	252

Robust standard errors in parentheses. * p<0.10, ** p<0.05, *** p< 0.01.

TABLE B.6 *Controlling for different levels of product differentiation*

	(1)	(2)	(3)
Intra-industry trade	0.340**	0.344**	0.343**
	(0.164)	(0.163)	(0.164)
Average firm size	−0.000	−0.001	−0.001
	(0.001)	(0.001)	(0.001)
Industry concentration	0.007***	0.007***	0.008***
	(0.003)	(0.002)	(0.003)
Industry size	0.000	0.000	0.000
	(0.000)	(0.000)	(0.000)
Average tariff (MFN)	−0.081	−0.079	−0.092
	(0.054)	(0.056)	(0.056)
Imported intermediates	−0.391**	−0.352*	−0.376*
	(0.196)	(0.204)	(0.213)
Related-party trade	−0.366	−0.309	−0.322
	(0.291)	(0.291)	(0.298)
Low substitutability	0.276***		
	(0.097)		
Medium substitutability		−0.184**	
		(0.080)	
High substitutability			−0.067
			(0.078)
Sector fixed effects	−0.299***	−0.274***	−0.266***
	(0.102)	(0.100)	(0.101)
Constant	0.756***	0.864***	0.846***
	(0.222)	(0.233)	(0.229)
Observations	257	257	257

Robust standard errors in parentheses. * $p<0.10$, ** $p<0.05$, *** $p<0.01$.

TABLE B.7 *Examining the relationship between lobbying, IIT, and comparative advantage*

IIT (mean-centered)	0.545***
	(0.191)
RCA	0.219**
	(0.089)
RCA × IIT	−0.872***
	(0.335)
Average firm size	0.001
	(0.001)
Industry concentration	0.005**
	(0.003)
Industry size	−0.000
	(0.000)
Elasticity of substitutability	−0.009*
	(0.005)
Average tariff (MFN)	−0.063
	(0.055)
Imported intermediates	−0.394*
	(0.208)
Related-party trade	−0.278
	(0.300)
Sector fixed effects	−0.193*
	(0.103)
Constant	0.968***
	(0.210)
Observations	254

Robust standard errors in parentheses. * p<0.10, ** p<0.05, *** p< 0.01.

TABLE B.8 *Regression table: Lobbying expenditures*

Dependent variable	Total domestic lobbying amount (10)	Total firm lobbying amount (11)	Total association lobbying amount (12)
Intra-industry trade	−0.327***	−0.073	−0.301***
	(0.100)	(0.088)	(0.089)
Average firm size	−0.000	−0.000	−0.000
	(0.001)	(0.001)	(0.000)
Industry concentration	0.001	0.003**	−0.003***
	(0.001)	(0.001)	(0.001)
Industry size	0.000***	0.000***	0.000
	(0.000)	(0.000)	(0.000)
Elasticity of substitutability	0.008*	0.007	0.003
	(0.005)	(0.005)	(0.002)
Imported intermediates	−0.012	−0.016	0.016
	(0.109)	(0.111)	(0.068)
Related-party trade	0.452**	0.167	0.412**
	(0.175)	(0.139)	(0.180)
Average tariff (MFN)	−0.023	0.013	−0.030
	(0.039)	(0.031)	(0.038)
Sector fixed effects	−0.413***	−0.317***	−0.125**
	(0.062)	(0.046)	(0.059)
Constant	0.710***	0.323**	0.472***
	(0.167)	(0.125)	(0.164)
Observations	313	313	313

Robust standard errors in parentheses. * p<0.10, ** p<0.05, *** p< 0.01.

TABLE B.9 *Regression table: Lobbying expenditures including average firm size instead of industry size*

Dependent variable	Total domestic lobbying amount (1)	Total firm lobbying amount (2)	Total association lobbying amount (3)
Intra-industry trade	−0.299***	−0.048	−0.294***
	(0.101)	(0.091)	(0.088)
Average firm size	0.001**	0.001***	0.000
	(0.001)	(0.000)	(0.000)
Industry concentration	−0.001	0.002	−0.003***
	(0.001)	(0.001)	(0.001)
Elasticity of substitutability	0.006	0.005	0.002
	(0.005)	(0.005)	(0.002)
Imported intermediates	0.038	0.031	0.029
	(0.113)	(0.112)	(0.070)
Related-party trade	0.619***	0.322**	0.456**
	(0.189)	(0.155)	(0.180)
Average tariff (MFN)	−0.018	0.017	−0.029
	(0.040)	(0.032)	(0.038)
Sector fixed effects	−0.423***	−0.327***	−0.128**
	(0.064)	(0.048)	(0.060)
Constant	0.736***	0.347***	0.478***
	(0.170)	(0.126)	(0.165)
Observations	313	313	313

Robust standard errors in parentheses. * p<0.10, ** p<0.05, *** p< 0.01.

B.1 DYNAMICS OF CHANGES IN IIT IN NET-EXPORTING VERSUS NET-IMPORTING INDUSTRIES

First, recall that IIT is measured using the Grubel-Lloyd index:

$$IIT_i = 1 - \frac{|X_i - M_i|}{(X_i + M_i)}, \tag{2.1}$$

where IIT_i is industry i's level of intra-industry trade, and X_i and M_i are measures of exports and imports of industry i.

When $X_i = M_i$, $IIT_i = 1$ and all trade is intra-industry.

When X_i or $M_i = 0$, $IIT_i = 0$ and all trade is inter-industry.

In a net-exporting industry, $X > M$. As M increases, the ratio of X to M decreases and the value of IIT increases, as shown in the example below. In this example, industry i exports 100 units and imports 50 units:

$$IIT_i = 1 - \frac{|100_i - 50_i|}{(100_i + 50_i)} = 0.67. \tag{B.1}$$

As industry i's imports increase to 75 units, we see the following:

$$IIT_i = 1 - \frac{|100_i - 75_i|}{(100_i + 75_i)} = 0.86. \tag{B.2}$$

Thus, in a net-exporting industry, an increase in imports relative to exports results in an increase in IIT.

Conversely, in a net-importing industry, $X < M$. An increase in IIT is the result of X increasing relative to M, as shown in the example below. Consider an industry i that exports 25 units and imports 100 units:

$$IIT_i = 1 - \frac{|25_i - 100_i|}{(25_i + 100_i)} = 0.4. \tag{B.3}$$

As industry i's exports increase to 50 units, we see the following increase in IIT:

$$IIT_i = 1 - \frac{|50_i - 100_i|}{(50_i + 100_i)} = 0.67. \tag{B.4}$$

Appendix C

Appendix to Chapter 5

TABLE C.1 *Summary statistics: Imported intermediates and industry size are measured in millions of euros*

	Mean	SD	Min	Max	N
Actor type	0.45	0.5	0	1	843
Intra-industry trade	0.53	0.3	0	1	821
Elasticity of substitution	8.10	15.07	1.16	131.5	804
MFN Tariff, trade-weighted average	5.33	12.95	0	191.8	779
Imported intermediates	33,502.16	19,824.08	4,206.66	161,916.92	842
Industry concentration	0.0003	0.0006	7.28e−06	0.006	762
Industry size	8.79e+10	7.51e+10	1.03e+09	4.68e+11	753

TABLE C.2 *Effect of IIT on the likelihood that lobbying actors are firms: Main models*

	(1)	(2)
IIT	0.226***	0.285**
	(0.085)	(0.115)
Elasticity of substitution		−0.151*
		(0.090)
Tariffs		−0.143
		(0.088)
Imported intermediates		0.108
		(0.167)
Industry concentration		0.167*
		(0.093)
Industry size		0.221**
		(0.089)
Constant	−0.173	−4.821**
	(0.504)	(2.117)
Random effects:		
Event-level variance	0.884	0.493
Observations	821	680
Log-likelihood	−508.8	−425.9
AIC	1023.7	867.7
BIC	1037.8	903.9
LR test Prob > x^2	0.000	0.000

Standard errors in parentheses. * p<0.10, ** p<0.05, *** p<0.01. Likelihood ratio test vs. logistic regression.

TABLE C.3 *Robustness check: Standard logistic regression with robust standard errors*

	(1)	(2)
IIT	0.312***	0.350***
	(0.071)	(0.090)
Elasticity of substitution		−0.173*
		(0.090)
Tariffs		−0.0805
		(0.080)
Imported intermediates		0.415***
		(0.157)
Industry concentration		0.128
		(0.092)
Industry size		0.186**
		(0.087)
Constant	0.158*	−7.164***
	(0.096)	(1.794)
Observations	821	680

Robust standard errors in parentheses. *p< 0.10, **p< 0.05, ***p< 0.01.

TABLE C.4 *Robustness check: Standard errors clustered by consultation-actor*

	(1)	(2)
IIT	0.312***	0.350**
	(0.121)	(0.151)
Elasticity of substitution		−0.173
		(0.115)
Tariffs		−0.0805
		(0.186)
Imported intermediates		0.415
		(0.440)
Industry concentration		0.128
		(0.163)
Industry size		0.186
		(0.144)
Constant	0.158	−7.164
	(0.233)	(5.025)
Observations	821	680

Cluster-robust standard errors in parentheses. *p< 0.10, **p< 0.05, ***p< 0.01.

TABLE C.5 *Proportion of industry lobbyists that are individual firms*

	(1)	(2)
IIT	0.268***	0.370***
	(0.087)	(0.122)
Elasticity of substitution		−0.190
		(0.119)
Tariffs		−0.272**
		(0.107)
Industry concentration		0.354***
		(0.123)
Industry size		0.491***
		(0.140)
Imported intermediates		0.462**
		(0.207)
Constant	−0.0430	−13.00***
	(0.121)	(2.416)
Observations	453	353

Robust standard errors in parentheses. *p< 0.10, **p< 0.05, ***p< 0.01.

TABLE C.6 *IIT interaction with RCA*

IIT	−0.257
	(0.246)
RCA	0.070
	(0.257)
RCA × IIT	0.656**
	(0.279)
Elasticity of substitution	−0.128
	(0.092)
Tariffs	−0.191**
	(0.092)
Imported intermediates	0.0578
	(0.169)
Industry concentration	0.188**
	(0.093)
Industry size	0.256***
	(0.090)
Constant	−5.038**
	(2.147)
Observations	680
AIC	862.4
BIC	907.6
Log-likelihood	−421.2
LR test Prob > x^2	0.000

Appendix D

Appendix to Chapter 6

TABLE D.1 *Summary statistics of final sample: Tariff analysis*

	Mean	SD	Min	Max	N
Trade-weighted average AHS tariff	4.15	14.13	0	277.26	6,155
IIT	0.52	0.27	0	1	6,155
Import penetration	0.25	0.25	0	0.99	6,155
Export dependence	0.17	0.18	0	0.88	6,155
Product differentiation	0.86	0.21	0.25	1	6,155
Particularism	8.66	3.08	1	11	6,155
Government ideology	1.68	0.86	1	3	6,155

TABLE D.2 *Summary statistics of final sample: NTM analysis*

	Mean	SD	Min	Max	N
Trade-weighted average AHS tariff	2.57	8	0	513	114,167
AVE of NTMs	28.36	52.78	0	997.49	114,167
IIT	0.46	0.32	0	1	114,167
Imports	158,380.26	1,204,541.90	0	139,440,515.05	114,167
Exports	162,503	1,203,131.66	0	121,468,057.08	114,167
Product differentiation	0.66	0.46	0	1	114,167
Particularism	6.10	3.62	1	11	114,167
Government ideology	1.77	0.90	1	3	114,167

TABLE D.3 *Main models and robustness: Tariffs*

	(1) OLS with Newey-West standard errors	(2) OLS with Newey-West standard errors	(3) Multilevel mixed-effects regression
Lagged IIT (4 years)	-0.032^{***}	-0.032^{***}	-0.065^{*}
	(0.011)	(0.011)	(0.039)
Export dependence	-0.098^{***}	-0.108^{***}	-1.460^{***}
	(0.029)	(0.028)	(0.086)
Import penetration	0.015	0.033^{*}	0.608^{***}
	(0.022)	(0.019)	(0.065)
Product differentiation	-0.019	-0.021	-0.211^{***}
	(0.014)	(0.014)	(0.045)
Particularism	-0.002		
	(0.002)		
Government ideology	-0.006		
	(0.004)		
Lagged tariff	0.956^{***}	0.954^{***}	
	(0.005)	(0.005)	
Constant	0.094^{***}	0.063^{***}	1.229^{***}
	(0.021)	(0.015)	(0.151)
Random effects: Country-level variance:			0.468^{***}
			(0.103)
Observations	6155	6762	6770

Standard errors in parentheses. * p<0.10, ** p<0.05, *** p< 0.01.

TABLE D.4 *Regression table: The effect of IIT on AVEs of NTMs*

	(1) OLS with Newey-West standard errors	(2) Multilevel mixed-effects regression
Lagged AVE of NTM	0.478***	
	(0.003)	
Lagged IIT (3 years)	0.201***	0.207***
	(0.020)	(0.022)
Imports	0.098***	0.132***
	(0.003)	(0.004)
Exports	0.015***	0.025***
	(0.003)	(0.003)
Product differentiation	0.059***	0.016
	(0.012)	(0.013)
Particularism	−0.067***	−0.094**
	(0.002)	(0.043)
Government ideology	0.106***	0.118***
	(0.007)	(0.009)
Lagged AHS tariff	0.090***	0.174***
	(0.007)	(0.008)
Constant	0.220***	0.619**
	(0.027)	(0.302)
Random effects: Country-level variance		0.802***
		(0.111)
Observations	87,635	87,635

Standard errors in parentheses. * p<0.10, ** p<0.05, *** p< 0.01.

References

AFL-CIO (2013). Comments on the Transatlantic Trade and Investment Partnership. Available from www.regulations.gov/document/USTR-2013-0019-0266. Accessed March 5, 2023.

Alliance for American Manufacturing (2013). Request for Comments Concerning Proposed Transatlantic Trade and Investment Partnership. Available from www.regulations.gov/document/USTR-2013-0019-0270. Accessed March 5, 2023.

Alliance for American Manufacturing (2015). AAM Statement on TPP Agreement. Available at www.americanmanufacturing.org/press-release/aam-statement-on-tpp-agreement/. Accessed December 19, 2022.

Alt, J. E., Carlsen, F., Heum, P., and Johansen, K. (1999). Asset specificity and the political behavior of firms: Lobbying for subsidies in Norway. *International Organization*, 53(01):99–116.

Alt, J. E., Frieden, J., Gilligan, M. J., Rodrik, D., and Rogowski, R. (1996). The political economy of international trade: Enduring puzzles and an agenda for inquiry. *Comparative Political Studies*, 29(6):689–717.

American Automotive Policy Council (2010). Comment from Charles Uthus, American Automotive Policy Council. Available from www.regulations.gov/comment/USTR-2010-0031-0037. Accessed February 10, 2023.

American Automotive Policy Council (2013). Submission of the American Automotive Policy Council in Response to the Office of the United States Trade Representative's Request for Comments on Negotiating Objectives with Respect to Japan's Participation in the Proposed Trans-Pacific Partnership Trade Agreement. Available from www.regulations.gov/comment/USTR-2013-0022-0064. Accessed February 10, 2023.

American Iron and Steel Institute (2010). Comments Concerning the Proposed United States-Trans-Pacific Partnership Trade Agreement. Available from www.regulations.gov/document/USTR-2009-0041-0061. Accessed January 16, 2023.

American Shrimp Processors Association (2010). Comment from Terence Stewart, American Shrimp Processors Association. Available from www.regulations.gov/document/USTR-2009-0041-0075. Accessed December 20, 2022.

American Sugar Alliance (2010). Submission of the American Sugar Alliance. Available from www.regulations.gov/document/USTR-2009-0041-0124. Accessed January 16, 2023.

Amiti, M. and Davis, D. R. (2012). Trade, firms, and wages: Theory and evidence. *The Review of Economic Studies*, 79(1):1–36.

AMTAC (2010). Comment from Augustine Tantillo, American Manufacturing Trade Action Coalition. Available from www.regulations.gov/document/USTR-2009-0041-0039. Accessed December 20, 2022.

Anderer, C., Dür, A., and Lechner, L. (2020). Trade policy in a "GVC World": Multinational corporations and trade liberalization. *Business and Politics*, 22(4):639–666.

Antweiler, W. and Trefler, D. (2002). Increasing returns and all that: A view from trade. *The American Economic Review*, 92(1):93–119.

Aspinwall, M. and Greenwood, J. (2013). *Collective Action in the European Union: Interests and the New Politics of Associability*. Routledge.

Baccini, L., Dür, A., and Elsig, M. (2018). Intra-industry trade, global value chains, and preferential tariff liberalization. *International Studies Quarterly*, 62(2):329–340.

Baccini, L., Osgood, I., and Weymouth, S. (2019). The service economy: US trade coalitions in an era of deindustrialization. *The Review of International Organizations*, 14(2):261–296.

Bailey, M. A., Goldstein, J., and Weingast, B. R. (1997). The institutional roots of American trade policy: Politics, coalitions, and international trade. *World Politics*, 49(3):309–338.

Balassa, B. (1966). Tariff reductions and trade in manufacturers among the industrial countries. *The American Economic Review*, 56(3):466–473.

Baldwin, R. and Lopez-Gonzalez, J. (2015). Supply-chain trade: A portrait of global patterns and several testable hypotheses. *The World Economy*, 38(11):1682–1721.

Baldwin, R. E. and Martin, P. (1999). Two waves of globalisation: Superficial similarities, fundamental differences. Working Paper 6904, National Bureau of Economic Research.

Barber, B., Pierskalla, J., and Weschle, S. (2014). Lobbying and the collective action problem: Comparative evidence from enterprise surveys. *Business and Politics*, 16(2):221–246.

Bastiaens, I. and Postnikov, E. (2020). Social standards in trade agreements and free trade preferences: An empirical investigation. *The Review of International Organizations*, 15:793–816.

Beaulieu, E., Benarroch, M., and Gaisford, J. D. (2011). Intra-industry trade liberalization: Why skilled workers are more likely to support free trade. *Review of International Economics*, 19(3):579–594.

Belloc, M. (2015). Information for sale in the European Union. *Journal of Economic Behavior & Organization*, 120:130–144.

Berkhout, J., Beyers, J., Braun, C., Hanegraaff, M., and Lowery, D. (2018). Making inference across mobilisation and influence research: Comparing top-down and bottom-up mapping of interest systems. *Political Studies*, 66(1):43–62.

Bernard, A. B., Eaton, J., Jensen, J. B., and Kortum, S. (2003). Plants and productivity in international trade. *American Economic Review*, 93(4):1268–1290.

Bernard, A. B., Jensen, J. B., and Lawrence, R. Z. (1995). Exporters, jobs, and wages in US manufacturing: 1976–1987. *Brookings Papers on Economic Activity. Microeconomics*, 1995:67–119.

Bernard, A. B., Jensen, J. B., Redding, S. J., and Schott, P. K. (2007a). Firms in international trade. Working Paper 13054, National Bureau of Economic Research.

Bernard, A. B., Redding, S. J., and Schott, P. K. (2007b). Comparative advantage and heterogeneous firms. *The Review of Economic Studies*, 74(1):31–66.

Bernhagen, P., Dür, A., and Marshall, D. (2015). Information or context: What accounts for positional proximity between the European commission and lobbyists? *Journal of European Public Policy*, 22(4):570–587.

Bernhagen, P. and Mitchell, N. J. (2009). The determinants of direct corporate lobbying in the European Union. *European Union Politics*, 10(2):155–176.

Betz, T. (2017). Trading interests: Domestic institutions, international negotiations, and the politics of trade. *The Journal of Politics*, 79(4):1237–1252.

Beyers, J. and De Bruycker, I. (2018). Lobbying makes (strange) bedfellows: Explaining the formation and composition of lobbying coalitions in eu legislative politics. *Political Studies*, 66(4):959–984.

Bhagwati, J. N. and Patrick, H. T. (1990). *Aggressive Unilateralism: America's 301 Trade Policy and the World Trading System*. University of Michigan Press.

Bidwell, P. W. (1956). *What the Tariff Means to American Industries*. Council on Foreign Relations. Harper & Brothers

Birchfield, V. (2015). Negotiating the TTIP: Comparing US and EU motivations, oppositions and public opinion. Working Paper GTJMCE 2015-2, Georgia Tech Jean Monnet Centre of Excellence.

Blanchard, E. and Matschke, X. (2015). US multinationals and preferential market access. *Review of Economics and Statistics*, 97(4):839–854.

Blanes, J. V. and Martín, C. (2000). The nature and causes of intra-industry trade: Back to the comparative advantage explanation? The case of Spain. *Weltwirtschaftliches Archiv*, 136(3):423–441.

Blanga-Gubbay, M., Conconi, P., & Parenti, M. (2025). Lobbying for globalisation. *The Economic Journal*, 135(666), 487–518.

Boehmke, F. J., Gailmard, S., and Patty, J. W. (2013). Business as usual: Interest group access and representation across policy-making venues. *Journal of Public Policy*, 33(1):3–33.

Bombardini, M. (2008). Firm heterogeneity and lobby participation. *Journal of International Economics*, 75(2):329–348.

Bombardini, M. and Trebbi, F. (2012). Competition and political organization: Together or alone in lobbying for trade policy? *Journal of International Economics*, 87(1):18–26.

Bouwen, P. (2002). Corporate lobbying in the European Union: The logic of access. *Journal of European Public Policy*, 9(3):365–390.

Brawley, M. R. (1997). Factoral or sectoral conflict? Partially mobile factors and the politics of trade in imperial Germany. *International Studies Quarterly*, 41(4):633–654.

Brülhart, M. (2008). An Account of Global Intraindustry Trade, 1962–2006. World Development Report Background Paper, World Bank.

Brülhart, M. and Hine, R. C. (1999). *Intra-Industry Trade and Adjustment*. Palgrave Macmillan.

Brülhart, M. and Matthews, A. (2007). EU External Trade Policy. In El-Agraa, A., editor, *The European Union: Economics and Policies*. Cambridge University Press.

Broda, C. and Weinstein, D. E. (2006). Globalization and the gains from variety. *The Quarterly Journal of Economics*, 121(2):541–585.

Broscheid, A. and Coen, D. (2007). Lobbying activity and fora creation in the EU: Empirically exploring the nature of the policy good. *Journal of European Public Policy*, 14(3):346–365.

Brutger, R. (2024). Litigation for sale: Private firms and WTO dispute escalation. *American Political Science Review*, 118(3):1204–1221.

Bunea, A. (2014). Explaining interest groups' articulation of policy preferences in the European Commission's open consultations: An analysis of the environmental policy area. *Journal of Common Market Studies*, 52(6):1224–1241.

Bunea, A. and Baumgartner, F. R. (2014). The state of the discipline: Authorship, research designs, and citation patterns in studies of EU interest groups and lobbying. *Journal of European Public Policy*, 21(10):1412–1434.

Buonanno, L. and Dudek, C. M. (2015). Opposition to the TTIP in the EU and the US: Implications for the EU's "Democratic Deficit". Available at https://core.ac.uk/works/18889000/. Presented at the 2015 meeting of the European Union Studies Association, March 5–7, 2015, Boston.

Busch, M. L. and Reinhardt, E. (1999). Industrial location and protection: The political and economic geography of U.S. nontariff barriers. *American Journal of Political Science*, 43(4):1028–1050.

Caddel, J. (2014). Domestic competition over trade barriers in the US international trade commission. *International Studies Quarterly*, 58(2):260–268.

Cadot, O., Gourdon, J., and van Tongeren, F. (2018). Estimating ad valorem equivalents of non-tariff measures. No. 215, OECD Trade Policy Papers.

California Cling Peach Board (2010). Comment from Sarb Johl, California Cling Peach Board. Available from www.regulations.gov/document/USTR-2009-0041-0076. Accessed December 20, 2022.

California Olive Association (2010). Comment from Bill McFarland, California Olive Association. Available from www.regulations.gov/document/USTR-2009-0041-0008. Accessed December 20, 2022.

Capaldo, J. (2014). The Transatlantic Trade and Investment Partnership: European disintegration, unemployment and instability. Working Paper No. 14-03, Global Development and Environment Institute, Tufts University.

Carey, J. M. and Shugart, M. S. (1995). Incentives to cultivate a personal vote: A rank ordering of electoral formulas. *Electoral Studies*, 14(4):417–439.

Cebeci, T., Fernandes, A. M., Freund, C. L., and Pierola, M. D. (2012). Exporter dynamics database. World Bank Policy Research Working Paper, No. 6229.

Chan, A. T. and Crawford, B. K. (2017). The puzzle of public opposition to TTIP in Germany. *Business and Politics*, 19(4):683–708.

Chase, K. A. (2003). Economic interests and regional trading arrangements: The case of NAFTA. *International Organization*, 57(1):137–174.

Chase, K. A. (2008). Moving Hollywood abroad: Divided labor markets and the new politics of trade in services. *International Organization*, 62(04):653.

Chase, K. A. (2009). *Trading Blocs: States, Firms, and Regions in the World Economy*. University of Michigan Press.

Chodor, T. (2019). The rise and fall and rise of the Trans-Pacific Partnership: 21st century trade politics through a new constitutionalist lens. *Review of International Political Economy*, 26(2):232–255.

Chorev, N. (2007). *Remaking US Trade Policy: From Protectionism to Globalization*. Cornell University Press.

Coalition for a Prosperous America (2016). Business Associations Urge Congress to Avoid Lame Duck Vote on Trade Deal. Available from https://prosperousamerica .org/business-associations-urge-congress-to-avoid-lame-duck-vote-on-trade-deal/. Accessed December 19, 2022.

Coen, D. (2007). Empirical and theoretical studies in EU lobbying. *Journal of European Public Policy*, 14(3):333–345.

Coen, D., Katsaitis, A., and Vannoni, M. (2021). *Business Lobbying in the European Union*. Oxford University Press.

Conybeare, J. A. C. (1991). Voting for protection: An electoral model of tariff policy. *International Organization*, 45(1):57.

Curran, L. (2015). The impact of trade policy on global production networks: The solar panel case. *Review of International Political Economy*, 22(5):1025–1054.

Davis, C. L. (2003). *Food Fights Over Free Trade: How International Institutions Promote Agricultural Trade Liberalization*. Princeton University Press.

de Backer, K. and Miroudot, S. (2014). Mapping global value chains. SSRN Scholarly Paper 2436411, Social Science Research Network, Rochester, NY.

De Bièvre, D., Beyers, J., Hanegraaff, M., and Poletti, A. (2016). International institutions and interest mobilization: The WTO and lobbying in EU and US trade policy. *Journal of World Trade*, 50(2):289–312.

De Bièvre, D. and Eckhardt, J. (2011). Interest groups and EU anti-dumping policy. *Journal of European Public Policy*, 18(3):339–360.

De Bièvre, D. and Poletti, A. (2020). Towards explaining varying degrees of politicization of EU trade agreement negotiations. *Politics and Governance*, 8(1): 243–253.

de Melo, J. and Nicita, A. (2018). Non-tariff measures: Scope and overview. In de Melo, J. and Nicita, A., editors, *Non-Tariff Measures*. UNCTAD.

Dellis, K. and Sondermann, D. (2017). Lobbying in Europe: New firm-level evidence. Working Paper No. 2071, European Central Bank.

Destler, I. M. (1992). *American Trade Politics*. NYU Press.

Dinlersoz, E., Greenwood, J., and Hyatt, H. (2014). Who do unions target? Unionization over the life-cycle of US businesses. Working Paper Series 20151, National Bureau of Economic Research.

Dixit, A. and Norman, V. (1980). *Theory of International Trade: A Dual, General Equilibrium Approach*. Cambridge University Press.

Drope, J. M. and Hansen, W. L. (2004). Purchasing protection? The effect of political spending on U.S. trade policy. *Political Research Quarterly*, 57(1):27–37.

Drope, J. M. and Hansen, W. L. (2006). Does firm size matter? Analyzing business lobbying in the United States. *Business and Politics*, 8(2):1–17.

Drope, J. M. and Hansen, W. L. (2009). New evidence for the theory of groups: Trade association lobbying in Washington, D.C. *Political Research Quarterly*, 62(2): 303–316.

Drutman, L. (2015). *The Business of America is Lobbying: How Corporations Became Politicized and Politics Became More Corporate*. Oxford University Press.

Dür, A. (2008). Bringing economic interests back into the study of EU trade policy-making. *The British Journal of Politics & International Relations*, 10(1): 27–45.

Dür, A., Bernhagen, P., and Marshall, D. (2015). Interest group success in the European Union: When (and why) does business lose? *Comparative Political Studies*, 48(8):951–983.

Dür, A. and De Bièvre, D. (2007). Inclusion without influence? NGOs in European trade policy. *Journal of Public Policy*, 27(01):79–101.

Dür, A., Eckhardt, J., and Poletti, A. (2020). Global value chains, the anti-globalization backlash, and EU trade policy: A research agenda. *Journal of European Public Policy*, 27(6):944–956.

Dür, A. and Elsig, M. (2011). Principals, agents, and the European Union's foreign economic policies. *Journal of European Public Policy*, 18(3):323–338.

Dür, A. and Lechner, L. (2015). Business interests and the Transatlantic Trade and Investment Partnership. In Novotná, T., Telò, M., Morin, J.-F., and Ponjaert, F., editors, *The Politics of Transatlantic Trade Negotiations: TTIP in a Globalized World*. Ashgate Publishing, Ltd.

Dür, A., Marshall, D., and Bernhagen, P. (2019). *The Political Influence of Business in the European Union*. University of Michigan Press.

Dür, A. and Mateo, G. (2016). *Insiders versus Outsiders: Interest Group Politics in Multilevel Europe*. Oxford University Press.

Eckhardt, J. (2013). EU unilateral trade policy-making: What role for import-dependent firms? *JCMS: Journal of Common Market Studies*, 51(6):989–1005.

Eckhardt, J. (2018). Business-government relations in EU trade politics. In Khorana, S. and García, M., editors, *Handbook on the EU and International Trade*. Edward Elgar Publishing, Cheltenham, UK.

ECS International (2013). Comments of Jeff Edwards, ECS International, Inc. Available from www.regulations.gov/document/USTR-2013-0019-0128. Accessed February 20, 2023.

Egger, H. and Kreickemeier, U. (2009). Firm heterogeneity and the labor market effects of trade liberalization. *International Economic Review*, 50(1):187–216.

Ehrlich, S. D. (2007). Access to protection: Domestic institutions and trade policy in democracies. *International Organization*, 61(03):571–605.

Ehrlich, S. D. (2008). The tariff and the lobbyist: Political institutions, interest group politics, and U.S. trade policy. *International Studies Quarterly*, 52(2):427–445.

Ehrlich, S. D. (2009). Constituency size and support for trade liberalization: An analysis of foreign economic policy preferences in congress. *Foreign Policy Analysis*, 5(3):215–232.

Ehrlich, S. D. (2018). *The Politics of Fair Trade: Moving beyond Free Trade and Protection*. Oxford University Press.

Ehrlich, S. D. and Jones, E. (2016). Whom do European corporations lobby? The domestic institutional determinants of interest group activity in the European union. *Business and Politics*, 18(4):467–488.

Eichengreen, B. and Leblang, D. (2008). Democracy and globalization. *Economics & Politics*, 20(3):289–334.

Eising, R. (2007). The access of business interests to EU institutions: Towards élite pluralism? *Journal of European Public Policy*, 14(3):384–403.

Eisner, M. A. (2000). *Regulatory Politics in Transition*. JHU Press.

European Commission (2018). Joint U.S.-EU Statement following President Juncker's visit to the White House. Available at https://ec.europa.eu/commission/presscorner/detail/en/STATEMENT_18_4687.

Fontagné, L., Freudenberg, M., Péridy, N., et al. (1998). Intra-industry trade and the single market: Quality matters. No. 1959, Centre for Economic Policy Research (CEPR) Discussion Paper Series.

Fontagné, L., Orefice, G., Piermartini, R., and Rocha, N. (2015). Product standards and margins of trade: Firm-level evidence. *Journal of International Economics*, 97(1): 29–44.

Fort, T. C. and Klimek, S. (2018). The effects of industry classification changes on US employment composition. No. 18-28, CES Working Paper.

Frieden, J. A. (1991). Invested interests: The politics of national economic policies in a world of global finance. *International Organization*, 45(4):425–451.

Frieden, J. A. (1992). *Debt, Development, and Democracy: Modern Political Economy and Latin America, 1965–1985*. Princeton University Press.

Fromartz, S. (2006). Who lobbies for small manufacturers on China? March 1, 2006. *CNN Money*.

Garst, W. D. (1998). From factor endowments to class struggle. *Comparative Political Studies*, 31(1):22–44.

Garst, W. D. (1999). From sectoral linkages to class conflict. *Comparative Political Studies*, 32(7):788–809.

Gawande, K. and Bandyopadhyay, U. (2000). Is protection for sale? Evidence on the Grossman-Helpman theory of endogenous protection. *Review of Economics and Statistics*, 82(1):139–152.

Gawande, K. and Hansen, W. L. (1999). Retaliation, bargaining, and the pursuit of "Free and Fair" trade. *International Organization*, 53(1):117–159.

Ghodsi, M., Gruebler, J., and Stehrer, R. (2016). Estimating importer-specific ad valorem equivalents of non-tariff measures. Working Paper No. 129, The Vienna Institute for International Economic Studies.

Gilligan, M. J. (1997a). *Empowering Exporters: Reciprocity, Delegation, and Collective Action in American Trade Policy*. University of Michigan Press.

Gilligan, M. J. (1997b). Lobbying as a private good with intra-industry trade. *International Studies Quarterly*, 41(3):455–474.

Goldberg, P. K. and Maggi, G. (1999). Protection for sale: An empirical investigation. *American Economic Review*, 89(5):1135–1155.

Goldstein, J. (1988). Ideas, institutions, and American trade policy. *International Organization*, 42(1):179–217.

Goldstein, J. L., Rivers, D., and Tomz, M. (2007). Institutions in international relations: Understanding the effects of the GATT and the WTO on world trade. *International Organization*, 61(1):37–67.

Götz, M. (2019). The representation of SME interests in the TTIP negotiations: A German case study. In Dialer, D. and Richter, M., editors, *Lobbying in the European Union: Strategies, Dynamics and Trends*. Springer, pp. 363–374.

Grübler, J. and Reiter, O. (2021). Characterising non-tariff trade policy. *Economic Analysis and Policy*, 71:138–163.

Greenaway, D. and Milner, C. (1986). *The Economics of Intra-industry Trade*. Basil Blackwell.

Greenwood, J. (2017). *Interest Representation in the European Union*. Palgrave Macmillan.

Grieco, J. (1990). *Cooperation Among Nations: Europe, America, and Non-Tariff Barriers to Trade*. Cornell University Press.

Grimwade, N. (1989). *International Trade: New Patterns of Trade, Production, and Investment*. Routledge.

Grossman, G. M. and Helpman, E. (1994). Protection for sale. *The American Economic Review*, 84(4):833–850.

Grossman, G. M. and Helpman, E. (2005). A protectionist bias in majoritarian politics. *The Quarterly Journal of Economics*, 120(4):1239–1282.

Grubel, H. G. and Lloyd, P. J. (1975). *Intra-industry Trade: the Theory and Measurement of International Trade in Differentiated Products*. Wiley.

Grundke, R. and Moser, C. (2019). Hidden protectionism? Evidence from non-tariff barriers to trade in the United States. *Journal of International Economics*, 117: 1143–157.

Gulotty, R. (2020). *Narrowing the Channel: The Politics of Regulatory Protection in International Trade*. University of Chicago Press.

Hamilton, D. S., and Quinlan, J. P. (2022). *The Transatlantic Economy 2022: Annual Survey of Jobs, Trade and Investment between the United States and Europe*. Foreign Policy Institute, Johns Hopkins University SAIS/Transatlantic Leadership Network.

Hanegraaff, M. and Poletti, A. (2021). The rise of corporate lobbying in the European Union: An agenda for future research. *JCMS: Journal of Common Market Studies*, 59(4):839–855.

Hankla, C. R. (2006). Party strength and international trade. *Comparative Political Studies*, 39(9):1133–1156.

Hansen, W. L. and Mitchell, N. J. (2000). Disaggregating and explaining corporate political activity: Domestic and foreign corporations in national politics. *The American Political Science Review*, 94(4):891–903.

Hansen, W. L., Mitchell, N. J., and Drope, J. M. (2005). The logic of private and collective action. *American Journal of Political Science*, 49(1):150–167.

Hansen, W. L. and Prusa, T. J. (1996). Cumulation and ITC decision-making: The sum of the parts is greater than the whole. *Economic Inquiry*, 34(4):746–769.

Hansen-Kuhn, K. (2016). Leaked TTIP memo shows EU targeting US government contracts. Institute for Agriculture & Trade Policy. Available from www.iatp.org/blog/ 201604/leaked-ttip-memo-shows-eu-targeting-us-government-contracts. Accessed March 4, 2023.

Hanson, B. T. (1998). What happened to fortress Europe?: External trade policy liberalization in the European Union. *International Organization*, 52(01):55–85.

Harley, C. K., editor (1996). *The Integration of the World Economy, 1850–1914: The Growth of the World Economy*. Elgar.

Helpman, E. (1981). International trade in the presence of product differentiation, economies of scale and monopolistic competition: A Chamberlin-Heckscher-Ohlin approach. *Journal of International Economics*, 11(3):305–340.

Helpman, E. (1987). Imperfect competition and international trade: Evidence from fourteen industrial countries. *Journal of the Japanese and International Economies*, 1(1):62–81.

Helpman, E. (2011). *Understanding Global Trade*. Harvard University Press.

Helpman, E., Itskhoki, O., and Redding, S. (2010). Inequality and unemployment in a global economy. *Econometrica*, 78(4):1239–1283.

Helpman, E. and Krugman, P. R. (1985). *Market Structure and Foreign Trade: Increasing Returns, Imperfect Competition, and The International Economy*. MIT Press.

Henisz, W. J. and Mansfield, E. D. (2006). Votes and vetoes: The political determinants of commercial openness. *International Studies Quarterly*, 50(1):189–212.

Hiscox, M. J. (2001). Class versus industry cleavages: Inter-industry factor mobility and the politics of trade. *International Organization*, 55(1):1–46.

Hiscox, M. J. (2002a). Commerce, coalitions, and factor mobility: Evidence from Congressional votes on trade legislation. *American Political Science Review*, 96(3): 593–608.

Hiscox, M. J. (2002b). *International Trade and Political Conflict: Commerce, Coalitions, and Mobility*. Princeton University Press.

Hoffa, J. P. (2017). Withdrawal from TPP the Right Choice for U.S. Trade Policy. Available at https://teamster.org/2017/01/hoffa-withdrawal-tpp-right-choice-us-trade-policy/. Accessed February 20, 2023.

Huneeus, F. and Kim, I. S. (2018). The effects of firms' lobbying on resource misallocation. MIT Political Science Department Research Paper, 2018–23.

Ikenberry, G. J., Lake, D. A., and Mastanduno, M. (1988). *The State and American Foreign Economic Policy*. Cornell University Press.

Ingersoll Rand (2013). Comments on the Transatlantic Trade and Investment Partnership. Available from www.regulations.gov/document/USTR-2013-0019-0232. Accessed February 20, 2023.

Irwin, D. A. (1995). Industry or class cleavages over trade policy? Evidence from the British general election of 1923. Working Paper 5170, National Bureau of Economic Research.

Jensen, J. B., Quinn, D. P., and Weymouth, S. (2015). The influence of foreign direct investment, intrafirm trading, and currency undervaluation on US firm trade disputes. SSRN Scholarly Paper ID 2665328, Social Science Research Network, Rochester, NY.

Jeong, G.-H. (2009). Constituent influence on international trade policy in the United States, 1987–2006. *International Studies Quarterly*, 53(2):519–540.

Johnson, J. W. and Wallack, J. S. (2012). Electoral systems and the personal vote. Harvard Dataverse, V1. Available from https://doi.org/10.7910/DVN/AMRXJA.

Kamal, F., McCloskey, J., and Wei, O. (2022). Multinational Firms in the US Economy: Insights from Newly Integrated Microdata. Working Paper Series WP2022-11, Bureau of Economic Analysis.

Kasahara, H. and Lapham, B. (2013). Productivity and the decision to import and export: Theory and evidence. *Journal of International Economics*, 89(2):297–316.

Kee, H. L., Neagu, C., and Nicita, A. (2013). Is protectionism on the rise? Assessing national trade policies during the crisis of 2008. *Review of Economics and Statistics*, 95(1):342–346.

Kee, H. L. and Nicita, A. (2022). Trade fraud and non-tariff measures. *Journal of International Economics*, 139:103682.

Kee, H. L., Nicita, A., and Olarreaga, M. (2009). Estimating trade restrictiveness indices. *The Economic Journal*, 119(534):172–199.

Kerr, W. R., Lincoln, W. F., and Mishra, P. (2013). The dynamics of firm lobbying. Harvard Business School Entrepreneurial Management Working Paper No. 12-034, Social Science Research Network.

Ketterer, T. D. (2016). EU anti-dumping and tariff cuts: Trade policy substitution? *The World Economy*, 39(5):576–596.

Kim, I. S. (2017). Political cleavages within industry: Firm-level lobbying for trade liberalization. *The American Political Science Review*, 111(1):1–20.

Kim, S. E. and Pelc, K. J. (2021). The politics of trade adjustment versus trade protection. *Comparative Political Studies*, 54(13):2354–2381.

Kim, S. Y. and Spilker, G. (2019). Global value chains and the political economy of WTO disputes. *The Review of International Organizations*, 14:239–260.

Kinzius, L., Sandkamp, A., and Yalcin, E. (2019). Trade protection and the role of non-tariff barriers. *Review of World Economics*, 155(4):603–643.

Knupfer, C. (2013). Counting on the American public to be informed on the TAFTA/TTIP talks?: Don't hold your breath. In Cardoso, D., Mthembu, P., Venhaus, M., and Garrido, M. V., editors, *The Transatlantic Colossus*. Berlin Forum on Global Politics, pp. 34–37.

Kono, D. Y. (2006). Optimal obfuscation: Democracy and trade policy transparency. *The American Political Science Review*, 100(3):369–384.

Kono, D. Y. (2008). Democracy and trade discrimination. *The Journal of Politics*, 70(4):942–955.

Kono, D. Y. (2009). Market structure, electoral institutions, and trade policy. *International Studies Quarterly*, 53(4):885–906.

Krueger, A. O. (1997). Trade policy and economic development: How we learn. *The American Economic Review*, 87(1):1–22.

Krugman, P. (2008). The Increasing Returns Revolution in Trade and Geography. Nobel Prize Lecture. December 8, 2008, Stockholm University.

Krugman, P. R. (1981). Intraindustry specialization and the gains from trade. *Journal of Political Economy*, 89(5):959–973.

Krugman, P. R. (1990). *Rethinking International Trade*. MIT Press.

Kuenzel, D. (2020). Non-tariff measures: What's Tariffs Got To Do with It? Economics Working Papers No 2020-006, Wesleyan University.

Ladewig, J. W. (2006). Domestic influences on international trade policy: Factor mobility in the United States, 1963 to 1992. *International Organization*, 60(1): 69–103.

Lakatos, C. and Fukui, T. (2013). EU-US economic linkages: The role of multinationals and intra-firm trade. DG Trade Chief Economist Notes 2013-3, Directorate General for Trade, European Commission.

Lakatos, C. and Ohnsorge, F. (2017). Arm's-length trade: A source of post-crisis trade weakness. No. 8144, World Bank Policy Research Working Paper.

Lipson, C. (1982). The transformation of trade: The sources and effects of regime change. *International Organization*, 36(2):417–455.

Liss, J. (2019). Social and political drivers of the reorientation of US trade policy: The case of US withdrawal from the Trans-Pacific Partnership. *Social Currents*, 6(3): 199–218.

Liss, J. (2021). Globalization as ideology: China's effects on organizational advocacy and relations among us trade policy stakeholder groups. *Review of International Political Economy*, 28(4):1055–1082.

Lohmann, S. and O'Halloran, S. (1994). Divided government and U.S. trade policy: Theory and evidence. *International Organization*, 48(4):595–632.

Long, J. S. (1997). *Regression Models for Categorical and Limited Dependent Variables*. SAGE.

Los, B., Timmer, M. P., and de Vries, G. J. (2015). How global are global value chains? A new approach to measure international fragmentation. *Journal of Regional Science*, 55(1):66–92.

Madeira, M. A. (2014). The new politics of the new trade: The political economy of intra-industry trade. In Deese, D., editor, *Handbook of the International Political Economy of Trade*, pp. 113–134. Edward Elgar Publishing.

Madeira, M. A. (2018). The politics of TTIP in the US: American industry, labor and public positions on transatlantic trade. *Asia-Pacific Journal of EU Studies*, 16(1): 31–53.

Magee, S., Lee, H., and Kim, J. (2019). Evidence and explanation for the tariff-lobbying paradox: Endogenous tariffs fall as protectionist lobbying rises. *Applied Economics*, 51(40):4368–4384.

Magee, S. P., Brock, W. A., and Young, L. (1989). *Black Hole Tariffs and Endogenous Policy Theory: Political Economy in General Equilibrium*. Cambridge University Press.

Mahoney, C. (2008). *Brussels Versus the Beltway: Advocacy in the United States and the European Union*. Georgetown University Press.

Mahoney, J. (2007). Qualitative methodology and comparative politics. *Comparative Political Studies*, 40(2):122–144.

Manger, M. (2015). PTA design, tariffs and intra-industry trade. In Dür, A. and Elsig, M., editors, *Trade Cooperation: The Purpose, Design and Effects of Preferential Trade Agreements*. Cambridge University Press, pp. 195–217.

Manger, M. S. (2009). *Investing in Protection: The Politics of Preferential Trade Agreements between North and South*. Cambridge University Press.

Manger, M. S. (2014). The economic logic of Asian preferential trade agreements: The role of intra-industry trade. *Journal of East Asian Studies*, 14(2):151–184.

Mansfield, E. D. and Busch, M. L. (1995). The political economy of nontariff barriers: A cross-national analysis. *International Organization*, 49(4):723–749.

Mansfield, E. D., Milner, H. V., and Rosendorff, B. P. (2002). Why democracies cooperate more: Electoral control and international trade agreements. *International Organization*, 56(3):477–513.

Martin, C. J. and Swank, D. (2004). Does the organization of capital matter? Employers and active labor market policy at the national and firm levels. *American Political Science Review*, 98(4):593–611.

Martinez, Jr., R. (2016). Machinists Union President Responds to TPP Signing. Available at www.goiam.org/news/machinists-union-president-responds-to-tpp-signing/.

Mayer, T. and Ottaviano, G. I. P. (2008). The happy few: The internationalisation of European firms. *Intereconomics*, 43(3):135–148.

Mayer, W. (1984). Endogenous tariff formation. *The American Economic Review*, 74(5):970–985.

McGillivray, F. (2004). *Privileging Industry: The Comparative Politics of Trade and Industrial Policy*. Princeton University Press.

McKay, A. M. (2011). The decision to lobby bureaucrats. *Public Choice*, 147(1): 123–138.

McMinimy, M. A. (2016). TPP: American Agriculture and the Trans-Pacific Partnership (TPP) Agreement. Available from Congressional Research Service at https://sgp.fas.org/crs/misc/R44337.pdf. Accessed December 19, 2022.

Melitz, M. J. (2003). The impact of trade on intra-industry reallocations and aggregate industry productivity. *Econometrica*, 71(6):1695–1725.

Melitz, M. J. and Redding, S. J. (2014). Heterogeneous firms and trade. *Handbook of International Economics*, 4:1–54.

Melitz, M. J. and Trefler, D. (2012). Gains from trade when firms matter. *Journal of Economic Perspectives*, 26(2):91–118.

Meunier, S. (2005). *Trading Voices: The European Union in International Commercial Negotiations*. Princeton University Press.

Midford, P. (1993). International trade and domestic politics: Improving on Rogowski's model of political alignments. *International Organization*, 47(4):535–564.

Milbrath, L. W. (1976). *The Washington Lobbyists*. Greenwood Press.

Milner, H. (1988). Trading places: Industries for free trade. *World Politics*, 40(3): 350–376.

Milner, H. V. (1999). The political economy of international trade. *Annual Review of Political Science*, 1999(2):91–114.

Milner, H. V. and Judkins, B. (2004). Partisanship, trade policy, and globalization: Is there a left–right divide on trade policy? *International Studies Quarterly*, 48(1): 95–120.

Milner, H. V. and Kubota, K. (2005). Why the move to free trade? Democracy and trade policy in the developing countries. *International Organization*, 59(1): 107–143.

Mizruchi, M. (2013). *The Fracturing of the American Corporate Elite*. Harvard University Press.

Motor & Equipment Manufacturers' Association (2016). MEMA Speaks Out for Regional Parts Suppliers on Trans-Pacific Partnership. Available from www.mema.org/mema-speaks-out-regional-parts-suppliers-trans-pacific-partnership. Accessed February 4, 2022.

National Association of Manufacturers (2010). Comment from Douglas Goudie, National Association of Manufacturers. Available from www.regulations.gov/document/USTR-2009-0041-0083. Accessed January 20, 2022.

National Association of Manufacturers (2013). Public Comments Concerning the Proposed Transatlantic Trade and Investment Partnership. Available from www.regulations.gov/document/USTR-2013-0019-0171. Accessed March 1, 2023.

National Electrical Manufacturers Association (2013). Letter to USTR, National Electrical Manufacturers Association. Available from www.regulations.gov/document/USTR-2013-0019-0187. Accessed February 20, 2023.

Neslen, A. (May 1, 2016). Leaked TTIP documents cast doubt on EU-US trade deal. *The Guardian*. Available at www.theguardian.com/business/2016/may/01/leaked-ttip-documents-cast-doubt-on-eu-us-trade-deal.

Nicolaidis, K. and Meunier, S. (2012). Revisiting trade competence in the European Union: Amsterdam, Nice, and beyond. In Hosli, M. O., Widgrén, M., and van Deemen, A., editors, *Institutional Challenges in the European Union*. Routledge, pp. 173–201.

Nielson, D. L. (2003). Supplying trade reform: Political institutions and liberalization in middle-income presidential democracies. *American Journal of Political Science*, 47(3):470–491.

Niu, Z., Liu, C., Gunessee, S., and Milner, C. (2018). Non-tariff and overall protection: Evidence across countries and over time. *Review of World Economics*, 154(4):675–703.

OECD (2002). OECD Economic Outlook No. 71 (Edition 2002/1).

Olson, M. (1965). *The Logic of Collective Action: Public Goods and the Theory of Groups*. Harvard University Press.

Olson, M. (1982). *The Rise and Decline of Nations: Economic Growth, Stagflation, and Social Rigidities*. Yale University Press.

Omega Flex Inc. (2013). Transatlantic Trade and Investment Partnership. Available from www.regulations.gov/document/USTR-2013-0019-0085. Accessed February 20, 2023.

O'Reilly, R. F. (2005). Veto points, veto players, and international trade policy. *Comparative Political Studies*, 38(6):652–675.

O'Rourke, K. H. (2003). Heckscher-Ohlin Theory and Individual Attitudes towards Globalization. Working Paper No. 9872, National Bureau of Economic Research.

Osgood, I. (2016). Differentiated products, divided industries: Firm preferences over trade liberalization. *Economics & Politics*, 28(2):161–180.

Osgood, I. (2017). The breakdown of industrial opposition to trade: Firms, product variety, and reciprocal liberalization. *World Politics*, 69(1):184–231.

Osgood, I. (2018). Globalizing the supply chain: Firm and industrial support for US trade agreements. *International Organization*, 72(2):455–484.

Osgood, I. (2021). Vanguards of globalization: Organization and political action among America's pro-trade firms. *Business and Politics*, 23(1):1–35.

Osgood, I., Tingley, D., Bernauer, T., Kim, I. S., Milner, H. V., and Spilker, G. (2017). The charmed life of superstar exporters: Survey evidence on firms and trade policy. *The Journal of Politics*, 79(1):133–152.

Owen, E. (2015). The political power of organized labor and the politics of foreign direct investment in developed democracies. *Comparative Political Studies*, 48(13), 1746–1780.

Owen, E. and Johnston, N. P. (2017). Occupation and the political economy of trade: Job routineness, offshorability, and protectionist sentiment. *International Organization*, 71(4):665–699.

Pareto, V. (1927). *Manual of Political Economy*. A. M. Kelley.

Penn United (2009). Comment from David Frengel, Penn United. Available from www.regulations.gov/document/USTR-2009-0041-0002. Accessed January 31, 2022.

Peterson, T. M. and Thies, C. G. (2012). Beyond Ricardo: The link between intra-industry trade and peace. *British Journal of Political Science*, 42(4):747–767.

Petri, P. A. and Plummer, M. G. (2016). The economic effects of the trans-pacific partnership: New estimates. Working Paper No. 16-2, Peterson Institute for International Economics.

Plouffe, M. (2017). Firm heterogeneity and trade-policy stances evidence from a survey of Japanese producers. *Business and Politics*, 19(1):1–40.

Postnikov, E. and Bastiaens, I. (2020). Social protectionist bias: The domestic politics of north–south trade agreements. *The British Journal of Politics and International Relations*, 22(2):347–366.

Powell, B. and Harrington, C. (February 4, 2015). TV News Shows Largely Ignore Historic Trade Negotiations. *Media Matters*. Available at www.mediamatters .org/msnbc/study-tv-news-shows-largely-ignore-historic-trade-negotiations.

Radhakrishnan, R. (2022). Public expenditure allocation, lobbying, and growth. *Journal of Public Economic Theory*, 24(4):756–780.

Rauch, J. E. (1999). Networks versus markets in international trade. *Journal of International Economics*, 48(1):7–35.

Ravenhill, J. (2017). The political economy of the Trans-Pacific Partnership: A "21st century" trade agreement? *New Political Economy*, 22(5):573–594.

Redding, S. J. (2011). Theories of heterogeneous firms and trade. *Annual Review of Economics*, 3(1):77–105.

Reynolds, K. M. (2013). Under the cover of antidumping: Does administered protection facilitate domestic collusion? *Review of Industrial Organization*, 42(4):415–434.

Ricardo, D. (1817). *On the Principles of Political Economy and Taxation*. J. Murray.

Richter, B. K., Samphantharak, K., and Timmons, J. F. (2009). Lobbying and taxes. *American Journal of Political Science*, 53(4):893–909.

Rickard, S. J. (2012). A non-tariff protectionist bias in majoritarian politics: government subsidies and electoral institutions. *International Studies Quarterly*, 56(4):777–785.

Rodrik, D. (2019). Globalization's wrong turn. *Foreign Affairs*, 98(4):26–33.

Rodrik, D., Haggard, S., and Steven B. Webb (1994). The rush to free trade in the developing world: Why so late? Why now? Will it last? In *Voting for Reform: Democracy, Political Liberalization, and Economic Adjustment*, pp. 61–88. Oxford University Press.

Rogowski, R. (1987). Political cleavages and changing exposure to trade. *The American Political Science Review*, 81(4):1121–1137.

Rogowski, R. (1990). *Commerce and Coalitions: How Trade Affects Domestic Political Alignments*. Princeton University Press.

Roncek, D. W. (1992). Learning more from Tobit coefficients: Extending a comparative analysis of political protest. *American Sociological Review*, 57(4):503.

Rose, A. (2005). Which international institutions promote international trade? *Review of International Economics*, 13(4):682–698.

Ryu, J. and Stone, R. W. (2018). Plaintiffs by proxy: A firm-level approach to WTO dispute resolution. *The Review of International Organizations*, 13:273–308.

Sambanis, N. (2004). Using case studies to expand economic models of civil war. *Perspectives on Politics*, 2(2):259–279.

Sampson, T. (2014). Selection into trade and wage inequality. *American Economic Journal: Microeconomics*, 6(3):157–202.

Santarelli, E. (1991). Asset specificity, R & D financing, and the signalling properties of the firm's financial structure. *Economics of Innovation and New Technology*, 1(4):279–294.

Schattschneider, E. (1935). *Politics, Pressures, and the Tariff*. Prentice-Hall, Inc.

Scheve, K. F. and Slaughter, M. J. (2001). What determines individual trade-policy preferences? *Journal of International Economics*, 54(2):267–292.

Schlozman, K. L., Burch, T., Jones, P. E., You, H. Y., Verba, S., and Brady, H. E. (2018). *Washington Representatives Study (Organized Interests in Washington Politics) – 1981, 1991, 2001, 2006, 2011*. Harvard Dataverse.

Schott, J. J. (2016). Understanding the Trans-Pacific Partnership: An overview | PIIE. In Cimino-Isaacs, C. and Schott, J. J., editors, *Trans-Pacific Partnership: An Assessment*. Peterson Institute for International Economics, pp. 9–22.

Schott, P. (2008). US Manufacturing Exports and Imports by SIC or NAICS Category and Partner Country, 1972 to 2005. Available from https://faculty.som.yale.edu/peterschott/international-trade-data/.

Schott, P. K. (2004). Across-product versus within-product specialization in international trade. *The Quarterly Journal of Economics*, 119(2):647–678.

Schuldt, R. F. and Taylor, J. E. (2018). Cartel attributes and cartel performance: The impact of trade associations. *The Journal of Industrial Economics*, 66(1):1–29.

Scott, R. E. (2011). Heading south: US-Mexico trade and job displacement after NAFTA. Economic Policy Institute Briefing Paper. Available at https://policycommons.net/artifacts/1414562/heading-south/2028826/.

Shaffer, G. C. (2003). *Defending Interests: Public-Private Partnerships in WTO Litigation*. Brookings Institution Press.

Shepsle, K. A. and Weingast, B. R. (1984). Political solutions to market problems. *The American Political Science Review*, 78(2):417–434.

Surge Suppression Incorporated (2013). Comments of Thomas S. Hogan, Jr., Surge Suppression Incorporated. Available from www.regulations.gov/document/USTR-2013-0019-0159. Accessed February 20, 2023.

Thies, C. and Peterson, T. (2015). *Intra-Industry Trade: Cooperation and Conflict in the Global Political Economy*. Stanford University Press.

Thomas, K. P. (1997). Capital mobility and trade policy: The case of the Canada-US auto pact. *Review of International Political Economy*, 4(1):127–153.

Tile Council of North America (2015). Testimony of Eric Astrachan, Tile Council of North America. USITC Hearing on the Trans-Pacific Partnership Agreement: Likely Impact on the US Economy and on Specific Sectors, January 14, 2015. Available from www.usitc.gov/press_room/documents/testimony/105_001_008d2.pdf. Accessed January 31, 2022.

Trefler, D. (2004). The long and short of the Canada-U.S. free trade agreement. *American Economic Review*, 94(4):870–895.

Trumka, R. (2016). TPP: A new low. Available from https://thehill.com/opinion/op-ed/267968-tpp-a-new-low/.

Tudela-Marco, L., Garcia-Alvarez-Coque, J. M., and Martí-Selva, L. (2017). Do EU member states apply food standards uniformly? A look at fruit and vegetable safety notifications. *JCMS: Journal of Common Market Studies*, 55(2):387–405.

Ugur, M. (1998). Explaining protectionism and liberalization in European Union trade policy: The case of textiles and clothing. *Journal of European Public Policy*, 5(4):652–670.

UNCTAD (2016). World Investment Report 2016: Investor Nationality – Policy Challenges. Technical report, UN.

United Auto Workers (2016). The trouble with the TPP. Available at https://uaw.org/solidarity_magazine/the-trouble-with-the-tpp/. Accessed March 2, 2023.

US Chamber of Commerce (2013). Statement of the US Chamber of Commerce on the Transatlantic Trade and Investment Partnership. Available from www.regulations.gov/document/USTR-2013-0019-0241. Accessed February 20, 2023.

US Council for International Business (2013). Submission to the U.S. Trade Representative on the Transatlantic Trade and Investment Partnership. Available from www.regulations.gov/document/USTR-2013-0019-0299. Accessed February 20, 2023.

USITC (2016). Trans-Pacific Partnership Agreement: Likely Impact on the US Economy and on Specific Industry Sectors. Technical Report 4607, US International Trade Commission.

USTR (2011). Trans-Pacific Partnership (TPP) Trade Ministers' Report to Leaders. Technical report, United States Trade Representative.

Verdier, D. (1994). *Democracy and International Trade: Britain, France, and the United States, 1860-1990*. Princeton University Press.

Verdier, D. (1998). Democratic convergence and free trade. *International Studies Quarterly*, 42(1):1–24.

Ville, F. D. and Siles-Brügge, G. (2015). *TTIP: The Truth about the Transatlantic Trade and Investment Partnership*. John Wiley & Sons.

Viner, J. (1950). *The Customs Union Issue*. Oxford University Press.

Vogel, D. (1989). *Fluctuating Fortunes*. Basic Books.

Walter, S. (2017). Globalization and the demand-side of politics: How globalization shapes labor market risk perceptions and policy preferences. *Political Science Research and Methods*, 5(1):55–80.

Walter, S. (2021). The backlash against globalization. *Annual Review of Political Science*, 24(1):421–442.

Waterhouse, B. (2014). *Lobbying America: The Politics of Business from Nixon to NAFTA*. Princeton University Press.

Weller, N. (2009). Trading policy: Constituents and party in U.S. trade policy. *Public Choice*, 141(1/2):87–101.

White House (2016). Statement by the President on the Signing of the Trans-Pacific Partnership. February 3, 2016. Press release, White House.

Winslett, G. (2021). *Competitiveness and Death: Trade and Politics in Cars, Beef, and Drugs*. University of Michigan Press.

Wintrobe, R. (1998). *The Political Economy of Dictatorship*. Cambridge University Press.

Woll, C. (2009). Trade Policy Lobbying in the European Union: Who Captures Whom? In Richardson, J. and Coen, D., editors, *Lobbying the European Union: Institutions, Actors, and Issues*. Oxford University Press, pp. 277–297.

Woll, C. D. (2006). Lobbying in the European Union: From sui generis to a comparative perspective. *Journal of European Public Policy*, 13(3):456–469.

Woolcock, S. (2005). European Union trade policy: Domestic institutions and systemic factors. In Kelly, D. and Grant, W., editors, *The Politics of International Trade in the Twenty-First Century*. Palgrave, pp. 234–252.

World Bank (2009). Reshaping Economic Geography. World Development Report, World Bank.

Wu, W.-C. (2020). Rethinking coalition size and trade policies in authoritarian regimes: Are single-party dictatorships less protectionist? *Party Politics*, 26(2):143–153.

Young, A. R. (2016). Not your parents' trade politics: The Transatlantic Trade and Investment Partnership negotiations. *Review of International Political Economy*, 23(3):345–378.

Young, A. R. (2017). *The New Politics of Trade: Lessons from TTIP*. Agenda Publishing.

Young, A. R. and Peterson, J. (2006). The EU and the new trade politics. *Journal of European Public Policy*, 13(6):795–814.

Zimmermann, H. (2007). Realist power Europe? The EU in the negotiations about China's and Russia's WTO accession. *Journal of Common Market Studies*, 45(4):813–832.

Index